ASK M[...]

my divorce

Women Open Up
ABOUT Moving On

edited by Candace Walsh

SEAL PRESS

Ask Me about My Divorce

Women Open Up about Moving On

Published by

Seal Press

A Member of the Perseus Books Group

1700 Fourth Street

Berkeley, California 94710

Library of Congress Cataloging-in-Publication Data

Ask me about my divorce : women open up about moving on / [edited by]
Candace Walsh.
    p. cm.
  ISBN-13: 978-1-58005-276-4
  ISBN-10: 1-58005-276-2
1. Divorced women--United States--Biography. 2. Women authors--United
States--Biography. I. Walsh, Candace.
  HQ834.A85 2009
  306.89'3092273--dc22
  [B]
                              2008051945

Cover design by Domini Dragoone
Interior design by Tabitha Lahr
Printed in the United States of America
Distributed by Publishers Group West

To my Salamandre

Contents

✳ Introduction

when i first started thinking about ending my marriage, I was terrified. Divorce was up there with death and taxes, right? It was a big baddie. I felt sadness at the loss of something to which my spouse and I had both pledged our everlasting commitment, *and* I also felt fear and foreboding about being in the "divorced" category.

Nuptial status can define us very much—whether we're married, never married, divorced, widowed, or remarried. We wander around with our bag of assumptions about what that means about the person who is any of those things. Especially when that person is "me."

Dictionaries generally define divorce as a legal dissolution of marriage that releases husband and wife from their marital obligations. The term comes from the Latin, *divertere*, which is to divert (to turn aside or turn from a path or course; deflect). To split. It's linked to versus, opposition, or turning and rotating (like the universe, like a ploughman turns the soil). That's what it means, literally. What else does it mean? It's up to you. Vertigo—dizziness. Version—your version of the story.

What's behind the divorce is really what people should think of in terms of what they have to grieve. Let's say that it wasn't what you thought it would be. Big time. You changed, your partner changed, *or* you stopped growing. Or you found yourself in a legal union with someone who defiled it by infidelity, verbal or physical or mental abuse, or just plain stubbornness and selfishness. Or you just stopped loving the person, the person stopped loving you, or you realized that what you thought you wanted was not actually what will sustain you for the rest of your life. *This isn't what I signed on for.*

You started hearing that little voice. "This isn't the right thing for me. I am not living my truth. I should really get out of here." And then you did the seventeen things we all do to not hear that voice of inner truth, because it would mean a great big change and many little ones.

After I moved out, I found the term to be so loaded with stuff that I didn't want to take on that I wouldn't even say it for a long time. I grieved the loss of the marriage, no doubt—but I didn't feel the extra badness that I thought I would. The air seemed purer. I had more free time. I did the dishes when I felt like it and didn't feel guilty because someone else had first. It was like moving off campus all over again, but without the long-haired roommate guy walking around in his towel. I had a fresh start.

When people asked me what was new, I said, "My ex and I are living in two houses now." Or, "He and I split up." Then I had to steel myself, because guess what was coming? "Oh, no! I am *so sorry!*" I wasn't. I wasn't sorry—I had just finished a big race, basically, crossed the finish line, and wanted a glass of water, a towel, a slap on the back, and to be asked, "So, how was it? How did it go? What did you learn? How do you feel? Give me a hug, girl!"

It reminded me of when my parents split. God bless them, they hung on for ten more years than they should have. They didn't want to traumatize me and wanted to be accepted in the eyes of their church and their families and friends. They didn't want to be "divorced." What did traumatize me was living in a house that was empty of a very crucial element: a healthy and mutually respectful love relationship. When they gave it up, I felt relief (because I knew it was inevitable) and space, and possibility, and peace flow in. And yet I encountered a bunch of grownups and peers pitying me, with prurient solicitousness. . . . The weight of their stuff around divorce had no place in my fragile little adolescent world, but I didn't know how to elucidate that, except to say, "You know, it's fine, it's better, actually."

Ask me about my divorce. You wanted to know about my college graduation, my first job, my new apartment, my engagement, my wedding, my honeymoon, my baby's birth. All rites of passage, all changes, all evidence of growth. As is this. And, maybe it's not the best moment, but, make space for the possibility that I have some cool things to share. Because it's been a wild ride, and I am learning new things every day. A friendship is about sharing what's going on for each of us, and if we stop here, at this point of where I am, well, then, that just leads to distance and growing apart, and now is not the time for more of that.

I learned to say, when asked what was new, "Everything's *good*, my marriage has ended, but it's a good thing; it's the best thing for us to do." A sandwich of good. It helped a lot. People relaxed at that point.

Of course, as you know if you are chilling with the big D, there *will* be people who drop off the face of the earth: the old friends you had as a couple but not as an individual. Always good to know who your friends really are, or, more charitably, which of your friends are completely triggered and weirded out by divorce. They might be back, after they stop hiding under the bed from your divorce cooties. As Marrit Ingman says in her essay, "It made me uncomfortable when . . . a couple I knew and regarded highly was calling it quits. I tried to never take it personally, but you can't hear about someone else's divorce without imagining it happening to you. It is proof of the mortality of marriage."

You can't take the deepest core of grief and loss away from something that has its unavoidable traumatic component, but divorce can lose the shame/fear/stigma frosting on its sometimes bitter cake. Because a lot of those bites are surprisingly sweet.

Marriage is a beautiful thing, when it works, *and* when it doesn't. When it works, it's made up of two people who love each other, sharing life's best and worst moments, fostering each other's growth, and having really great sex. When it doesn't, it *was* made up of two people who loved each other, shared life's best and worst moments, fostered each other's growth, and most likely had really great sex. So, instead of sitting with the last incarnation of it, which led to a split, I like to appreciate and be grateful for the whole, which gave me so much. It gave me the beautiful Manhattan wedding day, the French honeymoon, the honeymoon period, a summer on a sailboat, two gorgeous children, a sounding board, a hand in mine, and a lifelong friend who knows me better than most people. When it ended, it gave the two of us the opportunity to feel most deeply who we were in that moment, and then run with it . . . to flower and spread our limbs in all sorts of directions, until we found another place to put down roots. And, we did. Our kids have two extra adults in their lives who model different ways of being in the world, which broadens their definition of what it can mean to be an adult.

What follows: a spicy, riveting selection of essays from women from all walks of life. The words within will make you laugh, cry, nod your head, and shake your fist. The unifying thread is "I got divorced, and it rocked my world."

As Leigh Anne Jasheway-Bryant says in her essay, "If I'm happy, that's the kind of fairytale everyone should dream of."

*

Several Things I Know and a Few Things I Don't

*
melanie jones

i was twenty-six when my husband left on our second anniversary. It was New Year's Eve. I weighed approximately two pounds, not including the frizzy hair piled on top of my head. The bags under my eyes were like what people might take on monthlong expeditions to Everest. (Everest people have sherpas to carry their bags. I had to carry mine by myself. On my face.)

I don't know what the opposite of sexy is, but I think it was probably me.

But somehow, I functioned. I got up every day, put on clothing, and went to work—where the sales manager would look me up and down and say, "Best diet in the world, huh?" on her way to the coffeemaker. (She had been through three divorces. She would know.) My boss Jill's heartfelt advice was to get smaller pants.

A lot of people had suggestions, but I didn't really want them.

I was aware that my husband had just napalmed my life as I knew it. I was aware that I was a walking skeleton with unmanageable hair who had forgotten the many uses of eyeliner and mascara. I was also aware that I was probably facing years of therapy, lonely nights, and something called a "journey of recovery." But, I had already cried through our entire relationship, and now that it was over, I was sick of it. All that "five stages of grieving" crap could wait.

I just wanted to laugh.

If it was silly, bizarre, weird, or funny, I did it. I took merengue lessons with the old folks by the pool at a Mexico resort—where I wasn't sure whose butt was baggier, my butt or the butt of the old gal next to me.

I went to a sex toy party (even though sex was the last thing on my mind). The Elvira-looking hostess brought out a massive, floppy, flesh-colored "device" with a suction cup at its base. She dramatically licked the suction cup and slammed the thing against the wall where it rebounded hilariously. If it had a cartoon sound effect, it would be *wanga-wanga-wanga*.

I spent time with my sisters—attending a variety show where I ended up handcuffed to a magician—and savored a weekend in Huntington Beach, where the only music was James Brown, the only food was chocolate, and the only drink was champagne. I felt . . . good.

I didn't know that I was doing things like "being in the moment" and "living each day as though it were my last." Things that were probably in the self-help books people kept trying to give me. But, I was too busy enjoying my newfound freedom to care what it was called or what a book said about it.

In my secret thoughts, late at night in a bed that felt too big for me, this girls' night pajama party holiday was nice and all, but I wanted my life back. It was irrational, of course, and impossible. The so-called comfort zone that I craved was a marriage that had gone from bad to worse. My ex had moved on as soon as he walked out the door, taking up with another woman named Melanie. Which is just plain weird if you ask me. You'd think that's the last name he'd want to scream out in bed.

But, here is something I do know: a twenty-six-year-old divorcée cannot avoid dating. I was too young to give up on love, buy seventeen cats, and become a professional spinster. I was going to have to get back out there eventually. I just didn't want to. Or know how.

Several months after the Big D, ready or not, I waded into the shallow end of the dating pool. I worked as a magazine editor, so I did what any self-respecting journalist who is far too raw and vulnerable to start dating would do: I told myself it was research. I wanted to figure out this Relationship Conspiracy and how I got so brutally burned. Perhaps my research would help others like me prevent the soul-crushing pain of premature husband evacuation.

My first research subject was the Bulldozer. He worked in my industry, and I guess he'd had a crush on me for a while because when he found out I was single, he picked me up and started running down the street. For real. At the time, I thought that was funny (if not a little bizarre).

What wasn't so funny was when he asked my boss for permission to date me. Before he'd even asked me out. It was some weird gesture of mutant chivalry, I guess, but it felt more than a little invasive. Also invasive was his decision, on our second date, to grab a magazine, head into my bathroom, and make himself a little *too* at home.

There were other lab rats: Fart Boy (who let 'er rip on date number two), the Puppeteer (who lived in a puppet studio where romance meant an audience of Pinocchios hanging creepily from the ceiling) and the Swashbuckler (whom I caught kissing the coat check girl during one of our dinner dates). From a scientific perspective, I was gathering interesting data. From a romantic one, my experiments were failures.

But every week over cocktails, my group of friends would ask the token single girl (me) about her love life. And I'd tell them hilarious stories about the thirty-five-year-old whose mom still bought him all his clothes. Or the guy who waited until our fourth date to tell me about his fiancée. For some reason, at the time, it didn't occur to me that dating someone who's about to get married to someone else really wasn't very funny.

It was sad. And just ever-so-slightly self-destructive.

My friends, however, thought it was hilarious. They'd tell me I should do stand-up comedy or something with all my "material." But for some reason, dating stupid guys who did stupid things stopped being funny or fun. I was the butt of my own jokes and my life was the punch line.

These men were supposed to be *my* research subjects, but somehow, I got wrapped up in my own dating experiment. I was the one who felt like a lab rat, poked and prodded and zapped without warning.

I stopped frequenting nightclubs and started running. The group I joined was training for a half-marathon and I, for lack of any better ideas, joined in. As I gasped along on the weekly eight- or ten-mile runs, something started to happen. Muscles took shape under my skin and my eyes looked brighter. I felt more confident. My light-speed hyperanalytical type-A mind became peaceful and quiet. I was stronger. I was healthier. I was hooked.

On December 31, in twenty-four–below weather, one year after my husband left, I ran a five-mile race. It was a nighttime event, called the Resolution Run, and I didn't tell anyone I had entered. I toed the line and when the gun went off, I started out into the midwinter darkness. Every step I took moved me farther away from my old life and one step closer to a new one I didn't yet know.

I knew that laughing was part of healing, but that hard work was going to be part of it, too. I knew that friends can sometimes help you, but sometimes they keep you stuck in patterns that no longer serve. And I knew that running had made me stronger, emotionally and physically, than I'd been before.

The next morning, I registered for my first marathon. Running 26.2 miles scared me. I'd heard all the marathon horror stories of people puking or bleeding or soiling their shorts. A marathon was bigger than me. And at the time, it was more than I was capable of. I was going to have to dig deep and find resources I didn't yet know I had: to get stronger, to rise to the challenge.

I loved every minute of it. Running with nothing but the sun on my face and the sound of my own breath was true love for me—something more pure and clean than I'd ever shared with another person. I called my first marathon my 26.2-mile victory lap, and it absolutely was. I crossed the finish line and kissed my ex-husband goodbye.

Around the same time, the magazine where I worked was featured on the local TV station's morning show. As the editor, I answered questions about our annual dining awards while a local chef prepared his prizewinning dish. Standing there, bathed in light, with a microphone clipped to my shirt, I had an idea.

Running put me in touch with a sense of purpose that filled me with hope and possibility. I respected myself and I respected the people I ran with, knowing that they were on missions of their own. But in the dating world, it was every single woman for herself. On the surface, dating was about connecting, but everyone I met seemed just as lonely as I was.

There had to be another way. One where everyone chased their dreams, reached for their highest potential, and connected with others doing the same. Dating, but with a higher consciousness. I wondered if I could use what I knew to make a difference. And I wondered if I could make them laugh while I did it.

I pitched my idea to the TV station later that week. "We'll try it," came the reply to the email I sent the producer. Not a week later, I was back on the breakfast show, holding up a toilet roll with a single square of paper clinging pathetically to the cardboard tube. "This," I said, after a dramatic pause, "will not get you a second date." The entire studio howled with laughter and the cameraman could barely hold the camera straight.

They asked me back a few weeks later. Then they asked me back again and again until I was a regular Friday fixture, prepping singles on their way to the weekend with *Lust vs. Love,* or *Commitmentphobia and You,* or *How to Make the Friend-to-Lover Switcheroo.* I'd crack jokes and make faces but underneath all my funny one-liners about men who modeled in high school (lost cause), I was telling people to respect themselves, respect each other, and go after what they want in life.

Soon, I was asked to write a dating column in a local magazine. Then the TV station invited me to do a second segment for the evening show. I was the Dating Dame and people loved it. They'd stop me in the mall to chat. They'd offer suggestions. They'd ask for advice. Sometimes they'd scream, "The Dating Dame!" from across the street.

I had tapped into something, I could feel it. But I wasn't doing it justice. I had two minutes of television to sum up a giant aspect of human relationships, packaged and glossed up for the folks at home. A topic as complicated as Trust was reduced to three bullet points and a punch line. How was I going to make meaningful change with that? How was I going to help people find and follow their true purpose and attract like-minded people into their lives to create meaningful, evolved partnerships when all the producer wanted was stupid innuendoes and street interviews?

Another thing that bothered me was my image. People seemed to think I was some vixen, draping my fishnet-clad legs over bar stools and barflies five nights a week, when that wasn't me at all. My uniform in real life was more like running tights and sneakers. I didn't have time to drink cocktails all night—I was training for a triathlon and working on a book!

And no matter how many times I wove in messages about respect and friendship and common interests, people still thought their one-night stands were going to lead them to true love.

My mission to elevate the dating world wasn't working.

I took the message off the air and onto the stage, where I could say exactly what I thought and what I felt. Where trust wasn't a bullet point. Where it was real and raw and live. And where I would have to rely on myself more than I ever had before.

I wrote a one-woman show to be performed in a local theater the week of Valentine's Day. I would be up there alone, without a television screen to shield me. With no one to yell "Cut!" and give me another shot. It was a confession. It was a baptism. It scared the hell out of me.

The protagonist, Dating Girl, was a version of me at the beginning of my single life, (and probably a lot of single people in the world): hurting, clueless, and full of *Sex and the City* clichés about being single and fabulous.

Dating Girl put her faith in an online love calculator, hoping it would tell her how her relationship would work out. She offered "advice" that only revealed how afraid she was to be alone. She teetered around in heels and tight jeans, praying she was as put together inside as she was outside.

Along the way, fumbling through as best we could, Dating Girl and I figured out that happiness couldn't be found Out There until we discovered it In Here. That somewhere along the line, both of us had stopped running from How Things Should Be and started standing in How They Are. That when our dreams of a perfect marriage and a Hollywood ending faded, something else came into focus.

Standing there, alone, in the middle of a spotlight—my spotlight—I saw how far I'd come to get right here. I went through love and loss, laughter and tears, weakness and strength. I saw all of those things in this person I'd become. And though I didn't know what my next play would be about, I knew it was time to take a bow.

✳ Open Road
jessica cerretani

"*well, that's too bad,*" says my boyfriend, lifting a forkful of meat loaf to his mouth. "I'm sorry to hear that."

"Sorry?" asks Laura, our dinner companion. They're talking about an old college friend. "Did you ever meet her husband?"

"No," says Devin. "It's just, you know, she's divorced."

"Hell," Laura laughs. "I congratulate people when they tell me they're divorced." She should know. She used my divorce lawyer.

And Devin should know, too. After all, to the casual observer, he's the reason *I'm* divorced. He can see I've never been happier. But, on the surface, the dissolution of a marriage never seems like cause for celebration.

If you had asked me ten, or even five, years ago, if I thought my marriage would be one of the half that end in divorce, I'd have disagreed, then lectured you on the laziness of such couples, the ease with which they threw in the towel.

Like most children of divorce, I had vowed never to do the same. My own parents' split, when I was five, was a blur of unpleasant memories: unpaid bills, months of subsisting on canned food donations from our local church, two half-hearted suicide attempts by my mother, and long afternoons spent playing board games with a child therapist when I'd rather be home playing Barbies. For years I couldn't stand the mention of the word "divorce," couldn't bear to watch *One Day at a Time*, let alone *Kramer vs. Kramer*.

Yet twenty-five years later, I was reviewing legal papers in a tiny mouse-infested apartment, in contrast to the half-million-dollar home I shared with my husband. I was eating ramen noodles with a plastic fork as my friends suggested I throw a "divorce shower" to recoup the kitchen necessities I'd left behind. I was thirty-one, freshly separated—and actually enjoying myself. Clearly, this was not my parents' divorce.

As a child, not only did I know that I didn't want to be divorced, I also knew what I *did* want to be when I grew up: single, a successful writer, living in Boston or New York. But what I became was far from my dreams. I married Adam at twenty-five, after dating him for five years. We did live in Boston, but in a home he'd bought and paid for. Adam was good with money, so I let him handle our finances and mortgage. I worked as a ghostwriter for a famous doctor, but I didn't get a byline and the job didn't pay well. Still, I'd been with the company since right after college, and change seemed scary. I was stuck—and not just at work.

"God is in the details," Adam liked to say. He had trained as an architect; it was a Mies van der Rohe quote. This was a philosophy he carried with him when we renovated our house, as he carefully redid the trim around the doors and windows, which he thought I'd painted too sloppily. But when it came to our marriage, neither one of us had much of an eye for detail. We loved each other but weren't in love. We coexisted rather peacefully, like longtime roommates or brother and sister. He spent most of his time in his garage woodshop, fixing his sailboat. I spent most of my time on the couch. Despite all our talk, we *had* gotten lazy.

Still, I had always been someone who played by the rules. I liked safety and comfort. I lived in fear of failure and regret. I was afraid to take risks. I was that child who stood at the top of the high dive at the town lake and turned and climbed back down the ladder, refusing to jump.

Looking back at my own parents' divorce, the worst part wasn't the stigma attached to it or the sudden absence of my beloved father. The worst part, to me, was that everything now seemed so *hard*. My mother fought for custody of my sister and me, fought for ownership of our house—but it was the maintenance of all this that was difficult. They'd split in the midst of a major home renovation, and the outside of the house, a large, rambling thing, still needed to be painted. As an adult, I marveled at my mother's ability to balance on a ladder, three stories up, scraping and painting each summer. I knew before Adam and I had even filed separation papers that I didn't want the same fate.

"He can have the house," I told my lawyer, who had suggested we sell it and split the proceeds. It was his baby; he'd put the most work and money into it. I didn't want to be saddled with that responsibility and I was, remember, nothing if not lazy.

But it was more than that. I was happy with my little "Jess Cave," a cramped apartment that, if not exactly aesthetically pleasing, was all mine. I, who had once been terrified of being alone, now lived by myself—and, to my surprise, loved it.

Then there was the driving. "You can store some of your stuff at our house," my mother offered after I told her my new apartment had no storage. There was just one problem: My mother lives some two hundred miles away and neither one of us could drive long distances. Correction: We could, we just didn't. She hadn't driven much during her marriage decades earlier, and she didn't drive much now. I tooled around our neighborhood in Adam's Jetta, but I was terrified of taking the car on any major highway. I was, I realized, not unlike my late grandmother, who rarely got behind the wheel and whose husband drove her the few miles to her hair salon every week. I had envisioned myself a city girl, cosmopolitan, self-sufficient. The truth was painful: I was a passenger, not just in our car, but in my own life.

The week after my divorce was final, I took my check to the local Toyota dealership and left with a new Corolla. I was getting more and more comfortable with my drives to the supermarket and Target, but the trip to Connecticut for Thanksgiving was another story.

"Maybe you could drive partway?" I suggested sheepishly to Devin, who was accompanying me home to meet my family for the first time.

"It's your car, sweetie," he replied. "Why don't you just see how you do?" My new boyfriend was supportive of me in every way, but he didn't want to be my chauffeur—and I didn't really need him to be one. He sat next to me and I got in the driver's seat. I turned the key in the ignition and stepped on the gas.

I suppose it was this thrilling sense of freedom I was craving when I'd finally made the decision to end my marriage. Wait— that's an exaggeration. I never did make a conscious decision to get divorced. Instead, I approached the situation the way I had my entire life: with a heaping dose of passive-aggressiveness. If I was angry with a roommate, I left a note detailing my complaints. If I wanted to stop seeing a boy I didn't like, I didn't answer his phone calls. Anything to avoid confrontation.

With Adam, though, I'm not sure I even thought *that* much about my unhappiness. I didn't even think I was unhappy. Bored, yes. Feeling like my life would likely continue on the way it had for the next fifty years, yes. But if you asked me if I was unhappy, I would have uttered a shocked "No!"

In any case, a series of events soon converged to create a perfect storm for a bored, complacent wife. One day, my best friend, Karen—who happened to have been Adam's "best woman" in our wedding—asked me if I knew any single men. She wanted to set up a friend of hers. I only knew two single men, both of whom I worked with. Fred had a heroin problem. "Devin, I guess," I said. We arranged a happy hour group date.

"He's great," Karen crowed afterward. "He and Amy would be so cute together!" I'd never thought twice about Devin, a dark-haired man with an acerbic sense of humor. Suddenly we were friends. "He needs a girlfriend," said Karen, when it didn't work out with Amy. "I get the feeling he's a dirty, dirty boy."

The months rolled on. The presidential election came and went and Adam, unhappy about the results, began suggesting we move to France. Meanwhile, he was spending more time in the garage. I was spending more time with my friends. I've always had a lot of male friends, and Devin and I got along famously. But Karen was still there, too, joining me for dinner or shopping trips, and complaining about her own husband in a light, funny way that made it clear she was actually quite content with him.

Then Thanksgiving arrived and, as our families drove away that evening, Adam was back in the garage again, restoring his wooden sailboat. The circular saw he used rotated fast enough to easily cut through maple, oak, pine—and his thumb. The tough, calloused flesh gave way as easily as meat in a deli slicer. I drove him to the emergency room, racing down dark, winding roads, praying I wouldn't crash the car before he could get stitches.

Once at the ER, I waited while a doctor examined Adam's hand. The room was crowded with middle-aged women, also waiting for their husbands. Apparently Thanksgiving was a busy day. "What'd he do?" one of the women asked me, gesturing to Adam's empty chair. "Cut himself carving the turkey?"

"A circular saw," I told her, watching her eyebrows rise and her mouth open. "He almost cut his thumb off with a circular saw." The other women murmured; they were impressed.

"What the hell was he sawing on Thanksgiving?" one of them asked. "Shouldn't you two be with family?"

"He can see you now," said a nurse from the doorway before I could answer. I followed her down the hall to a room where Adam lay on an exam table, his hand extended above him while a doctor finished stitching him up. The doctor's pager buzzed and he excused himself.

I looked down at my husband as he started to cry, something I'd only seen him do once before.

"Oh, sweetie," I said. It was the first time in our decade-long relationship either of us had used such an endearment. I grabbed his good hand and squeezed. "It's okay. I'm here."

"No, I'm fine." He smiled his terse smile and gently pulled his hand from my grasp. "I'm just relieved, is all. I thought I'd lost my thumb."

On the drive home, I found myself daydreaming about Devin. A few days later, Adam, still bandaged, left for an extended business trip. And Devin and I shared a hotel room around the corner from our office, fulfilling every cliché in the book. I had finally jumped— without a parachute.

The affair lasted three weeks before Adam found out. That's right. I didn't tell him; that would be brave and mature. I don't know how he found out—perhaps from Karen. She had initially clapped her hands with glee when I confessed to her, but later, for reasons she never voiced, decided I was, in her words, "a terrible person."

For a man who'd been cuckolded, Adam took it surprisingly well. He wasn't happy about it, but he seemed to know our marriage had been over long before I cheated. "I guess I've got to let you go," he concluded. Then we watched an episode of *Law & Order* on the TiVo he'd bought me for Christmas four days earlier. And that was the end of my marriage. That night I moved into the guest room. Two weeks later, I moved into my new apartment.

Suddenly, everything changed. I was paying my own rent and bills. I was taking the bus to work and saving for a car. I was realizing I had to get a new job, not because Devin and I worked together, but because I needed to make more money. These changes weren't unlike those that my mother had faced so many years before. Yet I wasn't scared or sad. I was proud of myself. The difference, I suppose, is that I effected that change myself. My husband hadn't left me. I didn't have children.

"Stop telling people you're divorced because you cheated," my friend Terri finally said. She knew I didn't have regrets, but I had become honest to a fault. "An affair is just a symptom," she explained. "Not the disease." She was right. Who knows how long that "disease" would have lingered, though, until we finally pulled the plug? Another five years? Twenty? Fifty? I've read that infidelity is often a cry for attention and I think that's true. But in my case, it wasn't as much a cry for attention from Adam as it was for attention from myself.

Four years later, Devin and I are still together. Maybe someday we'll get married and have children, maybe not. All I know is that we're happy. As sweet as he is, though, he isn't the only reason for my joy. If we broke up tomorrow, I'd be sad—but I know I'd still have *me*. It's the me I always knew was there. I just had to shake things up to find her. Working as a successful freelance writer, speeding down the Mass Pike in my car, and paying the monthly mortgage on the condo I bought on my own . . . my married life seems very far away. "You set me free," Adam told me once after our divorce was final. And I set myself free, too.

✳

Sita's Eyes
✳ r. m. hora

raj always prided himself on having a well-dressed wife, and so with each year of our marriage, my wardrobe blossomed. I asked him once why he took such keen interest in my every sartorial need, and with his trademark three-time chin scratch he said, "You're pretty special, babe. Don't sell yourself short."

That's all a woman in love needs to hear, especially a woman who orgasms to shopping fantasies (that would be me). So as my friends continued to gasp in awe, I thanked the Gods for matching me with such a generous metrosexual.

Each year, as Raj left me for days at a time on the pretext of business trips, he scoured the depths of India to handpick exquisite silk saris to add to my already abundant collection. Jewelry? Rubies from Burma matched with diamonds from South Africa. Silver? Tea sets from the East India Company. Our home was a gallery of art and antiques from absolutely everywhere. For Raj it was an obsession; for me, it became a way of life.

In all my years of instant-gratification bliss, I did not see the writing on the wall. Probably because at some psychological level,

I chose to ignore the little nuances that became glaringly obvious indicators in retrospect . . . as to why a married woman with a very full schedule had a personal life empty and wanting of fulfillment. My sex life was sparse, and although I entreated Raj for intimacy, he invariably turned a deaf ear. He came back instead with couture, as if it were a consolation prize.

In year six, when my much loved childhood friend Hannah categorically asked me if I'd yet been able to determine whether Raj "enjoyed" women, I promptly dropped her.

Year seven, my fortieth birthday: I flew back home to San Francisco after a celebratory spa weekend with the girls. Upon reaching home, I threw open the apartment door, excited to tell Raj about the new seaweed therapy that had infused my skin and soothed my soul. But I was greeted with nothing. No art, no antiques, no European furniture. My living room had been stripped down to a bare shell. I burst into the bedroom to see that my beautiful sari collection had been minimized to less than a third of its original size. What *did* Raj leave me? A note on the bedside table. "You are a special person, so if life really does begin at forty, then it's time I set you free. I'm gay, I'm coming out of the closet and leaving you to settle down with the love of my life. Happy 40th Birthday!"

Gay? Leaving you for the love of my life? Happy 40th birthday? The words hit me right between the eyes. The love of his life turned out to be our house contractor. How could I possibly have a happy birthday now?

I fumbled through the phone book, looking for Hannah's number. Even after months of uncomfortable silence between us, she answered instantly when my name showed up on her caller ID. "You nailed it!" I shouted into the phone, hot tears rolling down my cheeks. I didn't have to explain further.

"Unleash your pent-up anger and sexual energy," she said. "Scream, yell—go find a lover. It's time to finally break free."

Separation and divorce are typically all that a woman needs to send shock waves through her system, but mine were underscored by the fact that I'd spent the last seven years coupling (albeit infrequently) with a secretly gay man. A weird sense of remorse reverberated through my nervous tissue. I couldn't help feeling like a complete failure as a woman.

Ironically, as Raj had always tuned in perfectly to my needs and emotions, he sensed my depression and reached out to talk. Six weeks and several gallons of coffee later, we met at a French bistro. "It's a bit of a jolt to the nerves," he said, "but you can hardly blame yourself."

"A bit of a jolt? Is that all you have to say?"

"I know, babe. . . . "

"Babe?"

Raj scratched his chin. "It's what I've called you for years."

"Yes, before you turned gay!"

Raj looked down at his plate and then straight into my soul. "I've been gay all along."

I knocked over my wine glass, staining white French linen a deep red. I glared at Raj, gripping my fork as though it were a trident.

"Why? Why now? Why lead me into failure . . . for all those years? And why did you have to abandon me on my birthday?"

Raj looked down at his plate. "I'm sorry, babe. I've been trapped myself by the stigma of being gay in the context of Indian society. I wanted to give you the most honest birthday present ever . . . to steer you out of the Sita syndrome."

The Sita syndrome. It occurred to me who I really was. No ordinary San Franciscan woman who goes through relationships, marriages, and divorce as a matter of routine like so many other American women, but Sita . . . the Indian woman whose life has no room for plurals. Even though an Indian woman might be perceived to be modern, urban, and cosmopolitan, the syndrome roots itself deep down inside her. Like Sita, the perfect woman (Lord Ram's wife in the great Hindu epic, *Ramayana*), the Indian wife is expected to give her virginity to one man and one marriage throughout her lifetime.

Right then, in the midst of crème brûlée, it dawned on me that accepting the Sita syndrome may have destroyed my entire potential for happiness. I was a victim of my own morals. And to what purpose? Even our common love for shopping backfired, as my ex-husband made off with most everything.

Ironically, though, I realized that Raj was not a selfish man. He understood me perhaps better than I understood myself. He divorced me because he had my interests at heart as much as his own: to finally free me from the Sita syndrome, so that I could pursue a life of intimacy with a man who could reciprocate. All of a sudden I felt that the door was finally open; all that remained was to go outside and look around.

Then came the Day of Reckoning. My family members arrived for dinner to express their love and support. "Take comfort in your *maayka*," Raj urged. "It might ease the transition to know that you still have family on your side." *Maayka* is a term that connotes "mother's home." It's where a wife goes for protection during difficult times, such as childbirth, sickness, or financial disarray. We come from a culture where a woman has not historically been a mistress of her financial or emotional destiny and hence looks for comfort to the society that produced her.

In theory, a daughter might derive strength from her parents. In an Indian context, a married daughter is only welcome as long as there is an understanding that she will eventually go back to her husband's home. Returning to *maayka* on a permanent basis is considered a matter of shame, a notion that has existed in our villages from ancient times. And although I would not physically move back to their home, the fact that I was a divorcée was shame enough for my parents.

My family, like others in India, assumed that in a turbulent marriage, the wife was the guilty party. In the *Ramayana,* Sita went through an ordeal of fire to prove that she had been faithful to Ram. Before we even sat down to the main course, I began to feel the heat.

"Even today, as women are out there working and all that, marriage remains a very traditional affair," my mother said. "You do know that marriage is entirely dependent on how much a woman makes her man want her?"

"Meaning what, mother? The man is gay!" I responded.

"That may be, but every wife has a hand in her husband's actions."

I gazed incredulously at the woman whom I imagined to be my first rung of emotional support. "Are you suggesting that I somehow turned him gay?"

"I'm suggesting that if you deprive a man of what he wants, then he might turn out differently from the boy he was raised to be."

"Mother, has it occurred to you that Raj might not have given me what *I* wanted?"

"What *you* want is a question mark, if approaching you is a no-entry zone."

A no-entry zone? I was shocked beyond measure.

"Is it so hard to see that I am a woman in midlife, absolutely desperate for sex?"

A snort of disgust from my first rung of support. "Spoken like a classic divorcée. This is the attitude that turns society away. Next, you'll be hiring an escort service!"

"You might reconcile by allowing his friend to move in," suggested my father. "It could then work out to be a manageable arrangement, perhaps."

This conversation went from the sublime to the ridiculous as my parents went on to dwell on the impact of my divorce on their own social standing. Did they truly believe that there is room in my life for my ex-husband and his male lover? How could maintaining social correctness include shacking up with Raj and the contractor?

"Think of the shame for Raj," my mother continued. "At the very least, you should try to be supportive of your husband."

I realized then that emotional support from my parents was not forthcoming. My inner voices advised me to embrace the circumstances and move on. But I remained indignant. Could we not have focused on my loss just this one evening, instead of turning it into a pity party for Raj? Who was I fooling? It is against the rules of Indian culture to give me permission to cry at my own party. Even Sita, the ideal woman, remains ideal only as long as she follows in the footsteps of Ram.

As I began to explore my newfound freedom over the next few months, grief and loss propelled me through a downward spiral. The baggage was immense and intensified by the following: A divorced woman is taboo in our society, both inside and outside of the geographical borders of India. Our friends and family presumed that I'd tapped Raj with a gay stick, and I felt the commensurate chill. Sunday morning phone calls, invitations to charity lunches, and social Friday evenings noticeably dried up. Even when I did make it to an event, the distance between other Indians and myself hung like a thick black cloud that refused to produce rain.

But then I heard a knocking at the door. It was Raj.

"Open the door to him," said Hannah. "He needs your help in getting through this as much as you need his."

She was right. Being gay is also taboo in Indian society. What was the purpose of our long friendship if we could not face the truth, align our agendas, and transcend this moment?

Raj and I began to talk about all the things that we should have experienced before we were forced into marriage by our families. For the first time, I realized just how scared he had been to face the truth all these years, and how much guilt he had suffered for pushing me into a corner. If I had to build strength to face rejection for being a divorced woman, Raj had to build strength to face being the person he was born to be. It was amazing just how much we had in common.

Together we waded through the thick marshes of our separate journeys. On the way, I finally began to see my surroundings unfold in silent lucidity.

Raj will continue to be my shopping buddy, my tax consultant, and my best friend. I finally broke out of the Sita syndrome and began to explore a world of non-Indian men who were waiting to woo me with wine and roses. None of them fit the image of the "perfect Indian man" but then when you go through the fire, you naturally come out with a whole new perspective on perfection. Breaking out of the Sita syndrome finally meant looking at the world from Sita's eyes, rather than the eyes of Indians who idolize her.

Today is my forty-first birthday. It is a year since I was set free by Raj, whom I thought was the perfect man. Sita proved her faithfulness to Ram by going through fire. When she emerged, however, she made the choice to leave him, bringing an end to the story of the *Ramayana*. When I emerged from my own fire, I made the choice to remain faithful not to Raj . . . but to his essence and to the latest incarnation of our relationship. Unlike the *Ramayana*, this is actually where my story begins.

Happy Divorce-iversary

kate mcdade

So many of my friends are hell-bent on mourning their wedding anniversaries. Not just my married friends—my divorced ones, too. I have to admit, I don't mourn; I celebrate the anniversary of my divorce. Not out of spite, but out of gratefulness for the grocery-bag-carrying and trash-taking-out life that I live. I write this on a rainy Sunday in Portland, Maine, where I live. I am in a trendy coffee shop called the North Star Cafe, that, rumor has it, Eli Pariser, of MoveOn.org renown, frequents. It's a bustle of happy folks ordering sandwiches and putting dirty plates in the big black bin on top of the trash can.

You wouldn't know that a few years ago, I didn't belong here. I was a gloomy shadow, glued to a wall behind my former husband, nicknamed "The Hippie." But I don't like to dwell on that, because in a few hours I must leave this place and travel to Boston to retrieve the kid, who has been spending the weekend with her dad. So for now, I sit and write, warm and cozy, enjoying my free time. Some funky ambient music starts playing at just the right decibel. And, oh yeah, one more thing. There is a smart, cute, and funny man with shiny green eyes with me. And our fingers just touched in the most romantic way.

I wore combat boots underneath my wedding dress. I was six months pregnant with The Hippie's child, and my feet were too swollen for the dainty white flats I'd brought with me from Boston. Our friends, who had come along with us from Boston to Vegas to witness the thirty-minute wedding ceremony, agreed that flame-stitched Tredair boots might be the perfect accessory for a pregnant bride. They were the "something old." And continuing with tradition, I wore borrowed blue nail polish.

The something new was the only thing I didn't plan. But it seemed all right, because the fetus inside me, who would later turn into my daughter, Nora, was probably growing eyelids, or something. There we had it, the new. Despite my quiet self-assurances that everything was perfect, I didn't send relatives the snapshots that revealed my boots.

Meeting The Hippie a few years prior was a fortuitous accident. By chance, we found ourselves in the same crowded, beer-soaked bar. It was a summer festival in Portland's Old Port neighborhood and The Hippie was on tour with his band. All I wanted to do that day was read, but my roommate had convinced me to get out of the house and visit my favorite bar. She had convinced me to do so by having loud, echoey sex, her door slightly ajar. So there I was, sitting in the back, on a sticky bar stool, reading C. S. Lewis's *Mere Christianity,* and doing my best to ignore the band, when one of their groupies struck up a conversation with me. The groupie said that the bassist was "very single" and a notorious catch. I looked The Hippie up and down. He did have very nice legs.

The Hippie bought me a Corona, and I relocated to Boston to be near him a few months later. Then we were renting a house together. Then the pregnancy happened. Then we were considering breaking up. I think it was Christmas Eve. We were on the bed in our upstairs bedroom, watching *South Park.* Our daughter, approximately the size of a fist, was squirming around inside me while I jonesed for a cigarette. I used to do this thing to get my mind off the cigarettes. I'd fantasize about leaving him, about renting my own apartment, and raising the baby on my own. *I can find a way to make this work. I don't need him*, I'd think. I was lost in a fantasy of myself as a single parent student, reading Machiavelli with my hair in a bun and glasses on, with the baby in a nubby hemp sling. The sling would probably be olive green. Or maybe I could make one out of one of those Palestinian scarves.

I realized he was talking to me. "Here," he repeated, pushing a small blue box embossed with "Shreve Crump & Lowe" into my hand. I think I stared in disbelief. This? This is what it felt like to be on the receiving end of a marriage proposal? I looked at The Hippie, no, not into his eyes, but at his face. Or the side of it. He was averting his eyes, probably thinking about making a Tuno sandwich. I broke the seal and was immediately bowled over by the rush of demons and horrible worldly truths that blasted from the box, and out, out, into the universe.

I will never want a cigarette as badly as I want one right now, I thought, amid the black swirl of evil spirits who were now trying to escape back to hell, probably. I tried it on. It was way too big. The heavy center diamond flopped, falling between my swollen fingers. Until I could get the thing resized, that diamond would always try to point down as if it longed to get back into the ground, and burrow toward whatever hellacious Ivory Coast diamond mine it came from. I sniffed it, imagining the smell of child laborers' sweat, and I said, "Okay." "But," I added, "um, I think you probably spent way too much on this thing."

"Wait, you said you wanted a serious rock or you wouldn't do anal."

"Yeah, but this looks like a Passat."

"Well, it nearly is a Passat."

"With leather?"

"No. But definitely a CD player. And electric windows."

i wore red pumps to my divorce; it just seemed right.
Pouncing on the opportunity to change my whole look, I bought
eleven pairs of red pumps, in all styles, from peep-toe stacked heel
to D'Orsay. I have been wearing them every day, just like that single
mom character in *Chocolat*. The kid was a few years old by the
time we finally got around to making our loveless nonrelationship
legal, but we didn't bring her to the divorce, because it would've just
seemed sadder. The room was empty but for me, The Hippie, the
judge, and the bailiff. We read our divorce vows to each other and
then the judge asked, "Is there anything else?" I told him I wouldn't
really feel like the marriage had been spiritually undone without
the seven-foot-tall Elvis who'd married us there to sing "Love Me
Tender," but replacing the word "love" with "divorce." The bailiff
snorted into his coffee. The Hippie said we could go get some Elvis
records to play backward, if we had time before we had to pick up
Nora from the baby sitter. The judge waited patiently for us to work
out who would pay for the record, since I didn't have any Elvis on
vinyl and neither did The Hippie, and then he pronounced us ex-
husband and ex-wife. And that was that.

Walking out of the courtroom, just two single folks headed
to the record store, it occurred to me how unceremonious getting
married and divorced can be. It had taken The Hippie and I just
over one hour, total.

That night, after I put Nora to bed, I did not cry or lament what
had been lost. I did not wish I could be back in that house in Boston,
every night with him on our hard mattress watching *Comedy Central*,
and every day suffering through vapid neighborhood mothers'
groups. I felt like celebrating my new legitimate singleness. It was
garbage night, so I took out the trash, slipping on a fabulous pair of
four-inch cherry red Mary Janes. It had been The Hippie's job to do
this, way back when. But I didn't feel sorry for having lost the service.
Out on the curb, I saw my neighbors' recycle bin and noticed that
they were throwing out a flattened box from a set of wine glasses. It
still had a tiny bit of silver wrapping paper attached. I wondered if

they were having a happy anniversary or a sad one. Once everything was fabulously arranged on the curb, I went inside and proceeded to design the coolest engraved divorce announcements that the world had ever seen. I would send announcements to everyone, especially the relatives who hadn't received wedding photos.

The next day, at the mall registry desk, I tried to register myself as a "divorcée." The customer service guy said, "There is no registry service set up for that. Now if you are a bride, yes ma'am. Babies, check. But we have nothing for divorced people. I dunno, maybe they have that down in Boston?"

There were so many things I would need for my new identity as a divorcée. Therapy. Silk blouses. Condoms. College. Maybe a set of Egyptian cotton towels with my initials embroidered on them in hot pink.

I decided to buy myself a "divorcement" ring. My left ring finger hungered for the ultimate antithesis to a wedding band. I searched for weeks before settling on a huge sapphire from QVC set in filigree. I decided in lieu of cards and gifts commemorating my rebirth as a single mom, I would cherish my single status, and never let it think—not for a moment—that I wanted anything else.

Things have been going very well as we approach the milestone of The Hippie's and my five-year divorce anniversary. The kid is able to read and write and has not taken up smoking or vandalism as a result of our failed matrimony. When she was three, she went through a short obsession with weddings and begged me to buy her a miniature wedding gown so that she could pretend to marry her dad. I said believe me, marriage is not going to solve all your problems. She was like, Mom, you of all people ought to know that it's not the commitment, it's the ceremony. Of course I understood completely. That's why I think it would be really excellent if The Hippie and I could bring everyone together and renew our divorce in honor of our divorce-iversary. We could do it on the beach. Or in one of the places where we used to argue a lot, like our old living room back in Boston. I suggested this to The Hippie and he demanded to know if it was something my attorney had planned, as a way of reinstating my transitional alimony. The nerve!

I said, "No, Hippie, this is just about the way I feel about you and the way you feel about me. We do not love each other. We do not love each other *very much* and we should share that with the people closest to us."

He said, "Can we talk about this later? I have another call coming in."

i am at the coffee shop with the delicious green-eyed man. We have ordered sandwiches and soup. Some jazz musicians are setting up on the little stage. The families are heading out and some chess players have taken over our side of the dining room. In a few minutes I will leave to go get my girl. The Hippie will be waiting with her at South Station. They will say goodbye from our bus queue and they will calmly embrace before he disappears off toward the trains. She will show me the "snow globes" she has made out of Poland Spring bottles and I will describe, with exaggerated humor, the calamity that ensued when I discovered that our kitten had destroyed an entire box of sugar I'd left on the kitchen counter. "It was while I was at a café, writing," I'll say.

"What were you writing about, dinosaurs?"

"Well, kinda. But it was more about how much fun I have taking out the trash and wearing red high heels. And most of all, it was about how much, every single year, I appreciate the life I have. With you."

I think of myself as a divorce success story. Not because I have pulled myself up by my Ugg straps, out of that painful, depressing hole that is single motherhood—not at all. If you want to look at it in terms of financial well-being, then my life is kind of an infinite pit of despair. And if you're looking for a fighting spirit, you're going to be disappointed. Because I am not some awe-inspiring survivor-of-a-failed-mega-commitment-turned-superhero. But, I do carry in my own groceries. And I take out my own trash. And it is me who checks to make sure the doors are locked every night and that the kid gets to school every morning. Somehow I manage to keep us happy. Plus? No anal.

My Arizona
theo pauline nestor

once, at a party, someone asked my friend laura where she grew up. She answered, "Oh, Arizona really," which I thought was odd, because I knew that she was from the East Coast. When I asked her about it later, she said, "I lived on the East Coast as a kid, but then we moved to Arizona, and that's when I grew up. My dad got sick and my parents needed me."

For some reason, I always remembered this, partly because I was struck by the truth of the idea that while growing up is a long process, many of us go through a galvanizing period that we enter as a child and come out the other side as an adult. For me—always a late bloomer—this growing up came at forty-two when my husband and I had a very sudden divorce.

Black Tuesday came without warning, as these dark days tend to do. You don't see it coming and later you realize how yes, yes, the signs had been there all along. My husband had a persistent poker habit that we'd struggled with early in our marriage, and at one point—six years earlier—we'd almost split up, but with the help of counseling and his determination to recover, we'd made it through.

As far as I knew, it was all in the distant past, until about four o'clock on this September afternoon, when I checked my bank balance over the phone. It started with a hundred dollar withdrawal that didn't make sense and over the next two days the trouble snowballed to tens of thousands of dollars that he gambled away. Within two weeks of Black Tuesday, we legally separated, and some months later, we divorced.

Up until then I'd done short stints of growing up here and there by facing challenges that scared me—grad school, marriage (turns out I was right to be afraid!), motherhood—but now I wasn't choosing the higher or the harder road. I was picking the one that *terrified* me. Luckily or unluckily, I already knew from watching my older sister's experience as a single mother that the relentless responsibility of one-handed parenting wasn't for me. But wanting out of my marriage *and* to live with my two children, I chose to be a divorced single mother, a state of affairs that has become my personal Arizona.

In *When Harry Met Sally,* Carrie Fisher's character explains to Sally that when you're married, you're stagnant and set in your ways, but single, you're more in the world. You try things, you experiment, you might order sushi even if you're the type of person who eats nothing but cheeseburgers. I think this is true. Since my divorce, I've started yoga, dined on Ethiopian food, installed a security system, enrolled in a continuing education Spanish class, and sipped tequila on the beach in Baja, all by-products of my newly single state in one way or another.

Divorce can be a time of a personal renaissance, even feverish individualism. At times divorce ushers in this ego-driven Me that zooms around town to a soundtrack of "Things are going to be soooooooooo much better now that I'm at the helm." In the first days of our split, I felt this heady sense of empowerment that came from knowing I was no longer signed on for all of my husband's problems, especially his reckless spending. My money was *my* money, what little there was of it. When I put money in the bank, it stayed there until I took it out. I vowed to have a zero balance on my credit card at the end of each month, a goal that seemed as impossible as defying gravity when I was married. I paid cash for nearly everything, keeping the crisp twenties in an envelope, on the back of which there was a list of where I spent what. So clean! So simple! So postmarriage thrilling.

But the thrill of this soon faded, in part because there was very little money to so meticulously manage, and in part because I quickly realized that while I was pretty good at keeping track of where money went, I had plenty of problems I didn't know how to deal with. The highlights of which would include: a molding basement carpet, unemployment, a laurel hedge about to bust out of the stratosphere, and an obstinate case of insomnia.

One day, while walking past my high shaggy lawn, I found myself reflexively thinking my husband should get out there Right Away and mow it. And then in a moment of startling clarity, I realized I had no husband, and if the lawn was ever to be mowed again, it would be me who did it. And there was more—it wasn't just the lawn—this was true for *all* my problems. They were now *my* problems. If I fixed them, great. But otherwise, my troubles would remain hovering in a crummy status quo or they would—as troubles are wont to do—compound and multiply. My life was my own in every positive sense of the phrase, but in every negative one as well. I had no one left to blame.

In Caroline Knapp's memoir *Drinking: A Love Story,* she describes a man early in his sobriety who finds himself shaking off alcohol's inertia. Slowly it dawns on him that he can do small things to make his life better. One day he realizes that the nonfunctioning spigot in his front yard could be fixed with merely a few simple turns of the wrench. Not long after, he's watering his now verdant front yard, amazed at the apathy that had held him in a choke hold during his drinking days.

When I read this passage not long after my divorce, I was struck by how well it described me in the aftermath of my marriage. I was stumbling out of a fog of "that's just the way it is" into a searingly bright world of problems that had grown from inattention. But I was also present to their vividly inherent solvability. I could paint dingy walls, complain to the principal, call a plumber, plant a bed of dahlias and lilies. I could make things better!

But I'm not a recovering alcoholic (or alcoholic, in case you're wondering). Why should this guy's experience match mine so well? A little light reading in the area of codependency quickly supplied the answer. Being married to someone with an addiction is much like having an addiction oneself: You're so focused on something you're powerless over—or in this case, some*one*—that you overlook all that you *can* change. Thus, the Serenity Prayer. Thus, my ever-increasing To Do list.

Yet I began to see that the roots of my It's-all-too-much-trouble mind-set predated my marriage. Whether it be from divorce or alcoholism in my family tree or some other source, I'm not sure. But I do know that I've had a long history with a tenacious form of apathy. I've had to force myself to vote, to keep my mind on task during meetings, to recycle, to take my complaints to the appropriate authorities. To give myself credit, I've done the right things that good citizens do most of the time, but always in the back of my mind a devil whispers, "What difference does it make?" It's an adolescent mind-set. Nothing to brag about, that's for sure.

And now the most obvious example of my juvenile foot-dragging was standing (shakily) all around me: the one hundred-year-old farmhouse I'd been waiting for someone (my husband?) to repair. As I made my daily circuit from the laundry room to the kitchen and the kids' room, I was assaulted by all that had to be addressed—curling wallpaper, leaky pipes, cracked single-pane windows, and stained linoleum from the Edwardian era.

The scariest place of all, though, was the house's bathroom, of the tiny '70s marbleized beige sink, stained ceiling, broken light fixture, threadbare carpet, and a teensy tiny cupboard far inadequate to the task of storing a growing number of girl things. My husband and I had spoken intermittently of a future renovation in the way some people speak of heaven—eventually the details would be revealed but until then we can only entertain dreamy images of what this halcyon place might look like.

But a few weeks after I discovered the toilet was dripping into the basement (remember the moldy carpet?), I was seized by an idea: I could renovate the bathroom. The usual thrumming chorus of *It-can't-be-done* started up accompanied by a soloist who sang out in trilling soprano *Where-would-you-even-start?* Then one day I was having my brows done (yes, some things *can* be fixed) and the Brow Woman was complaining about all the subcontractors who'd been working on her nightmare renovation. They left doors unlocked, arrived late, took lunch breaks that extended past the ten-minute pause allowed chain gang members—really, the litany of their shortcomings revealed much more about her high standards than their failings, I thought. Something inside me piped up and asked, "Was there any one of them who was good?"

Yes, and his name was John.

John arrived a few days later. He was as ill-prepared for me as I was for him, and in that way he was perfect. Unlicensed, unshaven, a cigarette perpetually in hand, John bid low and then glanced over at my daughters watching a movie on the couch and lowered the bid. He told me no matter what happened it would never cost me more. He was about forty but lacked that "professionalism" that is so often mistaken for maturity. He was awkward, unsure, tentative, but still he seemed to know what he was doing and, let's not forget, he had the stamp of approval from the Brow Woman.

You've probably heard this one before: Cheap, good, and fast— pick two because you'll never get all three together. So you can probably see where this is headed. Yes, it was going to be within my budget and in the end—just, wait—it would be the bathroom dreams are made of, but would the end ever come? Over the next few weeks, John became a fixture in my home, usually calling out my name in a plaintive tone whenever I was just about to write some profound sentence. When he wasn't in my bathroom, kitchen, or out on my porch smoking a Camel, we were making yet another run to the jumbo home improvement store. But it was there, in Home Depot to be exact, that I fell in love with the possibility of it all. The scent of fresh cut lumber, the whine of the saws, the dizzying selection of hooks, hinges, and sundry hardware lit in me a fire of potential of all that could be better in my world. Suddenly, life's chaos shook itself into a neatly placed order of fluorescent-lit aisles that stretched from doorknobs to eternity. *This* was the place, I could see now, where problems were solved. *This* is why men like these places. The answer to almost everything that troubled me—save unemployment and insomnia—was here, at the Depot.

The project took not the two weeks I'd originally imagined, but closer to two months. How this is possible I'm still not sure, although at one point John had to jack up the house(!) to make the bathroom floor level, and that cost us time (but, as he'd assured me, not a penny more than his original estimate). Finally the bathroom was finished, and it was the first time that my personality had manifested itself in porcelain and 1920s-inspired tiles, and the thrill was intoxicating. Every night I took a long bath in my soaker bathtub (two inches deeper than a normal tub!) and thought to myself: "Look what I've done." And then: "What else can I do?"

It's been over three years since then and almost five years since the Big Split, and a great deal has happened, some of it my doing and some just the forces of life madly at work. Today in my living room in Seattle, my boyfriend, my two daughters (thirteen and ten), and I are having a quiet writing time. On the sofa my adolescent daughter, Natalie, with the requisite shank of hair covering one eye, is sitting cross-legged over her journal, a few feet from my boyfriend, who's working on his book. Beside me on the loveseat is my ten-year-old, Jessie, whom I gather is writing a song, as every few minutes she mouths some lyrics and strums on an air guitar. It is a quiet Sunday morning except for the every-eleven-seconds-single-bark of the dog down the street and the dryer upstairs that is spinning our clothes together—socks, kids' underwear, and boyfriend's shorts, atoms of static electricity bouncing between our individual identities, pulling us into one.

An hour ago things were not so calm. Their dad is coming to pick them up this afternoon and during this coming week, my ten-year-old will leave for camp, so Kent and Jessie and I ran in different directions through the house gathering sunscreen, sleeping bag, riding boots (too small), and the other million things on the list while intermittently Natalie ran through to report various problems—she can't poop, her bicycle tire is flat, she doesn't have anything to wear. She's anxious, well, we all are. We always are on transition days when they go back and forth between the two houses, but Natalie is the family spokesperson for all our anxiety, the person who has to articulate all we don't want to admit. It's not easy.

And Jessie is the kid that deals with it all by trying to do everything right, which isn't easy either, especially at the age of ten.

When I left my husband almost five years ago, I had no idea how our family was going to evolve. The future was a black yawning hole. I either couldn't visualize at all, or it visited me as the Ghost of Christmas future—ominous, chain-rattling, and full of dark promise. A single mom, with sketchy job skills and two daughters in tow. The whole world is stuffed full of stories of just how fast the whole thing could go south. But it hasn't. I don't know quite how, sometimes, but we are making it—even thriving. Two nights ago Natalie read a beautiful piece about friendship, with boldness and poise in front of a crowded theater; Jessie has a green stripe belt in tae kwon do and the kindness of the Dalai Lama. And a few months ago, I published my first book.

Are things soooooooooo much better now? No, in some ways, life is still challenging, mostly because of the stress divorce has brought my children. But like the guy with the working spigot, I'm discovering I *can* make my life better. And, it *is* my life now.

*

Young Marvieds
sally blakemore

in 1967, the "summer of love," twenty years after my birth, women still had no real, practical human rights in the bizarre land of Texas. You were required to take your husband's name and couldn't qualify for a credit card unless it was through your husband. The '60s sexual revolution was just dropping anchor. I was happily living with my college boyfriend and going to undergrad in Fine Arts at the University of Texas at Austin. It all seemed so natural. Innocence overtook me, and I told my parents that he and I were sharing an apartment. Why marry? I liked my name and I wanted to keep it for my artistic identity.

My parents showed up at our garage apartment, in the form of an unannounced violent entry, my father's screaming fury so ferocious that my future husband jumped out of a second-story window and ran for his life. I, however, stayed alone, for three hours of screaming, humiliating attacks that they now call verbal abuse. My mother remained in the car, reading a *Family Style* magazine with her fingers in her ears.

After the angry scene, they wanted us to "Dress up! Act normal!" and they would "treat" us to dinner like nothing had happened. But my boyfriend declined to join us, and we went on without him. I remember putting pancake makeup on my crying eyes. Water and oil do not mix. I wondered, blinking blankly, "Who is looking out of these eyes?" I didn't recognize myself.

Twenty years later, sans eye contact, Mother confessed her experience of that day to me. She told me, as she traced her pearly beige fingernail over the skirt of her evening gown and flipped through a womenswear catalog, "I thought Dad was beating you, but there was nothing *I* could do. I didn't really know if you would come out alive."

My future husband's parents, from New York, were more sophisticated than mine. They had lived in Japan and Hawaii. They saw us as the twenty-year-old kids that we were. They thought I was cute and different. My family, wounded, uneducated Southern Baptists with no grip on reality, considered me an unclean, used whore and decreed that I needed to get married to be cleansed in the eyes of the world and the Lord.

I was too naive to realize I had my own life to live. My family was boundaryless, with no privacy. Their hypocritical values did not pertain to me at all, but I took them on. My boyfriend and I decided to take off to Santa Fe, New Mexico. We had to think about it. We felt tortured and slimed.

On the top floor of a beautiful old hotel, filled with Nigerians on an exchange tour, I broke down. The trauma had been bigger than I realized. He, too, was so confused by my father's overbearing demands and my hysterical begging for acceptance and "cleansing" that he at last agreed.

Back in Austin we felt the verdict had come down. There was really no choice. It was like being told by a doctor you were dying and you needed poison pumped into your veins. I arranged for Dr. Frank Buck, our veterinarian and friend, an ex-Episcopal priest, forty years our senior, to marry us. No romantic proposal, no ring, no cherished vows, just a new off-white bias cut dress whimsically printed with roosters, an appointment at the vet.

The old county courthouse smelled of cigars and marble floor wax. The clerk directed us to sign our names in an oversize book, its leather cover scuffed and branded with the shape of Texas. She swung a large plastic bag of corporate sample products for the "Young Marrieds" onto the white speckled Formica countertop. On the customer's side, the surface was worn through to the second layer, apparently by forearms reaching to get at the wedding bag. A dinner-plate-size, intertwined gold wedding ring set was printed on the front of it. A white dove flew toward the handle, holding white ribbons. Inside: a package of free "douche powder," a little box of Spic and Span cleanser, a pink kitchen sponge, a tiny bottle of Lysol, a box of some kind of cheesy macaroni "For the new cook!" and an envelope of mindless, dull recipe cards with pictures of "Man's Meals."

We drove to the veterinary clinic in silence, our documents in hand. As we climbed the cool concrete steps, we were met by a burly and comical Dr. Buck standing, covered in dog hair, on a bristly welcome mat. He hugged us and asked us to wait in a lovely Victorian living room. Mrs. Buck came in to offer us a cup of tea and a Bible.

As his wedding attire, my boyfriend wore his favorite blue jeans, off-white canvas patches ironed over the ripped-out knees. They looked like fresh flour tortillas. We both sat perfectly still, balancing our tea cups in silence.

Dr. Buck came into the room and we assembled by the bay window, which overlooked the large, lush, acid green yard. A stifling hot breeze barely moved the foliage. I was sick to my stomach; my palms were sweaty with fear and terror. I believed I truly was a whore. This little, stupid ceremony was not going to work the magic of cleansing and restoring my virginity for future use. Mrs. Buck, serving as our witness, stood beside us in a fretful kind of way, in her Sunday best.

"Dearly Beloved. . . . " The vet/priest spoke in a sort of haven't-done-this-in-a-while kind of way, clearing his throat and dabbing his bottom lip with an almost see-through handkerchief. Holding each other's sweaty hands, at Dr. Buck's instructions, we listened to each word. I could feel the calloused guitar fingers on my fiancé's hand and the ridges in his fingerprints.

Halfway through our ceremony, a frantic, screeching white station wagon careened over the curb and onto the shady grass. A chaotic family of two adults and three children sprang out, doors left open in their wake. We peered around Dr. Buck, whose back was to the window. He turned around as a white bulldog, wrapped in an old, blood-soaked blanket, was rushed up the stairs into his clinic. This dog was delivered like some kind of odd sacrificial lamb, right into my sacred wedding ceremony.

The beautiful, quaint old Texas living room, full of doilies draping mahogany furniture, redolent with the sour smell of decaying varnish, turned into an emergency ward for this dog that was hit by a car. They closed the upright piano. It had been a dust-free room. Dog hair flying, it was now filled with contrasting hysterias. It was a sign, but I was too young to recognize it.

At that moment, the vet/priest excused himself to tend to the injuries in a desperate surgical maneuver. His wife excused herself to prepare the surgical tools and change out of "my good dress!" My half-husband headed for the door. It was a reprieve—the cell had been sprung—and he was free! God saved us from my father's wrath. But out of confusion and integrity, we stayed. I still wonder: What if we had just run for our lives?

An hour later, the dog was saved. The relieved family apologized to us, the "happy couple," for their bloody intrusion, and Dr. Buck moved on to resuscitate our ceremony.

The ceremony ended with a kiss. We joined the Bucks in the kitchen. A little flowers-and-fruit oilcloth dressed a small table by the window, which was topped by an old brown plastic radio. Now in a housedress, Mrs. Buck made us a fresh cup of tea. Dr. Buck had some old postcards of his home veterinary clinic. He said we could send one to our parents to let them know we had tied the knot. We both wrote with a nearly dry blue ballpoint pen on the glossy surface. The ink came and went as we wrote, "We are married!" The vet/priest put a stamp on the card and mailed it for us. The elder couple, arms around each other's hips, stood in the doorway waving at us as we left.

We were exhausted, emotionally. There was no celebration, no honeymoon, just a sick kind of depression. We went home to our dogs and took a nice walk to clear our heads. A day later, at 8:00 A.M., we awoke to my father standing at the foot of our marriage bed. He had let himself into our rented house and stood screaming, "Is this your husband? Is this your husband?" He knew full well it was my husband.

"I will pay for the divorce!" he decreed.

A window jumper no more, my husband threw my father out: A very insane father, full of guilt for his own life's secrets and choices that he projected onto me, his scapegoat.

Although it had not been our decision, my husband's parents were delighted they had a new daughter. My father calmed down after a year, although he never apologized. By then my husband and I were having difficulties. We had had no real plans for the marriage. Neither of us wanted children. We were both struggling to define ourselves as artists and individuals.

In 1972, my father told me about a painting contest he heard about on ham radio at 4:00 A.M. Sponsored by Deutsche Welle, the prize was a trip to the Munich Olympics. I won it. I wanted to go to Germany alone, but my husband paid his own way and joined me there. He became ill immediately on arrival, and I left him at the hotel and started my tour without him. I had no compassion at this point. I was turning into my mother.

The trip to Germany was heartbreaking and exhilarating, for many reasons. I had never been to Europe before. I encountered terrorism for the first time in the form of Black September. A pilgrimage to Bergen-Belsen made me fall on all fours in a gasping sob that lasted for three hours straight. A person recognizes when something is dead or revivable.

It was time to return to Austin reality. At the airport, my husband's ticket was not yet confirmed, and mine was. I left him there, and as I boarded the plane, the sound system played "Stand by Your Man" by Tammy Wynette. I was numb from too much irony. I would later learn about synchronicity.

Just as we were about to take off, he appeared at the door of the plane. We decided on the return flight that we would divorce. My young husband knew the marriage was moribund and said, "Bring me the papers and I will sign them."

It was gut-wrenching, and I had no one to talk to. My poor mother had no compassion, as we've noted. After my father's initial response, he had finally gotten used to his daughter's odd husband. I took refuge with my mother's twin sister, and her worldlier, flapper sister who both showed me compassion and kept a sense of humor concerning the situation. My aunts told me, "People get divorced every day. It just didn't work out." They knew nothing of the outburst that forced us into marriage. No one talked about that.

So I filed for a divorce. Got a lawyer, "irreconcilable differences" was the cause. We wanted it over fast. We had no money. I wanted my dogs, stereo, and art supplies, and my guitar and accordion. He wanted his mandolin and nothing really but to get the hell out of the mess.

The day before my court date, my lawyer tried to commit suicide and failed, which delayed our divorce for six months. After her recovery, she contacted me. She was so shattered and weak I had to hold her up as she entered the courthouse.

The divorce was granted. My husband packed his boxes and found a nice apartment. I remember standing in the doorway of our rental house as he walked toward the curb. Simultaneously, I felt both relief and loss. Looking back at me as he lumbered away, he asked, "Do you think we can still have sex sometimes?" "No," I said. And it was over.

I have now been married, for thirty years, to my third husband. My second divorce is another chapter completely. My first husband is like a cousin to me. We are still some kind of "family," more so from being artists and sharing our youth together than any kind of marriage vow. He just remarried at sixty-one, and he and his new wife will come visit us next year. Sometimes friendship is much stronger than marriage.

That dog survived my wedding and my lawyer survived my divorce. My ex and I survived all that pressed us into marriage, and we fortified ourselves through our exit of same. My family's agony is understood now, and forgiven. People have flaws and they act within their flaws. I have learned that anything real that comes from being alive is sacred.

Broken Stove House
elisabeth kinsey

i'm watching my ex-husband's cat, still half my cat, a big fuzzy hairball of a Maine coon named Randall, while my ex is on one of the first vacations in his life. He traveled to Vietnam with a friend—for the food. I remember begging him about four years into our marriage, "Can we just have spaghetti instead of pho?" Don't get me wrong, I love the stuff (a staple noodle soup in Vietnam)—I can even eat it twice a week. But he was passionate.

As I push open the heavy, resistant front door, Randall recognizes me and acts like I never left five years ago. He saunters over to the orange rug and plops down, presenting an overstuffed belly to rub.

I'm always shocked to enter my old house and find it exactly how I left it, except much dustier and more cluttered. If I had kept the house, I would've redecorated or sold it and moved. When a friend of ours asked my ex why this house looked like a "Beth Museum," he said, "Men will take any decorating scheme if it's already there, regardless of whether it's their ex-wife's, or Bozo the Clown's."

I looked around at what used to be our dining room, devoid of my grandmother's dining set, or any replacement. The wall sconces I bought at Pier 1 were still perfectly even—I used a level to hang them. Although, now a cobweb linked them. The small loveseat I re-covered with sage green damask and matching pillows sat nakedly against the wall, unused. All my plants, in every room, were kept up, but their leaves had grown mangy and out of control. Not to mention the living room—its state was in so much of a time warp that I expected some other, duplicate "me" to turn the corner at any moment.

This house was still full of me. He just lurked there, eating, watching TV, and hanging out with that ghostly clone Beth who doesn't clean or buy anything new. I remember reading in our bed on Saturday mornings, while the birds sang in our back yard. He brought me coffee and left me to my own devices for hours. He read the newspaper and watched Saturday afternoon movies—and would have done that all day if I didn't insist on driving to the mountains.

His instructions are on the yellow legal pad left behind for me. It lists myriad ways to open broken doors tentatively so as not to break them completely, thus keeping them somewhat operational. That is, until they fall off their hinges. When they do, he'll be pushed into that extraterrestrial world of action. Perhaps he'll have some old pangs of feeling. What does this remind him of? His wife, who always made him do things.

I am guilty of that. I can slip into that married person I was, in this kitchen. I can see her, feverishly wiping the counter to catch every crumb. When we were first married, I walked into that house with an extreme need for order stemming from my own cyclonic family of six kids, all trying to be heard. "Please, God, bring me a beautiful black horse," was my childhood prayer every night, kneeling by my bed. The horse would carry me away to a clean Utopia where my stuff would never be touched and always be in the same place and condition in which I left it.

That came out in therapy. My dynamic with my ex (I'll call him Bob) followed in the footsteps of my role model (sorry, Mom). She talked when people were talking. She also asked my father to fix household items and when he didn't, she stormed out of the house. Then we'd experience an hour or two without parents and my mother would slink back, do the chore herself, and that was that. When Bob cooked, he was the typical chef. At the restaurant, a chef pitches the dirty dishes into a bin that Manny washes. I became Manny. I protested at first. "There are crumbs on the counters." "I'll get them later," Bob would say. His "later" didn't match my "later" (within twenty minutes), and I would angrily wipe up the crumbs.

I didn't know these types of actions, small though they appeared, strung into a long necklace of complaints that ended up as a noose around Bob's neck. By the time the weekend came around and I'd angrily cleaned each speck in our house, my straightforward query, "Can we go to Estes Park?" ended up being the last straw, and rage was all he had left for reaction.

I always wanted to leave after these fits. Once, he held my arm so tightly that it caused a bruise in the exact shape of each fingertip. He made it up to me, though, by cooking an amazing meal, therefore vindicating himself, washing the slate clean, and starting the engine over (though he still did not clean up).

I wasn't always able to look back at those times and acknowledge my part in this crazy behavior. I didn't get to this objectivity without walking through fire.

randall jumped on the kitchen counter. i never used to let him do that. I snooped around. There was the bread machine I bought, still untouched. And the Picasso print on the wall we fought over. That was an issue we brought up in couples therapy. Bob was angry I bought it.

"What is worth spending your money on?" I'd asked.

And the answer I always got was, 'I dunno.'

Then our therapist, George, would paraphrase for him, "I think maybe Bob is feeling frustrated that you both can't come to an agreement on your finances or budget, right, Bob?"

Then Bob would nod "Yes."

"Oh good. You can translate his 'I dunno.' That's great. Can we take you home with us and you can continue to translate for him while we draw up a budget?"

after another explosive fight where i threw a vase into the driveway and threatened to drive to the state line so I wouldn't be in the same state as him, I went to see George alone. I'd asked him, "Do normal people live in filth and never go out on the weekends?"

He asked me a hard question back.

"What is normal? Better yet, what would a perfect life look like?"

I used to nanny on and off, supporting myself through college, in a wealthy neighborhood. While the little, overly-smart towhead five-year-old poured me fake tea, I'd look out the tall window at the mansion across the street, their landscaper bending down to dust a random piece of cut grass off the curb. I related this house to my therapist.

"Everything in its place and when something breaks, they buy a new one." That's one glimmer of what happiness looked like to me.

"Is that important to you?" George was not smug, only professional.

"Can I just say, it's the only thing that *is* important to me?" Then I related the stove story.

Our '60s "original" stove that came with the house broke in several ways after about three years of use. It was bad, but for years, we got by with the two burners that barely worked. When we were down to one burner hardly lighting even with a lighter, Bob managed to admit that we needed a new stove. At that point, I thought I might be with the wrong person. It reminds me now of Virginia Woolf's *To the Lighthouse,* where the sweet English child asks every day, (and I'll paraphrase) "Are we going to the lighthouse today, mommy?" This trip, promised every morning, never materializes in the book. That would be our stove. "Are we getting a stove this weekend?" Except I wasn't sweet. More like annoyed and crazed.

"It's not the stove. It's us. We are ineffective, unmoving, and don't communicate at all." The day I uttered this in George's office is the same day I started moving my stuff out of our broken stove house. But this was after we bought the new stove and had our last Christmas party.

Every year, since Bob became a chef, he would cook for our friends. It started out as a wine tasting, where everyone brought wine that went well with the dishes he prepared. Then, by the fifth year, it was just Bob slaving away, me running around cleaning cobwebs and getting out punchbowls, and our guests—coming to the best free gourmet Christmas party ever. That last year, I wore tight red silk pants with roses up the side and a sexy bustier. Bob never even looked up from his mushrooms. There he was, hunched over our new stove, ignoring all of our friends. I scanned the room and saw our two good friends who had been married for years kissing and laughing. I'll call them Mary and Lou. Lou whispered in Mary's ear, and she laughed so hard, she almost spewed her drink across the room. Then they flagged down some of our other friends. I couldn't remember the last time Bob and I had laughed mutually about anything, let alone at a public event or party. I couldn't remember the last time I was successful at leading Bob out our front door into a social situation where he'd have to chitchat with other people his age.

After that, a bleak January set in and I wasn't sure what to do. I knew I had to get away. A Berliner friend invited me to visit her, and I bought a ticket immediately. In her high-ceilinged book-lined room, I slept lavishly, then made lists upon lists of goals. I stared at the small grocer across the street, spied on all those happy German people shopping for their daily dinner, and wrote a line in my journal that I still cling to. It might be overused, but it works for me. "A life unexamined is a life unlived." Yes, Socrates. I looked back at myself before Bob; how every step of my life maybe wasn't examined so much as reflective. Hearing my friends in the Berlin apartment on a Saturday morning vacuuming and laughing reminded me of mornings in high school when my brother and I would start the day with our favorite record, then both clean our rooms and maybe go to the mall later. This was all celebration; an engagement with life, where we woke up with a day and were eager to plan it out. How did I, a free-flying, goal-driven, somewhat kooky girl, end up with a stick-in-the-mud who couldn't assess his life if it were scrawled out in a book laid before him?

I didn't bring a watch to Berlin. I wrote in my journal that I wanted to let time go up, through the clouds, hover, and softly fall in the future somewhere. I actively got lost. I deliberately left my U-Bahn map behind me. (The leftover Bob critic in my head murmured words like "irresponsible" or "stupid.") My learned student German came out ill-timed and out of order, but I still got around. I remember feeling light and naughty. Light without the responsibility of directing Bob around Berlin, and naughty for purposely going against any and every logic offered by husbands and people needing to get somewhere. (Bob and I got lost in Venice on our honeymoon. When we finally found San Marco square, we were both so exasperated that I hit him with my umbrella. I didn't even know the phrase "red flag" at that point.)

Lost in Berlin, I found a music shop that sold new and used instruments on a tiny cobbled street. A woman in heels, a skirt, and suit jacket came out, her hair in a pinned blond bun. She clutched a small case and had wedged sheet music under her arm. She smiled and said, "*Tag*," and I returned the greeting. All of a sudden, I was included. I went in to the music shop. It was all I thought it would be. Cheery, quaint, the light slanting in and haloing the woodwind instruments. I walked straight over to the clarinets. Mine broke long ago, right after high school. The shopkeeper, somewhat interrupted, set down his paper and pushed back his glasses. I think he asked me if I needed any help. I shook my head and picked up a case. I asked in my best German if it was wood or plastic. He nodded and shot out a slew of fast information about the clarinet. Needless to say, I bought myself that German clarinet. I felt like I stole it, as if I shouldn't be allowed to have something foreign, so full of potential and fun. It wasn't expensive, but I felt like no money in the world could get it from me. It would be with me the rest of my life.

It took me five hours to find the right street, but I got back to my friend's apartment. The Volkspark with its meandering bike path led me there. *Entschuldigung* also got me through. The phrase translated means "Excuse me" but its root means "fault" or "guilt." It's true. I did carry a certain small guiltiness around with all this freedom, like a stone in my pocket with my husband's lost expression on it.

That was the one thing that kept me with Bob. The lost face he gave me when I left for the store every morning kept me in my marriage for three years longer than I should have been there. The thought of leaving him came with an image of Bob, huddled in the corner, utterly alone in the world, in a dirty and broken house. I felt responsible for his happiness and cleanliness. I couldn't leave him, or he'd die somehow. I wasn't sure how, but it was imminent. The Entschuldigung fueled my shower of gifts for him: white wine, cooking magazines, canisters of pressed German meats.

In the following weeks, my clarinet and I finally left that house. I scanned the living room and knew I was leaving dear things behind. Tears I'd never seen in all our marriage striped his face. He pointed and yelled while standing on that same black brick landing that was the deciding factor when we purchased the house. "I would never leave you," he said. "Even if you were the awfullest person on earth, I wouldn't leave you." He did say "awfullest". Then as an afterthought, "Why did you bring back wine if you knew you were leaving me?" I didn't have an answer. I still felt that rock in my pocket.

In my new, tiny, cheapo apartment, sitting on the floor, I wrote a list: "If anyone ever wants to marry me again." It was a bitter yet honest rant. Here it is verbatim:

You can marry me if . . .

* you don't call me "cunt."
* you don't get mad when you've been awakened because you're snoring.
* you know how to do laundry. (And you know where the laundry basket is.)
* you remember that I'm sleeping at 6:00 A.M. and are quiet.
* you care when I'm sick and check on me now and then to make sure I'm alive—and perhaps even drive me to the emergency room.
* you shave at least three times a week.
* you have your teeth cleaned at least once a year. (And have cavities filled.)
* you go to the doctor when you're very ill or let me take you.
* you go to the doctor, at any time.
* you get your hair cut at least biyearly.
* you know how to fight (i.e., when you're feeling angry, you don't hurl names at me but analyze the feelings of anger and make a list, therefore, turning the fight into a discussion of feelings).
* you don't just identify the newspaper recycling bin but put newspapers into the newspaper recycling bin.
* you know that I have cleaned your lunch plate and it wasn't elves that came in the night and left the kitchen sparkling, therefore motivating you to learn to put your dishes into the dishwasher.
* you have goals.
* you know what a goal is.
* you want to do things for me and aren't put out when I ask for a favor every now and then.
* you let me have a dog.

I needed this list to refer to for the future because every day, for weeks, I thought, "Did I do the right thing?" Another girlfriend going through divorce helped me through some crying jags. "Yes, you did the right thing. Remember the list," she said, and recited it back to me.

After being free for five years, my new list would throw off the whole notion of marriage. It's a social construct. Yes, it can be a special ceremony to reveal strong bonds of love and friendship. But I don't need it now. The person I am today is like a ten-year-old let loose, sitting on a public park lawn with her clarinet, hair unwashed, and barefoot. She doesn't *need* a guy for approval, nor does she necessarily need any material stuff. Her layers of grime, family "shoulds," and past marital shame, like a too tight dress, came off through support from friends, reading, and from therapist George's help.

Now, I have the things that previously marked me as a "selfish" person, like my writing and my office. I garden too long and collect too many cookbooks. I have grand plans and never enough time to pack them in.

I indulge myself now by taking creative writing as a major for my master's degree, even though in the back of my head I hear Bob's voice, "You want fries with that?" I also revel in thanking my boyfriend for taking out the trash, mowing the lawn, and filling the window washer fluid in my car. He's the kind of guy who pulls up to let you off at the entrance when it's raining. I'm not saying I don't have those dark-coated demons come out to tell me I'm not worth anything, to tell me I don't matter. That still happens, but I try to catch myself and write it in a journal.

at bob's house, randall jumps down finally and nudges his dish. He's happy enough, wandering around in his own ingrained rituals. His belly gets rubbed by all manner of people and he gets fed his Friskies Tender Beef Chunks at around nine o'clock every morning. Even though the sink counter in the bathroom is almost to the point anyone would call "filth," the sink itself is maintained, probably because enough washing of hands gets the grime down. It's usable. It works. It's not to the point where my ex turns on the faucet and nothing comes out. In that case, a cosmic fog would descend again, and he'd have memories of other times when forces would push him to motion, where things would get accomplished and he'd feel somewhat unsettled, and then resentful.

I left the house, careful not to shut the screen door, as the broken lock would jam everyone out forever. I turned a blind eye to the piles of weeds that overtook my expensive, manicured landscaping. A fleeting picture flashes, one of me helping him out, clearing weeds, planting pansies, little bits of color in his life that he could enjoy again. But then it's gone. It's not my responsibility.

My obligations are many these days: homework, friends, a Mastiff named Pasha, and two kittens that constantly fight. I have a sweet person in my life who helps me learn about myself daily. My biggest obligation is to myself. To go barefoot, kick off my shoes, and feel that cool, textured grass against my post-divorce skin. The grass is what it is. There are no double meanings, no games, no saying one thing to mean the other. Just grass against my feet, a clarinet, and me.

Marriage Is a Job

leigh anne jasheway-bryant

let's face it, marriage is a job.

In the beginning, to get either a job or a spouse, you have to dress better than you normally do, hide your true personality long enough to make it past the first interview, and keep secret the big things that you're sure will be deal breakers. You know the things I mean. Like the fact that you can't take a bath because your Elvis thimble collection has taken up residence in the tub. Or that little quirk you have where you save your cats' hair in Zip-Loc baggies that you label by cat and hide in shoe boxes in your closet.

If you do make it to "I'm hired!" or "I do," with both a job and a relationship you usually get a honeymoon period, during which no one really expects you to know what you're doing. You get to take it slowly and learn along the way. It feels like heaven, but it doesn't last an eternity. Not even half an eternity.

When you work in an office, you often get a nameplate to let people know who you are. As a woman, if you choose to change or hyphenate your name, you could actually use a nameplate to remind yourself who you are. Your wedding ring is like a business card—it announces to the world that you are now working as Mrs. Somebody, which is a completely different job than the one you had when you were Ms. Somebody. There's less flirting and more tearing your hair out over how to pay bills, for example. You have to report both your new job and your new marriage to Social Security.

And anyone who has managed to stay married longer than (insert your favorite short celebrity marriage here) can tell you that everyday married life can be just as boring and frustrating as the 9-to-5 world. There are power struggles, people behaving like children (they may, in fact, BE children), changes in management, walkouts, conversations about what constitutes sexual harassment, etc. There isn't a married person in the world who hasn't dreamed of not clocking in for a day—or a week or a decade.

Why is it then that with all the similarities between marriage and jobs, when someone decides to change careers, we admire her ambition and encourage them to follow their bliss, but if someone makes the same choice about a spouse, we feel sad and disappointed? Why do we say "failed marriage" but not "failed occupation?" I myself have had three careers and three husbands (in both cases, I still have the third). For the most part, whenever I have announced that I was changing jobs, people have been happy for me. No tears were shed, no one suggested I seek counseling, learn to be more agreeable, or just buckle down and give it another four or five years. Which, of course, is exactly what happened when I announced my divorces.

My first career was as an "Economic Analyst" for a bank. That sounds so '80s, doesn't it? Well, it was. The title was short for "We needed another woman in the department to make it seem like we're not sexists, and this one had the right education and didn't seem like she'd cause too much trouble because she's young and naïve." That title was way too long for my business cards. Oh, wait, I didn't get business cards. Maybe THAT was the problem. Every day I trudged downtown to the bank wearing a navy skirt suit with a matching bow tie. This was the era of women dressing like men so we'd be taken seriously in the business world. The then-famous book *Dress for Success* had just come out, and women everywhere were wondering just how big their shoulder pads would have to be for them to get ahead in the business world. And whether they'd need to stuff a sock in their undies. What the book's author didn't tell us was that we were dressing for her success, not ours. I was just out of college and didn't know any better, so I went along for the ride. These days, I'd just laugh and beat a hasty exit. With age does come some wisdom. Or at least the option to refuse doing things that are stupid just because someone tells you to. I did what the bank asked me to do—worked long hours for little money and no acknowledgment and pretended that my male boss with the Narcissus complex was as talented and good-looking as he thought he was. It was an Oscar-worthy performance on my part, although I was not recognized by the Academy. I managed to stay married to the job for eighteen months. During that time I learned a few things about myself: (1) I'm not fond of people who take credit for my work, (2) Panty hose suck, and (3) Bosses who criticize your job performance in their office, then feel you up in the elevator, are fairly easy to get good letters of reference from, especially if you know the guys who run the elevator video camera.

My friends were thrilled when I decided to leave that job. "About time!" was the most common reaction. Even the people I worked with at the bank (minus the touchy-feely boss) threw me a "We knew you could do better!" party.

My first marriage lasted ten years and had many of the exact same problems as my first job. Only I didn't get paid to show up as a wife every day. I didn't even get my two fifteen-minute breaks and sick leave. Or my own phone.

It's interesting how all these years later, my mind sums up both my first job and my first marriage with one single event. On the job, it was having to draw tiny charts that reflected which way the economy was headed that week (which back then was up, up, up). We did have a computer, but it couldn't do anything except spit numbers out. Make a chart? That required a human being. The one moment in my first marriage was when my then-husband asked me to "help" write a user's manual for a computer software program he and his partner had developed to help people keep track of their finances. I took one look at how boring the whole thing was and suggested I use humor to keep people from falling asleep. Hubby scoffed at the idea. Had I then the chutzpah I have now, I'd probably own the whole *Dummies* franchise. Despite all the problems, when my first husband handed me my pink slip—just as I was about ready to turn in my letter of resignation—no one I knew jumped for joy. This, despite the fact that both "About time!" and "We knew you could do better!" would have made great party themes. My friends mourned the death of my marriage. I wanted a party; I got a wake.

my second career began when i was twenty-six and had just finished grad school. I became a health educator at a major university. There was a lot to love about the job, not the least of which was that unless I had a management meeting during the day, I didn't have to wear a suit or panty hose. I had a computer that could actually do things, like make charts and communicate with other people. My boss was a woman who didn't need me to think she was the sexiest thing in the office. I just had to help her not fall asleep in meetings. For the most part, my job consisted of telling everyone who worked for the university to eat their vegetables, get more exercise, and for god's sake, wear a condom! I loved that. Of course, there were tough things about the job, too, like trying to talk tenured faculty members into giving up smoking in their offices when they knew full well there was nothing I could do to stop them. This was long before cell phone cameras and YouTube. It's so much easier to blackmail people these days! I had to appeal to their sense of justice and fairness—if no one else could smoke at work, wasn't it unfair that they got to? Can I say that was not a persuasive argument to people with a twenty-plus-year tobacco addiction?

I stayed committed to that job, in sickness and in health, for twelve years. At that point, I started to feel like it was getting stale and unchallenging. Besides, after ten years, you are privy to all the office politics and no one wants to be around politics of any kind for more than a decade. When I decided to pack up my belongings and head across country for a career to be identified later, once again my friends and family were thrilled. They thought I was adventurous, audacious, fearless, a role model. "Look at her," they'd say to their children, "She's not afraid to jump into the unknown and create a new life for herself!"

What I wouldn't have given for just one person to think I was a role model when I announced divorce number two. After all, I was freeing myself from a man who was nine years younger and still talked to his mother long-distance several times a week. Which is not all that odd, unless you understand that most of their conversations were about his days in elementary school and junior high. "He's bound to grow up some day," someone told me, "just stay with him and see." When he moved back to his mommy's house after our divorce, I felt somewhat vindicated. Still, no one told their daughters that my choosing to be free of his mother's apron strings was worthy of role model status.

I'm still in career number three—I write, teach, and perform comedy, both at night in a bar for drunk people and during the day in hotel meeting rooms for sober people in suits and ties who actually remember some of what I say. No one tells me when to get up or what to wear. No one feels me up on the job, not even the UPS man, not even when I beg. My coworkers are dogs, so the backbiting at work is literal instead of figurative. I like that. My friends and family are thrilled. They want to be me when they grow up.

I've been at this job for fifteen years and apparently it agrees with me. So far, there are enough rewards (although most of them are not financial) that I don't yet see an end in sight. I am also on marriage number three. Maybe three times is a charm. Maybe not. We're separated and "working" on things. See, marriage IS a job. I have to turn in a report to our therapist tomorrow. I mentioned the fact that things might not work out to one of my women's groups last night and jaws dropped all around the table. "But you've been married less than five years!" one said in shock. "Aren't you afraid to grow old alone?" another chimed in. Both are in relationships, and when they see one crumble, perhaps they worry more about the foundations of their own. Or maybe it's the PC thing to say. Better than "Hey, no fair, I want a divorce, too!" I guess.

I'm fairly certain that if I do end up with the divorce trifecta, no one will want to be me when they grow up. Which is a damn shame. Because if I'm happy, that's the kind of fairytale everyone should dream of. I've learned a lot from my jobs and my marriages, and it all can be summed up as this: Life goes on. And as long as you're learning something . . . anything . . . your job and your marriage probably still have a few good years in them. But it never hurts to keep your resume polished.

*

Schooled

* sonja herbert

i stand in line with graduates much younger than i am. my mortarboard is slipping, but I don't care. I feel as if I'm floating, and I can't seem to quit smiling. I've made it. Like my younger fellow students, I have graduated from being dependent to having power over myself. I've become my own person, something I couldn't be in my marriage.

The announcer calls my name, and I walk onto the podium. The department head, one of my professors, shakes my hand and holds the diploma out to me. I smile and blink at the flash from the ceremony photographer.

On my way back to my seat, I search the crowd and spy the smiling faces of my six children, sitting together. My oldest is going to be a graduate himself, and the youngest two are still in preschool. They wave at me, their eyes alight with pride. Their love warms my heart. Both their father and my ex–sister wife sit with them. I feel warm and supported, more so than I felt for many years in my marriage. I marvel at who I've become since then. I am the master of my own household now, with no sister wife to bring stress and discord into my life. As I sit down again, my mind flashes back to the shy little girl I used to be.

i was raised in a traveling carnival in post-world war two Germany. Every week, our caravan traveled to yet another fair in a different town, where I helped put up and run our attractions. I went to school for only eight years.

When I was twenty-three, I met my American husband, who had much more schooling than I. I was excited about the chance of starting a new life in a different country. Soon after we were married, I went with him to the United States. In the beginning, we had so much fun together. He helped me understand the cultural differences between my home country and the United States, introduced me to hamburgers and malted milk shakes, and laughed at my "cute" German accent.

After the first three children joined the family, however, things changed. We had always believed in the Holy Scriptures and faithfully went to church every Sunday. Our neighbors, who belonged to a polygamist religion, introduced us to their way of thinking. When they explained their reasoning for God wanting men to have more than one wife, I couldn't doubt the truth of their assertions, since it was written in the Bible, and to my mind the Bible was absolutely true. Eventually my husband suggested we join this church, and I followed him, with much religious zeal, and no understanding of what I was getting into.

Shortly before we joined the polygamists, one of my husband's friends died in an airplane accident and left a young widow, one year younger than I. She had blue eyes and curly blond hair, as compared to my brown eyes and dark hair. We comforted her and had her over at our house a lot. She also learned about our new church and joined when we did. Before I could fathom what it would do to my life, this young woman joined our family as my sister wife. Suddenly, my husband hardly noticed the children and me. I had to schedule time to be with him, and when we were together, his mind was elsewhere. He also started making all the decisions. I realized it was mainly to keep peace between my sister wife and me, but nevertheless, it made me feel small and dependent.

When jealousy darkened my soul, I suppressed it, but the joy was gone from my life. As my family expected, I cleaned the house every day, took care of the children, cooked breakfast, lunch, and dinner for the growing family, wiped baby butts and noses, took kids to and from school, and tried to live in peace with my husband and sister wife.

Now that my children and I are alone, life seems lighter, in spite of the added responsibilities. The house gets cleaned whenever it's dirty enough to bother me, and the children help. I never enjoyed cooking, and after the divorce I taught the children to cook. I still cook breakfast before the kids go to school, but for dinner we eat simply. I still wipe noses, but the kids walk to school now, and I am there when they return. Our home is more peaceful. No more demanding sister wife, or a husband who doesn't understand or doesn't care how much work it is to run such a large household.

At times, while I was married, I felt like a child, not capable of running my own life. I had no control over the household money. Sometimes my husband told me to collect from the farmers what they owed him for the welding he did on their equipment. Then I packed up the baby and the preschooler and drove the car to the outlying farms, handing out my husband's bills and hoping to get paid for them. On such days, I didn't have time to do the chores at home, and when my sister wife came in from work, she complained about the mess. She and my husband had to wait for their dinner, and that didn't make them any happier. But I knew it was important to collect the payments, or there wouldn't be enough money to feed us all. Most of the time, too little came in, but my husband didn't worry. He enjoyed his work, and if somebody paid us, he would pay a bill or two. When his customers didn't offer to pay and our finances grew really tight, I asked for credit at the grocery store.

Eventually I applied for food stamps. It was against my husband's will, but I did all the grocery shopping and had to feed the family.

When my last child was born, the electric company cut off our power, because my husband hadn't paid the bill for several months. During that winter, my eldest son kept the fire going in the woodstove during the day, and at night I wrapped the new baby in a crocheted blanket and took her to bed with me.

Now, after the divorce, I still don't have a lot of money, but the children and I get along. Up to now, I earned money as a teaching assistant and by typing papers for other students. The money was enough, because I also had good scholarships, and we were careful. Now that I've graduated, I hope to soon have a teaching position in a nearby high school or middle school. We're warm in the winter and comfortable in the summers. We rarely go out to eat, but we experiment in the kitchen, and I encourage even the little ones to cook. I hang the laundry in the furnace room to dry and so save the money that would otherwise go to the dryers at the laundromat. I get around on my bike and leave my car parked as much as I can.

As a single mother, I have control over the children and how they are being raised. When I was married, that wasn't always the case.

My sister wife couldn't have children. At times, she was angry at the little ones, and often she expected them to be able to do things they weren't mature enough yet to do.

I remember how upset she was when I was pregnant once again, with my fifth child. One day, at the end of that pregnancy, she confronted me in the living room. The children were in bed, and I was ready to tackle my biology homework at the dining room table. My husband was talking on the telephone in the kitchen.

"I can't believe you got yourself pregnant again," she said. "Don't you have enough children yet?"

I shrugged. "I've got to do this homework. Talk to him about it," I said and returned my attention to my textbook.

"You think you're so much better than me, just because you can have all those children," she said and left.

A few days later, after she had gone to work, I returned from taking my eldest to middle school in the neighboring town. I unbuttoned my two-year-old's coat and was taking off mine, when my husband came up to me.

"I'm on my way out," he said. "But I wanted to talk to you first. How about you let your sister wife raise the new baby when it's born? That will make her happy and will make it easier for you. After all, you have your hands full with the others."

My heart stood still. I felt like I needed to obey my husband, but something deep within me rose up. "There is no way," I answered. "I can't do that and won't do it. Don't ever ask me something like that again."

He dropped his eyes to the floor and said, "Okay. I was just asking." Then he grabbed his coat and left.

As time passed, my older children watched my husband and my sister wife, and I watched them. I realized my sons were probably learning that it was okay for men to dominate women. And the girls likely identified with me and my sister wife, and as they watched our marriage play out, they couldn't help but learn that, as women, their fate in life was to be dominated. I knew things had to change if I wanted my boys and girls to be successful, competent human beings.

In our religious group, I was taught to obey my husband and do whatever he wanted me to do. He suggested that I attend the nearby college full-time so I could get a degree. "Then you could contribute to the family, too," he said. I looked at the two preschoolers sitting among wooden blocks, paper, and crayons on the floor, thought of my two grade-schoolers, and wondered how I could possibly accomplish that. But on the other hand, my heart skipped a beat at the chance to get out of the house and do something for myself. In the beginning, because I wanted to improve my English, I'd taken classes off and on between having babies, and I soon realized that studying was easy for me. I had always enjoyed the classes and the new things I learned. However, attending full-time with four children and one on the way was a different story.

"Sounds good to me," I answered. "But I won't be able to keep things up the way I do now if I start taking classes seriously."

"That's all right. We'll help," he said and dismissed me.

I still tried to keep the house up and take care of runny noses and dirty diapers, but our home wasn't as clean anymore, and even though my sister wife complained, she had to pitch in when she came home from work. I studied while cooking and cleaning and after the children went to bed, while the other two adults of the family watched TV. At times, exhausted from a long day, tired, and discouraged, I was ready to throw in the towel and postpone my education. But I kept going and getting good grades.

One day, a few days after my husband suggested that I should let my sister wife raise my fifth child, something happened that eventually changed my life. As I attended Philosophy 101, the class discussed the merits of reading to make informed decisions instead of reading to sound educated. The instructor impressed upon us the importance of deciding for ourselves whether something written can be considered true or not. He brought home the fact that not everything that's written is necessarily true.

Yes, I thought, patting my pregnant belly. *Maybe not everything my religion and my husband tell me is true.* When I was a child, living in my parents' traveling carnival, I had no religious education. My parents scoffed at anything religious, telling us children that churches existed only to take money from the gullible. However, my parents also taught us to never question authority. They made it clear they thought that we were not smart or good enough and shouldn't trust our own decisions.

As a teenager, however, I did make a decision on my own. I joined a religious community, and there I also learned to exercise my faith and believe without questioning the scriptures and the leaders of the church. Because of my early upbringing, that was easy for me. Even years later, when living in polygamy became difficult, I never doubted the wisdom of the church leaders, until that day in Philosophy 101.

I thought about the discussion in philosophy class for a long time. Eventually, I realized that maybe God had given me the power to think so I could make my own decisions. *And maybe,* I thought, *maybe it is alright to doubt my religion and to challenge what the leaders tell me.* As time went by, I saw how restricted my life was. Maybe God wanted something better for me. Two years later, when my youngest child was a baby, I was finally brave enough to talk to my husband about my religious doubts. He shrugged them off and told me to see a doctor. He thought my strange behavior and thoughts might be hormonal.

When he blithely ignored my concerns, I felt completely abandoned. Since the arrival of my sister wife, I had grown more and more emotionally distant from my husband. Not only did he not help with the children, he also left me to my own devices financially and withdrew his emotional support. I finally mentioned divorce.

"If you would get a job and leave the polygamists," I said, "maybe we could work this out. Otherwise, I want a divorce."

"If you really want to leave," my husband said, "then go. She," he said, referring to my sister wife, "needs me more than you do."

His words cut deeply. I was the wife of his first choice, the mother of his children. What happened to the love we had for each other before he had another wife? Maybe he thought I wouldn't go, but his hurtful words made me even more determined.

The college I attended had awarded me a large scholarship, and if I kept getting food stamps and typing papers for other students, I knew I would be okay financially. I found a small, inexpensive house for rent in my college town and moved in with my six children. In the mornings, when the older children went to school, I walked the little ones to their nearby baby sitter and then walked to campus. Every second weekend, my oldest son took his siblings in the car to see their dad, which gave me time to catch up on my studies and the household. A year after the move, on the day of summer semester finals, my divorce, too, was final.

In spite of the divorce, my relationship with my ex seems better now. He is more aware of my needs, and he is there for me and the children. When our car broke down, he found us a new one, and he cared enough to come to my graduation. I think he now recognizes what he lost when the kids and I left him.

Today, my oldest son is working on a degree in physics and computer science. My oldest daughter is finishing high school and plans to work for a company that will pay for her computer engineering classes. My second son is about to graduate from middle school, and the three little girls are successful in elementary school and preschool. My children are happy and at peace. The younger ones hardly remember when they lived with their dad and my sister wife. That's how it should be. Today, I live to show my girls what an education can do for a person's life, and what power a woman has, even if she's alone and raising six children.

Sitting among my fellow graduates at the university, I realize I haven't just earned a degree, I also earned official recognition of the fact that I am a valuable person and am able to make decisions for myself and my children.

Now that I have finished my studies, things can only improve. I've already begun to apply for a teaching position at several schools, and I'm confident I will be able to support my family. The kids and I will again be in school together, but this time, I'll be a teacher while they engage in their studies.

I turn and wave at my children. The worst is behind us. The divorce has brought its share of trouble and stress, but it has also brought a measure of peace and self-esteem to me, that formerly undereducated little girl from Germany.

There from Here

candace walsh

"so, are we divorced?" asked will. i was seated on his girlfriend's overstuffed brocade-print sofa, in the home they shared, which was populated full-time with her things, his things, many of my kids' things (they live there half-time), and things, like the set of dishes from my bridal registry, that will always be a little bit mine.

"Um, yeah," I said. "The divorce has been final for two months."

"Oh," he said, genially. "I didn't know."

So it goes.

He didn't know we were divorced, but I did. And when we were married, he didn't know we'd divorce, but I did. I didn't want to know. I drank wine nightly to soften the edges of it. I read long novels back-to-back, to live other lives, not my own.

I woke up one day when our daughter was a year and a half. As my sleepiness drained away, it left me with the dreamlike impression of a casita. It was there as if it had always been there, but its presence was new to me. From then on, I lived in the main house, but my heart was out in the casita. My heart paced back and forth, waiting for me. The casita had a Provençal blue front door, a room with thick mud walls painted a rosy pink, and warm wood floors and windowsills.

In my real life, I lived in a house with shiny, stippled walls colored month-to-month tenant white. The *talavera* counter tiles rose and fell, glaze worn away at the edges, grout stained and pitted. The house's walls were made of "penitentiary brick," the heated air was forced, the front yard fence was made of long, variegated shavings of thick dark tree bark—the kind of fence a Black Forest witch would lash around her hut.

In my real life, we didn't have a car, were new to town, I had no friends, and no job. Will worked long hours. On good days, I'd take my daughter for open-ended walks around town. On bad days (and these came in stretches), I stayed home, day after day, glued to the Internet and in bed reading, serially popping our two kid videos into the VCR, making desultory lunches, nursing.

It was fall, and the piñon-sharpened air sank into my nostrils as I pushed my daughter through town in her stroller. It was warm and then cold, and then colder. Sometimes I stopped at a cowgirl-themed restaurant and had a two-margarita lunch before pushing my daughter and myself home. The waitress shot me looks because she thought I was going to get in a car, half in the bag, with my toddler. "I don't have a car, and I don't know anyone, and I'm miserable, and I promise to look both ways," I thought but didn't say. I felt bad.

It was a perfect time to ruin a young marriage that was already staggering. When Will and I argued, he flew into rages that lasted for hours, lacerated my wife-heart, and propelled him through the house after me, pushing on doors that had no locks. He didn't care that our wee one was present, didn't care that I was sobbing and had no car, no money, no friends, no way out. He had a problem. And now it was my problem, too.

When I met him, I was an East Village girl-about-town with lots of friends and a big, close-knit family. Within two years I was in Northern New Mexico getting screamed at nonstop with not one person for thousands of miles to turn to. His rages were like shrapnel inside me. His contrition was like plaster that frosted smoothly over the pockmarks. It was big, unctuous, heartfelt, defiling.

But I was invested. There was still passion, because I believed he could stop it. There was passion in the arguing, in the penitence. There was engagement. There was the dream, and my pride. The dream began in a bar on Bleecker Street, next door to the little shop that I ran for my friend. It was filled with vintage children's clothing, and I banged away at my first novel when there were no customers. I had to stop and start, to stop and start. It was good practice for being a mother who writes. I went next door for a beer after work, and he started talking to me. I thought he was the kind of deeply nice and handsome man whom I could marry, if I weren't too busy nursing a broken heart. But he saw something in me, something beyond that skittering inner state. And we fell in love.

It proceeded through a whirlwind romance, an instant cohabitation, a wedding written up in the *New York Times* Vows column. It was the dress, the guests, the first course of melon wrapped in prosciutto. My mother and father happy that I was settled, with a fine man who would take care of me. A honeymoon in Burgundy and Paris, a stay with his Tante Paulette, because like many dream men, he was part French and had relatives in Europe. It jetted on, a summer with a sailboat, a conception, a baby, and then 9/11's infinite rupturings. A year spent on Long Island, in the loving yet dysfunction-dappled bosom of my family. A rough commute, not enough money, our move to Santa Fe. A fresh start.

A half year into that, he went back East for business for a weekend. I stayed and cleaned the house, and watched a lot of television, and even pay-per-viewed some porn one late night. I came hard watching girl-on-girl sex (funny how that had always been the most lubricious flavor of erotica for me) and fell asleep.

When I woke up, the casita was there, very real in my mind. And my love for him was gone.

(I learned years later that he haphazardly cheated on me that night in New York, with a new hire at his old company.)

My heart was empty. I called my mother, crying, to tell her. "That happens," she said. "The love will come back. Just wait, and pray." And I did. But what I also did was pretend. For seven years. And had our baby boy, who came into this world because my grandma died, which set me on a grief-fueled baby quest. Will was amenable.

Unlike the first pregnancy, which was thoroughly, tenderly nurtured by Will, this second one was riddled with Bad Signs. He was pissed off at me because it postponed my ability to contribute financially. He did not want to touch me, to rub out the aches and pains of pregnancy. He called me a cunt in front of his visiting mother, because I asked them to lower the television so I could sleep at 11:00 P.M. I had a secret crush on one of my midwives. I felt no need to maintain his sex life. I had a sex life of my own—after he fell asleep, while he snored beside me, I unapologetically pleasured myself once, twice a night, as I thought about women.

The baby came, the sweetest boy, in two and a half hours, at home, in the middle of an April night, by candlelight. My midwife's hands were pleasingly cool on my lower back as she applied counterpressure to soften the bite of transition contractions. I wanted her help, not his.

Two years went by. I put two and two together about a deceased relative who, when I was three and he was alive, violated me sexually over some months. And then I cried and cried. In between mothering, working part-time, renovating our first home, getting a straight C- in housekeeping, and going through the motions of wifehood.

And then I began therapy. I really liked my new therapist, and her Provence-inspired office, with the right kind of yellow walls. She had a partner, and not a man partner. Unwittingly, a harbinger of my next life, the afterlife part of me scrabbled to ascend to, while most of me played Will's wife, of the dinner parties, the house on the hill, the new station wagon. We were no longer poor and I was no longer friendless, and I had a job.

And shortly thereafter I fell in love with my therapist, much to my mortification, one autumn day, after I ran into her at a museum fundraiser yard sale. I had been thinking about her. It felt so good to think about her.

Her warm smile, the way she offhandedly resided in her body, her sweet smell, and eyes that brimmed with empathy. She saw me. That *was* her job. But, I had spent too long not quite being seen, by most anyone. They saw the mother figure, or the editor person, the commiserating, exasperated friend, the wife person who was supposed to, was supposed to, never quite, almost, I wish you had, why don't you ever, goddamnit.

I had my son on my back in a baby carrier, my daughter beside me, my hands full. I carried a plump celadon ceramic turtledove, $2 marked on it with grease pencil. She seemed to swim out of the crowd and stood before me, smiling.

There she was. Wearing makeup! Her hair done! With a pale green, fitted fleece vest and *jeans,* not the scrubs she wore in session. In the world. In my world. For a moment.

I introduced her to my children, flustered and pleased. My four-year-old daughter picked up a crone mask and stared at her through the eyeholes, impassive times two. I, tremendously self-conscious, my pulse beating in my eardrums, looked down, surprised to see the bird in my hands, to feel so bashful. She left me with pinked cheeks and a spinning heart.

And they're off.

All signs point to the conclusion that this quiescent woman of a certain age had no idea how to handle my Sagittarian, ruthless pursuit, my big-T transference, my ardor, my affect. I knew she didn't—because I did research. What research?

✴ *In Session: The Bond between Women and Their Therapists,* Lott
✴ *Deepening Intimacy in Psychotherapy: Using the Erotic Transference and Countertransference,* Rosiello
✴ *Between Therapist and Client: The New Relationship,* Kahn

* *The Love Cure: Therapy Erotic and Sexual,* Haule
* *The Patient Who Cured His Therapist, and Other Stories of Unconventional Therapy,* Siegel and Lowe
* *Bonding: A Somatic-Emotional Approach to Transference,* Keleman, and
* *The Impossibility of Sex: Stories of the Intimate Relationship between Therapist and Patient,* Orbach.

I read what therapists should do: point out the feelings so obviously felt by the lovestruck client. But, she did not. I was so incredibly keyed up, simultaneously ashamed and giddy. The thought of bringing it up myself was about as do-able as slicing off the skin on my arms and folding it into an origami crane. We emailed, and then she said we should not email. She accepted gifts and then said she could not accept gifts, and then she accepted gifts once more, because they were perfectly chosen, and I sensed she had also not been seen for so long. I was her coyote, and she was mine. It was unexamined Transference/Countertransference Bumper Cars, and it was not doing me a certain kind of good— the good that I had signed on for. But it was doing other, very needed things.

All the same, I couldn't trust her. I couldn't stop thinking about her. It was so hard to talk about therapy stuff when I felt so . . . I felt such a connection. I wished we could be friends. She said that after we did our work, she was not strict, it's a small town. You know.

So, I did my work. I made a list and ticked it off, except that one thing was not on the list: falling in love with your therapist and all of the rich, juicy fruitfulness that could yield if it was steered correctly back to healing. I worked through the stuff on my list and then I terminated. It was like giving my baby up for adoption so that I could hopefully find her someday.

I went away to Africa and India for work and as sort of a last hurrah with Will. My mother stayed with the children. My therapist and I emailed all the way through. We made plans to have tea when

I got back. I was flying high. I was a very bad wife and former client at this point, and I did not care. I was on this very particular crack, you see. It was an illicit drug, and it made me irresponsible and wild inside. I felt good again. Not just "good again," but better than I had ever felt. Right after feeling dully worse than I had ever felt for half a decade. I'd felt bad for so long that I thought bad was normal. And then it shifted.

We came back. Will and I began to have the conversation about divorce. The first one was preternaturally calm. The following ones were alternately furious, begging, hopeful, conditional, despondent, and furious again. We had one in the middle of the night, and I drove to a hotel because I knew that if I slept beside him, I would wake up too weak to follow through. The fellow who checked me in asked me if I were from out of town. I said "No, from here." He mercifully let the topic drop.

My room was unexpectedly Tuscan in decor. I called my sister, methodical and flip as I relayed the situation. I called another friend, and she soothed me about how little it might mess up my children after all. She reminded me that things were escalating with Will, and that was not good for the children to witness, ever ever.

I meditated and heard, in my mind's silence: "This is going to be bad, but it's the good kind of bad." I woke up with grief kneading my ribs and palpating my heart. I called my sister again, in hoarse sobs. "Oh," she said. "Oh, honey, the shock is wearing off. It's hitting you. It's going to be okay. For so long you've been so very quietly miserable."

I drove home, early, so the kids would wake up with me there. I cried on I-25, wild animal howls, loud and scary, because I could. No one could hear me, no one would worry.

When I came in, he was sitting on our big green couch.

"So," he said, "how do you feel now? More sure, or less sure?"

"More sure," I said.

"More sure," he repeated.

"Yes."

But we decided to stick it out for six months and go to marriage counseling. For the children. We owed it to them. In therapy, Will admitted that for years, he'd felt terrible, because whenever I'd go on a trip, he'd have this brief flare of a wish that my plane would crash. "Oh my God!" I said. "Me, too!" The survivor would be free of the marriage, *and* get sympathy.

Things were status quo–ish (read, miserable) when he surreptitiously scanned my journal and wrote my therapist a letter telling her of my feelings for her, out of spite. And she told me this, in a park, while we drank the chai that I made from scratch, while my daughter twirled in dance class down the street and my son climbed on the jungle gym. My body curled into the fetal position on the park bench.

For the last time.

Within an hour and a half, I was out of there. I picked up my daughter, drove to a friend's house, went online, and called the number for a guesthouse for rent. In the midst of the conversation, I realized that I was talking to a friend of a friend.

I walked into the place, looked around, and asked, "Can I move in today?"

"Sure," she said. I wrote her a check for three months on the spot.

After all those years of the casita hovering on the edges of my vision, I was standing inside of it. It did not have a blue door, but the bedroom walls were pink, its floor slate tile, and it looked out over a park. I could walk or bike to work, which I did, the air whapping my newborn face.

We were welcome to borrow my landlord-cum–new friend's two small dogs, Milk and Honey, whenever we wanted. I knew my children would need those little balls of fur, their loving, licking tongues and warm brown eyes, their wee nails clicking on the tile floor. The small dining room table's glass top was held up by bare-breasted, carved wooden caryatids. The couch and chairs were upholstered in comforting British floral fabric. I had landed.

"You deserve a future that's not contaminated," said my new therapist, whom I was thrilled to find perfectly nice, but nothing more.

So there I was, in the land of pure oxygen. I could lock my door and feel safe *inside.*

And I could take stock. I'd been partnered with men but dreamed about women. I remembered my proud five-year-old declaration, "I want to marry my best friend Stacy!" My parents were horrified, agape, as if I had just crapped on the living room floor. My years of religious indoctrination decreed that acting on same-sex attraction was wrong. Apoplectic, spit-flecked sermons on the topic to a congregation filled with people who couldn't see me now, who I was; I'd be shunned and also hounded. My inner scrabbling, *No that's not me that's not me that's not me.*

Repression exhausted me, but I didn't know why I was exhausted, because I'd been repressing since I was five. I ran out of reasons to repress my true self around the time I ran to therapy to heal myself. And here I stood. Ready.

It was time to go there. I would have committed to some kind of hardcore, excoriating therapy with Will if I hadn't known, too deeply, that at the end of the day, that was the way I most wanted to love and be loved, and that he deserved better, as did I.

Once again, I did research:

* *And Then I Met This Woman: Previously Married Women's Journeys into Lesbian Relationships,* Cassingham and O'Neil
* *From Wedded Wife to Lesbian Life,* Abbott and Farmer
* *Living Two Lives: Married to a Man and in Love with a Woman,* Fleisher
* *The Art of Meeting Women: A Guide for Meeting Gay Women,* Sacks
* And *The Straight Girl's Guide to Hooking Up with Chicks,* which I bought because Amazon reviews by lesbians said it was better than the lesbian-written sex books. Go figure.

The really great thing about dating women you meet online is that when you're both women, you actually do have a good chance of being friends if the chemistry thing isn't there. Therefore, I soon had a posse of about fifteen new women friends to show me the ropes of being in the girl-girl world. And they all had really great Josie and the Pussycats names. We went out to women's theme dances (from "Leather and Lace" to, informally, "Hemp and Handpainted Silk"), to a women's land commune to help remud an adobe house, and to potlucks with wide arrays of hummus on offer, and made snarky, gut-bustingly funny comments out the sides of our mouths about what we thought was the Lesbian What Not to Wear. Vests, for instance.

Gia and I went to our first dance together, burned up the dance floor, drank about four too many Cosmos each, and ended up separately being hit on by women who soon thereafter held our hair while we booted on different ends of the parking lot . . . and then *still* wanted to date us.

Nancy and I went out to dinner at a resort that had an outdoor swimming pool for the guests, which was closed, as it was late. "Want to sneak in and skinny dip?" Nancy asked. "No! Well . . . okay!" In we slid, giggling, our breasts bobbing chastely in the warm water. And yes, we did get busted.

My former therapist and I did do a few "friendlike" things, innocent things that for me were overwhelmingly charged. After not too long, she stopped responding to my overtures to have tea, or dinner, and I let it go. I grew weary of the elevated, toe-curling hyperarousal, parsing every damn thing she said six ways to Sunday. I was ready to graduate from the junior high of lesbian love; I was ready for something viable.

I made my friends and even got involved two times—enough to know that I really was on the right track and not just having some kind of "Screw men, I'm gonna go hide out in flannel pajamas foot-rub land" reaction. I *knew* I wasn't, but there was the worry. Both of these encounters ended badly, and with those endings, the deep sorrow of my divorce wound gushed out like Linda Blair's possessed vomit.

The first time, I hid my grief from Will. He had just been getting together with a woman. I knew because he'd stopped asking me daily if I thought that maybe we should get back together, and he'd been picking up the kids in the morning with sex hair. I could not go there with him. I felt weak and scared, and protective of my journey thus far. My grief fanned out inside me, immobilized me mornings when I could not for the life of me get out of bed, even to pee. I held it and huddled under the covers, fighting off the taunting, seductive desire to cut myself, just a little bit, someplace no one would see. Come on. I did not come on. I went on an antidepressant.

The second time, Will, who had gotten more serious since then with a lovely woman, called me, caught me in tears, and came over straightaway, a six pack of sympathy beer in hand. He sat beside me on the couch, wrapped his arms around me, and held me tightly as I unapologetically sobbed about the loss of someone besides himself. But more than I cried about that, I cried out my grief at my deepest fear: that I was inherently unlovable and flawed, incapable of being happy ever again; that I was like so many women of my mother's generation who divorced or had been widowed, and spent the rest of their lives monastically solo.

"You're a wonderful person," he said. "I married you! That's got to count for something. You and I split up, and it was the right thing to do, *and* there are lots of other people out there who will appreciate you and enjoy you for who you are. That woman was not right for you. You spent all this time settling for *our* relationship, which was not enough. That relationship was not enough either. I know you really wanted to be in a relationship with a woman after all of this upheaval, but don't sell yourself short. She doesn't drink, she doesn't eat this, she doesn't eat that, she can't stay up past eight, she doesn't want to have sex. . . . Candace, when there are more 'Don'ts' than 'Do's,' *don't*."

Those words helped, but more than that, it helped me to cry so hard and so freely, and cry on someone who did not really care that I was sliming the hell out of his nice dress shirt. Unlike many ex-lovers I'd wadded up like toilet paper and flushed out of my life, Will and I were bound to each other through our children, who made us find a common, respectful ground, and even though that was for the good of the children, it was (surprise!) good for us as well.

Will got me drunk in the middle of the day, ignored more than one cell phone call, and waited till our friend Susie could arrive to take over, all blustery indignation that someone could cut *her* best friend loose, comfort groceries in hand. Then Gia arrived, and we drank more and made lists of what I wanted in my next girlfriend, and just as importantly, what I didn't.

"Must *get* you and know that you are great," Gia said.

"Must be able to fall asleep where you are," Susie said.

"Yes to consciousness of what's reasonable," said Gia.

"She can't smell like soup," I said. "And she has to be a good dancer."

"She can't tell you how to parent," said Susie. "And she has to love your kids."

"Yes to a little bit of butch swagger," said Gia.

"Oh, yes," I said.

"And good nighttime skills," said Susie.

So it goes.

I'd moved out of the casita when the three months were up. I went to full-time at work and bought a new house with money from the one Will and I sold. I had a bunch of great friends, was very involved with my spiritual practice, and as I shared custody 50/50 with Will, had time to exercise, write, play, and cook up meals for friends. I was living the life I loved, at peace with where I was. It was nearly March, marking a year since I had moved into the casita. I decided to finally take a hiatus from dating, just to give myself a little down time, and space to grieve in case I needed to really fall apart. The year had been full. With actual lady relationships under my belt, I no longer felt I had all that much to prove. Chasing relationships down had not worked; it was time to put down my butterfly net.

February 27, I got an email from Match.com with "Your Matches." Oh, pshaw, I thought. Most of the time I didn't even open those. When I did, I'd see about fifteen women who were most certainly *not* my matches—instantly disqualified by bad mullet hairdos, their joyful employment in the trucking industry, or monikers like "I_love_snoopy." Match had been good for making friends. That was it.

But, what the hell. . . . I clicked on it.

Gah. A photo of the most adorable woman ever. She was *my type* . . . she looked at once intellectual, boyishly pretty, smartly dressed, witty, sexy, intelligent, kind, and gentle. All that from a photo the size of a postage stamp. Her profile text was probably going to show me that I was jumping to conclusions—but it did not. Our first phone call—that would break the spell. But it (all three and a half hours of it) did not. Nor did our first dinner, in which she was prettier, smarter, kinder, funnier, and more smartly dressed than her photo or profile text *or* phone conversation had led me to believe. Her hair was precociously silver, her eyes cornflower blue with ice flecks. Her smile was girlish, and also, a little bit rakish. Her vocabulary was killer, and her hands were sexy. She talked, and she listened. She laughed and made me laugh. There's no way, I thought. If I like her this much, and she's this perfect, she does not like me back. But she did.

After dinner, I asked her if she wanted a ride to her car, because it was snowing lightly, and I wanted to be kissed. She said yes. We parked in front of a store called Objects of Desire. We sat. We fidgeted. She leaned, infinitesimally and definitely.

She told me later that I moved toward her in slow motion. I just remember that I felt like the air was suddenly more tensile around me . . . that I had to lean through it deliberately, to get to her mouth with my own. It was the slowest . . . it was so slow, this kiss. First our lips grazed against each other, then seemed to land like birds on a certain branch of a tree. We kissed, and kissed, and kissed, while intangible things that have no name entwined around and inside us.

Many months later, I still want to be kissed, and she is still kissing me. With the softest, strongest, most knee-weakening kisses. She *sees* me, and not because it is her job. It's her avocation.

We are neither of us perfect, but we are imperfect together in ways that heal and gratify each other and ourselves. And in the ways (too many to count) that we *are* perfect together, the bliss rains down.

Even though both my quite traditional mother and my father would not choose this life for me, this very happy life, they have told me that they are happy that I am happy. And I am. Sitting here in my pajamas at 3:30 P.M., writing while she writes, right over there, in my blue drawstring miniskirt and her V-neck white T-shirt, her dogs asleep on the big green couch.

How sure are you now?

More sure.

*

The Love List
julie hammonds

it began, as so many things do in my life, with a list.

First, a list of losses: a seven-year marriage, a home, the feeling of security that comes when you know you belong to one particular person and place. After my husband told me he was done with our marriage and ready to move on, these losses were inevitable. In a few months, I would move out of our house; a few months after that, my job working for the governor of Alaska would end due to term limits. These losses would take place, whether I was ready or not.

Other losses would come as a result of choices I made, though at the time they seemed inevitable as well. Once my job ended, I would leave Juneau, the Alaskan city where we'd made our home as a married couple. I didn't know many things for sure, in the fog and grief of losing a marriage, but I knew this: I could not share this small town with my ex-husband. It was time to go, to make a new life somewhere else. Where, I didn't know.

Assessing these losses to come, I felt both exhilarated and terrified. No longer bound to a failing marriage, a demanding job, or the town I once loved, soon I could go anywhere, do anything, be anyone. Few people ever experience such freedom.

But the same changes that provided opportunity also scared me to the core. I liked being a wife, an Alaskan, a professional whose job title earned notice. I would let them go with enormous reluctance. Without them, who was I? Truly on my own, who would I become? One Saturday morning as a sourdough waffle baked and news chattered on the radio, I stood alone in my kitchen, chilled by the enormous changes to come. Time was passing; soon, I would move out of my house and lose my income.

Obviously, I would be better equipped to face the future if I made a plan. But how could I come up with one, when what I needed to plan for was not just how to support myself or where to live, but both?

Whatever the plan would be, I could not imagine building it around another job that drained me of energy for all but the most menial tasks when I got home. Such a life drove me to spend free time working through lists of chores, mistaking checked-off tasks for meaningful accomplishments. I had lived that way long enough, letting "must do" get in the way of what I wanted to do. Of the many things that killed my marriage, this chore-driven personality that placed pleasure last was a prime suspect.

My future life simply had to include more happiness. I could go without a big salary, a prestigious job title, even a house of my own. I was willing to give these up, if I could have just enough, and be happy.

Standing in the kitchen that rainy morning, I decided that any plan for my future had to begin in the fertile ground of love. Into my future life, I wanted to build activities I genuinely love to do. Surely a good job, a rewarding place to live, and every other component of a healthy new life would spring up naturally from such rich soil. But what were those things I loved, exactly? Years had passed since I last asked myself that question, or listened to the answers.

Beside my list of losses, it was time to make another, more joyful list: a love list.

I walked upstairs to my desk and pulled out six sheets of blank paper, a box of crayons, and a spool of clear tape. Taping the sheets together to form a poster-size rectangle, I attached them to the pantry door where I would see them each morning as I fixed breakfast. At the top of this big, blank paper I wrote a question: "What do you love?"

What do I love? Answering that question became a regular part of my morning ritual. Waiting for tea water to heat, I would stand pondering the list. When an idea popped into my mind, part of the fun was choosing which color crayon to use for any particular item. Taking long hikes was green, candlelight yellow, swimming in the warm ocean a soft blue. But what color was spending time with my family? Reading? Dancing?

I could use any color I wished — there were no wrong answers. There also were no boundaries to limit what I could add to the list. I could love an activity, a place, a person, an area of intellectual interest, an animal, or anything else. I could love something I did often, such as swimming. Or I could love—potentially, anyway—something about which I felt curious, such as the idea of learning to scuba dive. Anything was possible and everything was okay, on the love list.

Occasionally, another type of thought would pop into my head as I pondered the love list. These were always related to the big question of doing what I loved, but they didn't answer the question directly. A typical one read, "I do what I love because I respect myself." As I wrote these philosophical insights on the love list in firm black ink, they became bricks and mortar against which the rest of the list leaned.

The love list defied organization, although interesting connections linked items added on different days. "Love" and "solitude" rested side by side in strong red crayon. "Living in a harmonious home" was also inscribed in red, but "a home filled with love and laughter," a goal I was having trouble envisioning in my newly single condition, was written just below in brown.

As my list grew, the multitude of colors made it cheerful. And because it followed no order or particular format, anything that popped into my head fit right in. Some mornings, especially just after I posted the list, I added lots of items. Other mornings, nothing came to mind. What did it matter? Having the list posted so prominently affirmed the renewed importance of love in my life. Not romantic love with its vicissitudes; that was impossible to rely on at a time in my life when everything was in flux. I needed to know what I could count on, what would get me through. The love list provided stability and reassurance of my commitment to building a positive future. Big decisions had to be made, and soon. As I faced these decisions alone, I wanted to make them based on feeling as well as thought. This was new territory for me, in some ways. Sure, I had acted on emotion before. Much more often, I reasoned my way to a course of action. But I rarely succeeded in pairing emotion and thought to come up with decisions that felt as emotionally satisfying as they were sensible.

What to do next with my life? Where to go? Who to become? Big questions, fear-inducing. The love list on my pantry door reminded me of the importance of loving the answers. As I invited feelings into my decision-making process, I found myself much more satisfied with the results. No more second thoughts that were really first feelings, calling into question decisions already made. Now once I reached a decision, the decision stayed in place, not because I ignored my feelings, but because I had considered those feelings in making it.

I can't say it was easy. I'm the kind of person who prefers to gather every scrap of information before moving ahead. Better still, I like it when someone wiser than I am points out the best possible path. In this situation, though, no sage would fix my life for me. No partner would help me look at the problem from all angles before taking a step. No, it had come down to me, and the need to act. I would have to start with what I knew, and accept that there was no "right way" to plan the next phase of my life.

Slowly, I got used to the feeling of working on the high wire without a net. If I fell, nobody would catch me. The responsibility for making these big decisions, and living with their consequences, was all mine. Walking across the wire, I rarely looked down into the pit where the questions "What will I do without an income?" and "What if nobody ever loves me again?" waited with open jaws. Whenever I started to feel afraid, I would stand in front of my pantry door.

Those mornings were like arriving at a party where the guests are your closest friends, so delighted to see you they greet your arrival with cheers. Gazing at their familiar faces—*quilting,* written in red; *laughter,* in green; the name of my cat, Jazz, in purple—lifted my heart. The words *sea kayaking,* written in blue-green, reminded me of many memorable days on the water, including the time a humpback whale rose to blow about sixty feet away from my boat, startling me with its unexpected presence. A past composed of such ecstatic experiences simply could not become a future that felt as gray as the present day.

If I could hold on and trust the love list, color would come back to my world. As I had kayaked in the past, I would kayak again; as I had loved in the past, I would someday love again. There wasn't time to be afraid. In the next six months I would leave my house, go to my divorce hearing, close my office, and leave my hometown. Fear could come later.

on the love list, alongside all the activities i enjoyed or the topics I was curious to learn more about, the names of places I wanted to visit sprouted. I love seeing new places. I have driven throughout the United States and visited Southeast Asia, Mexico, and Canada. But I had never seen Australia and New Zealand, Japan, Ireland, or the European continent. As I looked at the love list for guidance about what to do next, the names of these places I might love to see became a chorus, calling to me more urgently with each passing day.

I did not want to work for a while, that much was clear. When my job ended in a few months, the thought of immediately seeking another in a new town depressed me. Job hunting is no fun, even when the other pieces that make up a life are stable. Mine would not be. Instead of returning to work right away, I dreamed of taking a serious piece of time away.

Could I afford a sabbatical? Yes, if I lived frugally. It would not be the wisest thing financially, to take a span of months in my prime working years and live off savings. It would not be prudent or practical. But I had done the prudent and practical thing for a long time. If I lived frugally, then went back to work when the sabbatical ended, the financial loss shouldn't hurt too badly over the long run.

Frugal by nature, in this instance I was forced to acknowledge that my emotional needs, impractical and messy though they were, outweighed the need to make money or protect my savings account. I needed to rest, to heal, to carve out a new life for myself. As I pondered the love list, it became clear I wanted to do this healing on the road. Travel would cost money as well as time. But I had enough of both, if I could give myself permission to use them.

That was my reasoning, but to be honest, I was just thinking my way toward the answer my heart already knew. My love list had become a signpost, and it was pointing to the road. I was deeply, sorely tired, and hurt by all the predictable but nonetheless personally painful aspects of divorce. I wanted to go wandering someplace far away, and do something besides work, and see what happened inside my heart.

Time is the great healer. I trusted that axiom—I had to. That other great healer, a new love, was nothing I could mandate or count on. So, in some ways, the idea of hitting the road and letting time pass was a medical decision—travel was the best medicine I could imagine. So, a sabbatical it would be. Where to go, and how much time to allow before returning to the world of work? A year—that sounded long enough to encompass the size of the healing to be done. Pieces of that year would be consumed in the tasks of moving my belongings from Alaska to a storage unit somewhere. I would also enjoy reconnecting with family and friends neglected while I lived so far away, whose names on the love list beckoned to me.

Inside that year off, I decided to spend six months on the road . . . and I decided to do it alone.

Six months is a long time. Nobody I knew could take that much time away from job and family responsibilities to go with me. But the truth is, although I eventually invited people to join me for small pieces of my journey, I never seriously wished for or asked anyone to come with me for the whole stretch. On the love list I'd written both "going solo" and "being alone." Honoring this aspect of my personality seemed important. I loved my own company, or had, once upon a time . . . the journey would offer space for reconnecting with that closest of travel companions, my own unique self.

Once I decided to travel, the remaining decision was, where? Because I'm the kind of person who likes a big challenge, an around-the-world journey first came to mind. I could buy one of those tickets that allows you to hop on and off planes anywhere they fly, as long as you proceed in one direction around the world.

The longer I thought about a circumnavigation of the world, though, the less excited I became. Like a student caught napping the night before the big test, I felt unprepared to understand the many cultures and countries an around-the-world traveler visits. And with my job becoming more intense as it neared the end, I did not have time for the research needed to prepare adequately.

So I narrowed my focus to Europe, a place I always wanted to visit. My sister had already enjoyed several solo trips there. A desire to get in on the fun (mixed with a bit of sibling rivalry, I'll admit) called me in the same direction. By going to Europe, I would achieve a goal of lifelong significance without feeling I had to spend a year preparing in advance for the trip. European literature, art, and language formed part of my cultural heritage. In some ways, I had been learning about Europe for years. Was I ready? No. But I loved the idea of a European trip. I could start with what I knew and learn the rest as I went along.

looking over the love list, i decided to combine a european journey with another of the things I love: the Spanish language. It was the first language of my beloved paternal grandmother Carlota, who was born in Mexico to parents of Spanish descent. I studied Spanish in high school and used it on visits to Mexico, as well as when talking with my grandmother. Wouldn't I love to recover my rusty language skills while I traveled?

As the trip came together, I decided to spend my first month in Europe at a Spanish language school in Spain. This would let me get my feet on the ground, in a country where I stood at least some chance of understanding the language. I would be lost in German- or French-speaking countries, but in Spain I could get by. Once I was used to the challenge of traveling in a country where English was not the first language, I would feel more comfortable exploring the rest of the continent.

And by "exploring," I do mean exploring. Buying my plane tickets ahead of time determined where and when I would reach and depart from Europe. Committing myself to Spanish language school locked in how I would spend the first month. Other than that, I would go without plans or reservations. I wanted to learn to lie back into the arms of the universe and just let things happen, and see how that felt. Never one to paddle in the shallows when I could dive into deep waters, I decided to practice by launching myself into new territory, alone and without an itinerary.

After months of living with the big questions, my answers slowly became clear, thanks to the love list. After my divorce, where would I go, and what would I do with myself? I would follow my love for the Spanish language and solo travel to Europe, that's what.

it's now been more than five years since the night i loaded my possessions onto a southbound ferry and left Juneau. My sabbatical included three weeks traveling solo and practicing my Spanish in Costa Rica, then five months in Europe. Along the way, I added more items to the love list: among them, the world's great art museums, the hill towns of Andalusia, and the theaters in London's West End.

Part of the reason I gave myself that time on the road was an intuition that I could best plan the next phase of my life while wandering. Immersed in experiences that gave me joy, my imagination would feel free to construct the happy future I craved. Intuition did not lead me astray. The dream of what to do next came as I hiked along the shore of an Austrian lake in midsummer: I wanted to write a book about my travels.

I spent the following winter in Arizona, writing every morning and swimming or jogging each afternoon, shaking off memories of Alaskan winters by indulging in the intense physical pleasure of being outdoors in sunshine. Those months spent writing stories gave me as much joy as the solo road itself did. My next paying job, the one I still hold, is a writing job; at last, I earn a paycheck for practicing the craft I've always loved.

In these five years I've bought a new home and found a kind man with whom to share it; all good parts of the story, and worth telling. But could I have done these things, if I hadn't given myself the freedom to explore the world on my own while my heart healed? Could I have done these things, that is, without the love list?

Maybe. But I wouldn't have wanted to. In the darkest days of my divorce, the love list focused my gaze on a future worth building, a life with joy at its heart. It forced me to take the things I love—and thus my own happiness—seriously, at a time when my life was about anything but being happy. Scrawling ideas on the love list in crayon gave me space in which to play, and because there were no wrong answers on that list I was gently forced along the right path. Months that might have been consumed by darkness and loss instead sparkled with the rainbow colors of crayons and the radiant light of love.

In the coming year, my partner and I are thinking about selling our home and moving out of Arizona. He wants to attend graduate school. I want to pursue freelance writing—preferably while gazing out through a window fringed by trees.

These are big changes we're facing, huge decisions. We don't yet know where we are going, or what will happen when we get there. But whenever we feel scared of the future, we both know just what to do.

Pull out the crayons.

Married to the Dance (Not the Dancer)

mary-charlotte domandi

j. left for his native country before sunrise. originally he was just going home for the holidays, but now he was going to stay. I drove him to my city's little airport, where a cat lounged out front, observing the early morning travelers. It scampered into the darkness as we passed through the glass door.

J was sadder than I was. In the end the split had been my idea. We hugged goodbye, no tears; I did not look back as he headed for his gate. A crescent moon rose before me as I drove home alone on the narrow county road. I felt an unaccustomed freedom of movement in my limbs, a sense that I was stretching into ample new clothes that finally fit my body. The tension of years of contraction, of having held myself in a space far too small, melted away before I reached my front door.

We met dancing. I had moved to New Mexico to go to graduate school and was trying to figure out what my life's work might be when suddenly and without warning I succumbed to an all-consuming, insatiable passion for Latin music. I spent my time listening studiously and ecstatically to the weekly salsa show on public radio, taking dancing lessons, and going to the one salsa club in town. The night we met, J and I danced together until the end of the last song; he dipped me and spun me and held me and led my body into movements I had never done before, that I didn't know I had in me. I followed him as best I could.

That was the beginning of my years of following. At first, following a man for any reason seemed wrong. I was a feminist, an Ivy League graduate; I'd read Western Classics at St. John's and made angry, funny art works about the misogynist passages in Plato. I had grown up dancing classical ballet, which required total self-control, and now I was doing a dance that was all about letting go, letting the man lead. I resisted. J insisted, "Just follow what I do, like this, like this."

One night, before we left my house to go dancing, J looked at me, looked at my closet, and asked, "Do you have anything more *form fitting?*" I did not. He began to buy me clothes, tight and feminine. I loved them. He had a good eye for women's clothing, for what would look good on me. I felt pretty and sexy in a way I never had before. The androgyny I had adopted as a defense against sexism began to fall apart. This man loved women, loved me, loved our differences. I slowly began to deconstruct the familiar and arrogant stereotypes about Latin machismo that many Americans held. Something ugly began to emerge: a specifically Anglo-American misogynist machismo that was, at its root, a deep, unspoken contempt for women, for femininity—a machismo in which there was no dance but only sports, in which sexuality was lascivious rather than joyous, in which the only way to success for women was to play by the man's rules in the man's world, competitively, sexlessly. I had internalized all this from my WASPy environs to the point where by age thirty I was plain, nearly invisible, and conflicted about how to move in the world, in my flesh.

Now I was being shown something else, a way of being a woman that was strong and feminine and sexual and free all at the same time, that was expressed in this joyous phenomenon called salsa.

It was utterly nonverbal. We danced, he led, I haltingly learned to follow and came to love following. It was a freedom of expression, a surrender that allowed my own movement to shine without the pressure of having to call the moves myself. I sensed at moments something both fleeting and breathtaking—in learning to follow in the dance, I was also learning to surrender to the larger, invisible dance of my own elusive destiny.

Not that the dance was always smooth. Sometimes J led too aggressively; sometimes he did not give me enough room to move. Sometimes, as I became a better dancer, he competed with me so that I would not outshine him. He never admitted this, but he criticized my dancing more and more the better I became.

I was not ready to get married when he asked me. I had loved him so ardently in the months after we met that he came to feel that I was a treasure, told me so, and proposed. We were in a theater, at the concert of one of the great salsa musicians of Puerto Rico. I was taken aback, and said "Maybe." Then "Yes." We eloped.

Now I was a wife. I had no models for this role, at least none that I liked. "Wife" was like a strange shirt with the armholes in the wrong place, too constricting around the neck, in a color that didn't suit my skin. I rationalized that the marriage wasn't real because we didn't sanctify it in a church. But I had said the words, "'Til death do us part." I was in. I wasn't at all confident that it would really last that long, but I was in.

I learned Spanish. I welcomed his parents into our small apartment; they spoke no English and stayed six months. It was astonishingly harmonious. They were ready to love me and never judged me. J adored his parents and they him. He had never had a rebellious adolescent period.

I asked him about this once and he said, "I love my parents; they gave me life. I would be happy to live in their house with them for the rest of my life."

"But didn't you rebel?"

"No, why should I?"

"Everyone does at some point," I maintained.

"Not in Peru," he said. "Not in my family. Why do you Americans make everything so difficult?"

I allowed him to change me. I came to accept my mother more deeply and easily because of his example. I opened myself to a domestic togetherness I had never known. All my previous relationships had been extreme, intense, passionate, and heartbreaking—whether I was on the giving or receiving end of the heartbreak. I had always thought that marriage would make me feel like a caged animal, bored, restlessly pacing a space too small. Now I loved coming home to my chubby Peruvian with the calm eyes and quick smile who loved his family and didn't waste time on unnecessary worries.

But . . . but . . . he also didn't want to work much. He taught dancing but never paid his share of the bills. He bought luxuries before necessities. He talked about the exploitation of indigenous people of the Americas by Europeans, and it seemed that he felt he was correcting the balance by living off me. He got depressed, missed his country, his work in tourism. We moved to Peru for four months. There he was happy. I took it all in, got to know his extended family, to love our amazing nieces, to feel the pace and vibe of his city. I tried to make it my own. I observed how happy the children were, how both ancient and modern culture were taking root inside them—they knew both the Inca dances and the Latin pop songs. The village ethic of taking care of others' children was still in place. It was a stark contrast to the sullen, restless faces of the American kids I knew, weaned on gadgets and high expectations.

And after a month I was bored. There were no bookstores, no movie theaters, little urban cultural life outside of tourism. I loved having the chance to practice my Spanish, but once I had broken through to a basic understanding of the language, most of the conversations I heard were banal. I noticed that the women, the wives, were starved for female friendship outside their families, and I made a few friends with women who were less than happy with their married lives. J didn't notice any of this; for him Peru was paradise.

We went to Machu Picchu, a place he knew very well, where he proudly guided tourists, telling them endless stories about the Incas. That day we were the last people allowed to climb up Huayna Picchu, the tall, steep mountain that towers over the archaeological site. By the time we reached the summit, all the other tourists had left and the gate below was closed. We were alone on a sacred Inca mountaintop, which, according to legend, was the residence for the high priest and the local virgins. J looked at me with a combination of tenderness and mischief and said, "Do you want to . . . to . . . we can conceive our child here."

I stared at him. "Now?"

"Yes. This is the place of my ancestors, this is a sacred place, and the child we make here will be very special. An Inca and a Gringa. A Grinca!"

We laughed. A door in my soul opened and I saw clearly in that moment that the child would be wonderful, as magical and beautiful as this place, with the best qualities of each of us—J's friendly and calm nature, my observant intelligence, and both of our endless humor and love of dance and music.

But I saw something else. J would lead, and I would follow, and my choices would be severely constrained. He would do what he wanted, when he wanted, just as his father did, and I would be expected to stay home and do most of the work, like his long-suffering mother. I saw the film running in my mind: I was stuck in his parents' house with a baby, bored, waiting for him to come home, hungry for intellectual stimulation or any work of my own. I would devote myself to the health and well-being of my baby, and then J would burst in and give it chocolate bars, even when I objected that chocolate wasn't good for a baby and I didn't want our kid's teeth to rot by the time it was twenty, like so many of the silver-toothed Peruvians, and I didn't want to mess with its blood sugar. J would scoff; he'd be Santa Claus and I'd be the bitch queen. And there would be no escape, except divorce, which would likely damage the child, as my parents' divorce had me. In an instant I saw the next decade of my life. I decided to leave the film in the can, and close it.

"I'm not ready," I said.

"Okay," he said wistfully, looking at me, still hoping. I took his hand and we sat on a stone overlooking the beautiful ruins below.

From then on I knew that I would not have a child with this man. The disadvantages of following him became more apparent all the time. In his own country he was more contented and less interesting. He was a family man with a job and wasn't looking for much more. There were, oddly, fewer opportunities to dance salsa than back in New Mexico. And although I still didn't know precisely what I wanted to do with my life, I knew it was something I wasn't going to find in Cusco, Peru. I grew moody and anxious to go home.

We returned to New Mexico, and I got a good job. He found little or no work and sat around in his underwear watching movies. We grew apart, had fights, tried to pretend that things were as they had been, held on to our dancing. But even the joy of dancing wasn't enough to hide the terrible new thing I saw: that if I was to find my life's work, which I was determined to do, he was going to hold me back. I had spent much time and effort getting to know him, his family, his work, learning his language, his culture, his dances. But the reciprocal effort had been spotty at best. I wanted to be not only loved but deeply understood and supported.

It was not to be.

I knew it was over on the day when we were visiting my mother in her small town by the ocean. The night was warm, the moon was full, and I asked him to take a walk with me on the beach. "I don't feel like it," he said.

"Please, J, it would mean a lot to me."

"No, I don't want to walk."

"Can you do it for me just this once? This is where I spent all the summers of my childhood and I want to share it with you and it's so beautiful tonight and I want to walk in the water which is warm because it's August and it's night and please, please come with me."

"No."

It wasn't a defiant No, it was a languid, I just don't feel like it No, a No that said, what I want is more important than what you want, to the point that I am incapable of noticing the hurt in your eyes. A No that said, I will never follow you. I am a man. I do what I want when I want.

That was it. A few months later he got on the plane. He had cried when I told him it was over between us. For the next two years he called and visited, trying to mend what was broken, saying, "My love, I didn't know what I had until I lost it," and "You are my Treasure, I need you."

I held my ground.

I am so much happier without him. But here's the beautiful irony: J was, inadvertently, the key to finding my life's work, but—just as I intuited—I could find it only when he was gone. The week that he left, I decided to make salsa my own. Because I no longer had a built-in dance partner, because I no longer had anyone to follow, to choose salsa CDs, to help me understand the language and culture, I felt I had to take strong measures. I went to Havana to study dance. I was swept off my feet by the intensity of Cuban music and Cuban people, their expression unmitigated by the homogenizing effects of commercialism. I met musicians from the very top bands in the country. If I had been there with J, he would have been the one to meet them while I stood quietly by, smiling and taking it in. Now I was doing it all myself. I returned to Cuba year after year, met a family that essentially adopted me. I internalized the dance to the point where they called me "La negra Americana."

Back home I was asked to be the Latin DJ at the local dance club. I got good at it, had a feel for musical segues, for getting people onto the dance floor. I got to know a large number of Latino immigrants, mostly young working-class men, and witnessed their spunk and humor and generosity and resilience. And I danced with them, danced and danced, some of the best and happiest dances of my life, dances so fully in the moment that the dance was dancing me.

Club DJing led to radio DJing. I volunteered at the public radio station on which I'd heard my very first salsa, the one that rocked my world. Within a week I was on the air, a trainee for the program *Salsa Sabrosa*. Within a year, I had a reputation as DJ Carlota, and a growing number of fans. I began to volunteer as a DJ at a second public radio station, which had a show of Latin music from all over the Americas and all over the world. I learned about Paraguayan harp music, about Tango and Fado and Flamenco and Samba and Cumbia and Bomba and Plena. I drank it all in; each new music was like falling in love, only without the drama. I missed my musical connection with J but was glad he wasn't around, as I sensed he'd have tried to take over in some way, to eclipse me with his great big presence.

I began to interview musicians in English and Spanish. I got a job doing technical work at the radio station, where I came to love the mission of public radio. I'd always listened to it, but now I was part of it. One day I looked down the hallway of the station, and it seemed very long; I realized that my life path was there.

But doing tech wasn't enough. After about a year, the woman who did the daily interview program, one of only two paid on-air jobs at the station, resigned to follow her true love somewhere. I applied for the job. I knew it would be mine, and I got it. And this turned out to be my life's work—I have become a successful radio producer and program host. Every day I thank destiny for giving me the chance to do something I love and that I'm good at. As it turns out, I'm really good at only two things: playing a Latin music set, and interviewing people. So was the marriage worth it? Hell, yeah.

Will I ever follow a man again? Other men have come and gone, I have accommodated myself to them, to their interests and passions, I have followed for moments, wondering if the dance would last for more than a song or two. But none of them was my equal; the song would end, and I would move on, not without suffering, but always sure that the ending was necessary and right. Not one has yet engaged me in a life dance that is truly balanced, fully mutual.

But the night is still young.

Bien-Divorcée

rozella kennedy

one day my family and i went to the animal shelter "just to look" at the puppies, and we fell deeply in love with one and took him home. We put him on a tiny leash and took him to the back yard to show him his "spot," and my husband and I shrugged with excited awe, as in, "Wow, now what do we do?" It was a "wow" somewhat similar to when we became parents, except of course with pregnancy, you have nine months to prepare physically and emotionally.

The day I left my first husband—I mean physically, for emotionally I'd been long gone—was the polar opposite of those kinds of moments. It was more of a "God help me; what do I *do?!*" The gestation period for this breakup had been long and tortuous, with ins and outs, cold sweats and chilling certainty. I finally made up my mind to leave, but I hadn't read any books about how to do it successfully.

I had met P in the way of a storybook romance: at a party during my junior year abroad, in France. All the girls had dreamed of this, and little ol' me actually nailed it: with a wonderful, sensitive young man who represented everything we had all mooned over. He and I fell very deeply for each other, and I stayed in Europe through the summer. I got the latest flight possible back to Boston to finish my senior year. He came to the States for Christmas break, and I went to France for Easter break, and he came back for the summer, and we worked hard and saved all our money so we could build a life together in Paris and live happily ever after. The plan was that we'd switch continents every seven years so both of us would have some time as the foreigner. We would be "Citizens of the World" and it was going to be very modern. We were very, very much in love.

Three years after I moved to Paris, we were wed. Our wedding day was wonderfully, cinematographically sunny, but I don't remember the date, or even the month. We didn't have a particular inclination to legalize our union, but there had been considerable pressure from my mother, who was unable to bear having a daughter who was "living in sin," and after finishing my master's degree at the Sorbonne, I had no legal right to remain in France. I had to persuade P to do it. I told him it'd just be a big party. He agreed, and we had a civil ceremony at the *Mairie,* a sumptuous multicourse feast, and we partied into the night.

Four years later, and the embarrassingly predictable seven years into our relationship, it was over. I was on a bus, from Bristol to London. It was the year of living "abroad" in England for him that ruined it all for us; he had no capacity to live outside of France, no ability to be so far removed from his *maman,* no grace about being the underdog who had to adapt to another language, no humor about any of it, and no future at all as a "Citizen of the World." In fact, what he did possess was a deeply seated French chauvinism that I could never have imagined.

I'm on this bus, Walkman playing the perfectly apt "Nothing Compares 2 U" by Sinead O'Connor, and my heart and throat are so tight I can hardly breathe. I wave goodbye from my window seat, and there are so many tears streaming down my face that the punk woman next to me turns in disgust. "Oh come on," she says, "you don't have to be so bleeding dra-ma-tic." Well, yes, I actually *do* have to be so bleeding dra-ma-tic, I motioned, pointing to my wedding ring (which my mom would later melt down into earrings) and making a slashing motion across my throat. Understanding my pantomime, she adapted to the gravity of the situation by not saying another word to me for the remainder of the trip.

I went to London, to the flat of a woman I had worked with peripherally, a few years before. She had just broken up with her boyfriend, and we spent that weekend complaining and commiserating together, except that five months really did not compare to seven years. Or did it? Perhaps it was actually more dra-ma-tic for her. Because when you are first in love like that, it's all so Technicolor and passionate, maybe that ending is worse. You're mourning all the fun times and not relieved to be relieved of the burdens: the taxes, the chores, the children to plan for (or *not,* in our case, thank you Jesus), the ho-hum heck of life.

I had been living on his continent for half a decade and now I was going to return to America. I had no job (though enough connections to at least get something menial), no home (but a safety net of friends and well-wishers to help me resettle), very conflicted feelings about living my life in flat English again, but sadly, most of all, no comforting familiar shroud of our youthful dysfunction. To assuage the terror, I decided to go numb. Just *do:* no thinking, no feeling.

The sheer mass of logistics that awaited me made this easy, and necessary. I had to ship my most important belongings to New York. I recollect that P's parents packed everything for me, because I left for New York directly from London after that weekend and never went back to Paris to say goodbye to anyone. My collegiate oil paintings, which were displayed in his bedroom, and which P's parents never liked, arrived years after that, after spending many years in a corner of their garage. One got ruined in transit and, like my first marriage, all that's left to preserve it are photos. I was not to return to Paris for fifteen years. Definitely sufficient time for me to forget a lot.

As life and memory like to play out, a weird historical inversion is much clearer in my mind: that summer after senior year of college, packing all my books into enormous burlap M-sacks that would be thrown on a boat and shipped slowly to Paris so I could begin my life as P's fun-loving *américaine* expat. As much as there was, during that weekend in London, great trepidation and numbness regarding the future, there was, in those late summer days of 1985, enormous exhilaration around our preparations. In our old album, there is another photo: him, supine on the bed in the room of the house we shared with three smelly male roommates after graduation (we were saving money!). Hundred-dollar bills surrounded him: our summer earnings, ready to be converted to francs so we could have this incredible life together in mythical, complicated Paris. Everything was so heady and conspiring.

but on this cold, march 1991 weekend in london, there was no excitement, just a sense of grim duty. I had decided to end it all that past November, after a silly fight where I decided to go on strike and act like him: lazy and listless and wanting to stay in bed till 3:00 P.M. watching TV. He spitefully took on my role, taking our dirty clothes to the Laundromat and doing the shopping. At the end of the day, neither of us was vindicated. He'd gotten the wrong food, and I was sore from lying around watching boring soccer. We felt stupid and sour. I told myself this was not how I wanted to go into my thirties. All signs pointed to *la sortie*.

On the plane back to New York, I felt like a failure, but not for the reasons you'd think. I would miss him, but I was determined to get over that eventually. I was mostly disturbed about having to live a regular life as a New Yorker all over again. We'd been back a few times, and I liked it better as a foreigner. So, for the first year back I resisted being American. I made friends with the kinds of conservative Euro-trash French banker types P and I would have shunned back in the days of our left-wing, postcollegiate bohemia. I only slept with Europeans (the first one, a portly Italian, looked much better in his pressed suits than in the buff). For several months, I felt completely alienated in my skin, lost amid my surroundings. I was going through the motions of living, feeling very little.

I had successes with that tactic, and many failures. One of the most acute failures manifested itself the way my deep conflicts always do: in my asthmatic lungs. Within my first month back, I had to be transported to the ER twice in one week. I was once next to a guy who had a collapsed lung. I overheard the doctors talking about his IV drug use. I felt sorry for him, but my woes still consumed me more. I think that was justifiable; there was no one to look after me.

Looking back on all this now with twenty years' reflection, I realize that I had never had anyone but myself to look after me; and in fact when I was married to P, I was the one doing all the looking out. People said, "It's amazing that you never had kids." I corrected them—oh yes, I did. I had him.

I am someone who squeaked through a lot of complicated circumstances that should have ruined me. They are too many and too disparate to account for here, but the bottom line was that their totality had burnished some sort of survivor instinct into my soul. I slowly began to rebuild a life. I became a star performer in one of the hippest funk-dance classes in New York. We were hot and fabulous. Older men vied for the right to buy me drinks at clubs. I had crushes and quite a few lovers. I tried my luck one summer with a French surfer (old pillow-talk habits die hard); dated a bunch of foolish guys; made tons of new friends; got exciting, low-paying jobs; went on vacations alone and made weeklong best friends; got better jobs; and fended off the advances of men I didn't like. *And* I am so grateful that life let me move on from that before it turned pathetic.

P and I still clung to each other emotionally for the first year of separate lives. That French surfer boyfriend proved to be an asshole. I hadn't dealt with a lot of asshole boyfriends in my life, because P was only the third or fourth man I'd ever been with. Because P and

I had vowed to maintain dignity and not totally negate what we had meant to each other by shunning each other for life, we agreed to "be there" for each other when the other really needed it. Let me say this: If you are going to get divorced, try to make it involve moving to another continent. You end up not abusing your privileges. Only one time did I call P to have him cheer me up after a breakup; after Surfer Dude (thank God, because if I had called him after every breakup, I'd still be paying off the phone debt today).

He listened to my complaints and told me quintessential friendly ex words: I was still a wonderful person and worthy of someone who would love me. I thanked him for his consideration. He said he was glad to be back in Paris where he could be himself. That was a revelatory line. I thought to myself, through my tears, "You loser, you never meant it about living in America with me. You cannot adapt!" And I felt this totally inane sort of patriotism all of a sudden. I hung up feeling definitively separated, completely emotionally detached. My foreigner was foreign to me.

Except for one dirty weekend in Florence, Italy. (I still had a flair for the grandiose gesture, I suppose.) My closest friend from college was there, and when I went to visit, P came down from Paris to see me. I was so jet-lagged and he was so nostalgic that we ended up sleeping together within moments of being alone. I'm not proud of it, but my motivation was knowing that an orgasm (should I be able to attain one, after all this) would have a sedative effect. He was amazed, because I had been working out so much and my tummy was flat. (For the record, such a period actually did exist in my adult life!) He told me he missed "the pillow." I thought to myself, "*Tant pis* for you, I'm a single New Yorker now, and the competition is fierce."

One night during that weekend, a crowd of us—my friend and her entourage of Italian pals, P and I, and some other hangers-on, gathered around a huge table for a late-into-the-night Italian dinner. I remember not being able to stop myself from flirting with a cute boy at the table. Over pasta and copious quantities of wine, I could sense I was rousing his curiosity. At one point he asked me how I knew that skinny guy at the end of the communal dinner table. "Oh," I remember saying, because it was still the truth, *"e il mio sposo."* Too much of a French movie for the Italian guy, I guess, because that ended our conversation for the night. P didn't seem to mind, or know what was going on. He certainly had no claim to stake. I took it all as a sign that I needed to stop pursuing casual sex.

Months became years, new friends and jobs ensued; I got another boyfriend who stayed around for a year and who burned my soul inside and out but grew me up.

France had definitely turned into the Old Country now; my first marriage receded into the stuff of anecdotal conversation-toppers. Oh, did you know I lived in Paris for seven years; my ex-husband is French. It made me a colorful party guest.

After the yearlong boyfriend, I geared my compass toward self-help. I did some intensive therapy and worked out some important things regarding codependency and communication. I may have written P a letter apologizing for having been immature. He wrote me about his life from time to time, too, but frankly, his handwriting has always been so bad I can't make out much of what he's trying to say.

I was just looking for someone to go to the movies with, and I ended up meeting a man with whom I have built an adult life. He was seeking permanence and meaning, just as I had only recently realized I was. Within a month, I moved in with him.

He knew about P, but it represented nothing to him, for he had his share of relationships behind him, too. One late afternoon, we were lying in bed and he presented a ring he had made out of sea grass. I said "yes." (We had already fantasized about how he might propose to me: One of our favorite improbable options was the corny scoreboard-at-the-baseball-game thing. P never understood even the basic rules of baseball and found it stupid. All the pieces of cultural shorthand that got lost between us probably made our relationship too literal.) My brand-new fiancé rushed off to get pizza and a split of champagne so we could celebrate. It was one of those still moments when you are just completely happy. Until a harsh fact slammed me out of my reverie: "Oh *damn,* I am still actually married!"

The paperwork involved in dissolving marriage number one was completely my responsibility, because P cared little for the institution, and so, be it dissolved or not, *pas d'importance.* I had seen a lawyer a few months after first moving back to New York, but he quoted an unattainable sum to me, some five thousand dollars. A good friend who was himself divorced hipped me to those D-I-Y books you could buy where you did all the forms yourself and it cost just a few hundred bucks. I didn't get the final notarized signature back from P until two or three days before my fiancé and I were leaving to the Caribbean for the vacation where we would be married. P meant me no malice in taking so long to return the paperwork. It was just his disorganized, sluggish way. I remember a mad-dash cab ride to City Hall before our flight out, striving to get to the clerk before they closed. I was prepared, anyway, to be a bigamist.

I got married again when I was a wiser woman, to someone from my own country, so we go through life's ups and downs with no fantasy escape hatch. He had a real life before he met me, and we merged ours together and have built terrific permanence and meaning. We had a daughter three years after getting married, and when she was one and a half, we moved to New Mexico. Now we have two daughters and two dogs and a life with some heck but a lot of love.

P's parents came to visit the American West the first year we lived out here, and my husband and I ended up inviting them to stay in a guest apartment in the complex where we lived. P's stepfather still spoke passable English, but his mother had completely given up now that I was gone, and my French was rusty at best, but we got by. It was fun, like dinner with an old college professor.

My husband was part of an opera project that took the three of us to London that same summer. P took the Chunnel up to meet my *petite famille*. I was distressed and saddened to find a bitter man before me. He complained that he was in a relationship that was ending poorly and with some measure of violence. (He is the ultimate pacifist.) He and my husband circled wagons somewhat warily, though my husband was actually honored to meet the man who had once loved me so fully, and who still held my memory dear enough to come up to London to bear witness to my new life. I told my husband that that made him sound rather heroic, and he joked that he is.

I felt very sorry for P. He felt sorry for himself, too, and made it clear that he envied my happy life, my family; he felt like a loser. We had a very somber lunch, and even my lightheartedness didn't lift the mood. This time on the plane to the United States, I was elated to be getting away.

In 2004, fourteen years after leaving Bristol, I returned to Paris for the first time, as a middle school French teacher with thirteen students in tow. I imagined it would be emotionally overwhelming to return to mythical Paris after fifteen years, and I warned my students not to be alarmed if I burst into tears when visiting certain monuments. But in the end, there were no tears. I was extremely happy and grateful to be there again. It was a simple joy of past familiarity, and a marking of the passage of time.

On my day off, P met me at the Picasso Museum (something we had never found the time to do together!). We had a delightful lunch and a wonderful time looking at the art, and I climbed on the back of his bicycle (he had become an ardent follower of the Green Party) and he rode me all the way up to his apartment, across the city. It was a gorgeous, sunny day, not unlike the one of our wedding, I suppose. The bike ride was very long, and the cobblestones hurt my butt. I was quite impressed by how strong he had become. He also had a little bit of a potbelly and thinning hair. I no longer had anything like a flat tummy, but I thought I still had a sense of cheap creative style. We must not have looked that different from all the regular people out and about in Paris that day.

To steady myself on the back of his bike, I put my arms around his waist, like one would do with a friend's husband in a conga line at a tacky wedding reception.

He seemed intent on impressing me with the order and affability of his life, and I was pleased to be gracious and obliging. We arrived at the apartment where he lived with his girlfriend of three years and their nearly two-year-old daughter. (How thrilled I was that he had finally accepted that settling down was not a form of bourgeois death!) His girlfriend was wary, but kind enough. I could tell this was not easy for her, and I wanted to reassure her that there was no reason to be uptight. I hadn't cared for him, in anything but the most diffuse way, in almost a decade. Those seven years together were consigned to memory and subsumed by our new lives. But, I just played it all off by being blithe and jovial, the Rozie of a thousand cocktail parties and a million glasses of *kir royale*.

Their baby was asleep. I peeked in to see her and I was choked with gratitude and admiration for this fidgety French woman who had given P what he needed out of life, and what had never been my role to give. His girlfriend, C, made a lovely dinner of crustaceans, and we drank wine and listened to Boris Vian records. P burned me a couple of discs of nostalgia music, which my own children find hysterically bizarre: all tubas and cha cha cha. He asked me to stay on, longer into the night, so we could all talk and make new memories of camaraderie over another bottle of wine. I was sleepy and had a full day of sightseeing ahead with my charges, so I got a cab and went to bed feeling just content at how beautifully everything had evolved.

Two years later, my family went to Paris, following my husband on a trip to meet with a French composer. My ex-in-laws took my husband to the Paris Bastille Opera. Okay—the fact that my ex-in-laws went on a "date" with my husband *is* right out of a French screenplay, I admit, but I know this was the ooh–la–la way we all needed for this to work itself out.

This winter P and C had another daughter. They sent us a birth announcement, which was very sweet. The daughter's second middle name is Rose. My husband wondered aloud if I thought they'd named her after me.

"Oh God, no," I replied. "Honey, I'm just an artifact in that family history."

And *nom de Dieu,* it is a dignified and pleasing role to occupy.

So Much Strong
samantha ducloux waltz

jacob, my friend's three-year-old son, held his arms at right angles and flexed his biceps until they quivered. "I am so much strong," he said and roared like a lion.

I squatted and looked into his sparkling brown eyes. I wished I felt as strong. In my conflict-torn marriage, my emotional biceps were like jelly.

True to my marriage vows as I understood them, I tried for twenty-two years to honor and obey my husband, praising his mechanical and artistic skills, often working full-time to help support the family, and working alongside him evenings as we built a house on ten rural acres. When we tried marriage counseling to alleviate our constant arguing, I accepted his blame for our problems.

But I could never please him, and I was miserable. One morning I counted the number of things he accused me of doing wrong between the time I got up and the time I left for work forty-five minutes later. I did twenty-five things wrong. Twenty-five. From using too much water in the bathtub to leaving crumbs on the counter when I made my toast.

Worse, I didn't protect my children from his frequent rage. "You didn't clean the tub," he snarled at Joel, our eleven-year-old, one Saturday.

"I saw him scrub it for twenty minutes," I protested, outraged at both Hal's incessant criticism of our younger son and my inability to protect Joel.

Hal glared at me, grabbed Joel's arm, and dragged him to the bathroom. "Stupid retard. You call this clean? Look at the soap dish."

Notice what he did do! I wanted to scream. But that would make him even angrier.

When Tami, my seventeen-year-old daughter, played the flute, Hal complained that her daily practice sessions at home weren't long enough. When she took voice lessons, she didn't sing loud enough at church. When reading, she chose the wrong books. She also chose the wrong friends.

Hal seemed to have more patience with our middle child, Ben, who enjoyed working alongside him on many projects. But occasionally I caught Ben downstairs crying, depression from the chronic discord in our home consuming him, along with the rest of us.

Why couldn't I roar like a lion? Flex my biceps like Jacob?

Tami was the first to stand up to her father. One day Molly, our old poodle, wandered into Hal's path as he crossed the family room to the couch, and he kicked her out of his way.

"Don't kick Molly," Tami snapped at him.

"Don't tell me what to do." Furious, Hal pushed her onto the couch and pinned her there, his hands gripping her wrists, the weight of his body pressing on hers.

Before I could intervene, Tami freed herself enough to kick him in the stomach. "Don't ever fucking touch me again."

It was time I stood up to him, too.

With the help of supportive friends and therapists, I started individual counseling. My diagnosis of clinical depression, caused by anger turned inward, frightened me. Hal had always belittled my feelings, but now I took them more seriously. After a few months, I added group counseling. Slowly I grew stronger.

Yet another round of marriage counseling failed to alter our pattern of endless arguing. One night I was sitting in my therapy group and a member said, matter-of-factly, "Have you considered divorce?"

My chest tightened, and my stomach clenched. Through all the years of arguments and insults, I hadn't considered divorce. My mother had stayed with my father despite his same-sex affairs. My church, the Church of Jesus Christ of Latter-Day Saints, taught that the sanctity of the family was more important than any personal consideration, and that a temple marriage was a prerequisite of getting into the celestial kingdom.

I saw divorce as an obvious, but still undesirable, option. I went home and broached the subject with Hal for the first time, in confidence.

"Your mother is thinking of breaking up the family," he told the children the next day, without warning. He gathered us all around a blackboard in the family room and cruelly drew lines and arrows that showed each child having to come to us both, individually, if they wanted or needed as much as a sandwich or a dime.

Joel didn't want me to break up the family. My heart wept with sorrow and regret as he assured me that he could lie face down on his bed and make himself forget any encounter with his father, whether it was a scolding or a slap. It might take as long as two weeks, but he could do it.

Ben wanted to stay on the property with his father if I left. He loved wandering our woods and thought his father needed him. How could I leave my beloved son behind?

Only Tami pushed for a separation.

I hesitated. Again, I thought of my mother's example, and of the church's teachings. Then, one night, when Joel was helping me prepare a quick dinner, Hal came into the kitchen. He said something to Joel that I couldn't hear. The next thing I knew he was shoving Joel against the kitchen cabinet. Wham.

Anger flooded my body, followed by resolve. I asked Hal to leave. He laughed.

It took another month of emotional muscle-building for me to retain a lawyer and make arrangements to move in temporarily with a friend. Tami and Joel went with me. Ben tried staying with Hal for a few weeks, but he soon chose to live with us.

I was getting stronger.

With money borrowed from my parents I bought a little house and began decorating it. The music of Mary Chapin Carpenter filled the rooms, and French doors opening onto the patio let in the early summer warmth along with a faint smell of lavender. Contentment expanded my chest as I chose which pictures to hang where, without fear of criticism.

I missed our former home with its view of the Tualatin Valley—a patchwork of farmhouses and fields broken by an occasional square of industrial gray or clump of residential development. I missed the way the branches of the trees formed snow-laden boughs over the driveway during Portland's occasional snowstorms, and the quiet that allowed me to hear entire symphonies of birdsong. Ben missed it, too, although he sometimes camped on the five undeveloped acres I retained from the divorce.

But what gains we made over the next months as our shoulders straightened and our faces relaxed! Joel played football for the first time, astonishing me because I'd never seen an aggressive bone in his body. During one game, he really caught fire. The coaches jumped to their feet, screaming, "Joel! Joel! Go Joel!" as he tackled one player after another and made a first down possible for his team. Of course I yelled the loudest.

Now, in the middle of the day, he lies face up on his bed, figuring out how to find the leak in the sprinkler system of our new home or how to fix the broken blender; not face down, to forget hurtful things.

Ben counted the days until the first snow fell. He wanted to snowboard, so when I overheard one of my students say he was selling his old board, I asked the price. I gave my student the best moment of his academic life when I bought the board, and I thrilled Ben.

Ben worked through some problems at school and widened his circle of friends. He began cracking jokes and soon had us all laughing daily.

Tami sang and danced in her high school production of *Oklahoma*. I doubt she would have had the confidence to audition before the divorce, since her father derided all her extracurricular activities. I loved seeing her onstage.

She brought friends to our new house, something she hadn't wanted to do before. She got a part-time job and excelled in her responsibilities there.

When the kids were busy with their activities, I hiked and bicycled with friends. I took up ballroom dancing, something I'd always wanted to do. I visited on the phone with friends and read books I'd longed to read but never had the time for.

I kept us all in counseling, knowing life would continue to lob us challenges. Divorce, with its losses and its gains, is only one possible stop on the journey of life. When challenges came, the kids and I would be ready to dig deep, understand how we felt about the issue at hand, and make choices consistent with those feelings.

life lobbed a big one.

"I'm sick of people at church saying bad things about you." Tami seethed, sitting beside me as we drove home from services, arms folded tightly across her chest. "They say you're a bad person for breaking up the family. They don't know you saved us."

At first I shrugged off her comment, assuring her there might be a few people judging me, but other members of the congregation, like several families in our new neighborhood, were becoming dear, helpful friends.

But her words sat heavily in my heart over the next months. The two women I thought were my best friends at church suddenly quit calling to chat and gave no explanation. I was relieved of a volunteer job teaching in the women's auxiliary, perhaps because I enriched lessons with materials from outside the church-approved lesson manual, but also perhaps because I set a bad example for the other women. The bishop who had lovingly counseled me about my divorce was replaced by a more austere minister. Monday through Saturday I felt increasingly happy with my single life and its opportunities for new friendships and new activities. Only on Sundays did I feel the gray weight of depression settling again on my shoulders.

Tami was the first to ask if she could quit attending. I agonized over her request. Our family had always gone to church, as did my parents before me, and their parents before them. My ancestors had crossed the plains pushing handcarts or driving covered wagons to help settle the Salt Lake Valley. Still, Tami was seventeen, and a major principle of the Mormon Church is free agency. So, I respected her choice.

The boys followed her out—first Ben, and then, a few months later, Joel. I knew my children would still be thoughtful, compassionate, moral people if they left the church. I had never believed that the Mormon Church is the one, true church, as it claims. My mother, though very active in the church, had taught me when I was young that all roads—Christian, Buddhist, Islamic, Zoroastrian, Hindu, whatever—lead to the same God. My children would find their own version of spirituality.

But I, personally, was in a real bind. I felt stifled and defective if I went to church, yet miserable and guilty if I didn't attend.

I'd always had fundamental disagreements with Mormon theology, such as denial of the priesthood to women, the church's stand on homosexuality as a moral issue, and the belief in polygamy as a celestial principle. The authoritarian feel to everything bothered me. On the flip side, some of the best people I knew were Mormon.

Their beautiful families filled the pews at church. Most of them welcomed me at church and visited me in my home, offering to help with anything, from fixing our screen door to bringing dinner. I believed in a God who answers prayers, though I was no longer convinced he/she was the anthropomorphic God Mormons worship. Above all else, I felt I *should* go to church.

I poked my biceps with one finger. How strong had I become? Strong enough to stay in a church of mostly good people whose beliefs I didn't share?

Or strong enough to leave a church I had been taught all my life I must attend?

I journaled obsessively for months, my heart torn in two. I had felt so resolute about leaving Hal. I could not get clarity on leaving the church.

My body finally made the decision. I began waking up acutely nauseated on Sundays. Despite the goodness of many members whom I still loved very much, I simply couldn't attend anymore.

I celebrated when my divorce was final. I celebrated when Joel tackled a guy twice his size, when Ben swooshed down a hill on his snowboard, when Tami sang a solo in *Oklahoma*. But I never celebrated leaving the church.

Strength means being true to myself. But it doesn't always mean being happy right this minute.

I think of Jacob proudly showing me his biceps. We now have something in common. I, too, am so much strong.

Travel Somewhere

teresa coates

it must be just about lunchtime; the cicadas are screaming again. Every spring, they crawl from the ground, rising from the silence of winter, to signal the change of the season here in northern Vietnam. Twice a day, the thumb-size males sing out in unison, shaking against the trees, creating a group love song that calls out to the ladies. I head into the kitchen to start lunch. There are only three walls in our kitchen—the fourth is open to the courtyard, barred to keep out intruders, but not the cacophony of sound or waves of summer heat. The bamboo shade billows up with the wind, cooling me slightly. It's early June, but the temperature is already well into the nineties.

I'd visited the outdoor market down the block soon after the sun rose, already heating up the air. Even in what might be called the cool of the morning, it is warm. Learning to sweat without humiliation is just one of the skills I've acquired since coming to Vietnam last December. I've also learned to use chopsticks for every food group, how to unintentionally offend the nice fruit seller at this market, and how to say "I don't understand Vietnamese" in fairly good Vietnamese.

I buy four foot-long carrots, two goose eggs, a small, chartreuse-colored squash, my daughter's favorite chocolate drink mix (Milo), a whole chicken (head and feet intact), and two fruits of the gods: Asian pineapple. The woman selling the small variety sits in the shade of an awning, her wicker tray filled two feet high with six-inch pineapples. I hold up two fingers in a peace sign, she grabs a pair, and I nod, *Yes, they're good.* She pulls out her cleaver, deftly peeling them and removing the dark eyes with swift chops of the knife. No matter how many times I've watched her, her skill always amazes me.

Back home, I pull out my small round cutting board and cleaver, though I'm not nearly as adept as the pineapple slinger. I chop vegetables while the chicken boils in a pot of sterilized water atop our two-burner gas stove. Sweat slides down my temple. I wipe it with the sleeve of my torn T-shirt.

"Stuart!" I call to my son in the next room. "Can you bring me the rice from the fridge?"

Our miniature gray refrigerator sits next to the bed that we share in our tiny studio apartment. Two kids and one mom in a twelve-by-twenty-foot room makes for some clever furniture arrangement, and the patience of Job, but it works.

Stuart, fifteen and nearly as tall as me, pushes the door open and pokes only his hand—bearing a plastic bag of cold, cooked rice—into the room.

I place it on the tiny counter space and get to work on assembling the fried rice: carrots, squash, onion, garlic, egg, and then I stir in the rice last. I mix in the soy sauce and pour it all into a large, brightly colored plastic bowl. We'll eat in the other room, circling the short coffee table that doubles as our dining table.

This isn't what I'd ever imagined for my life. As a teenager, I'd hoped to study fashion design. I wanted to learn how to sew and I wanted to leave Newberg, the small town I'd lived in from kindergarten to graduation. I'd never dared to dream this big . . . this *let's-get-rid-of-everything-and-move-to-a-foreign-country* big. This was a fluke, something that would have been impossible if my life plans hadn't gone awry.

My ex and I married when we were both nineteen, too young to realize just how much we didn't yet know about ourselves or each other. Just after our ninth wedding anniversary, he met Sarah—a sixteen-year-old who loved the Dandy Warhols, thrifting, and playing guitar as much as he did. I attributed his late nights, oh-so-private phone calls, and short temper to the band he'd recently formed, only to find out two months later that it was his girlfriend and not his bandmates who were keeping him away. Given the choice, he decided he'd missed out and wanted to try to be a rock star, to live life over—but this time without a wife or kids. So, he split. Just like that, I was on my own with two kids, all of one and six years old.

It'll be fine, I assured myself. *He'll miss having two kids around. We'll be a family again.* I kept that game going for the next six months before denial turned to anger, as Kubler-Ross's famous five steps of grief predicted. I pounded my fists against the pale cream walls of our apartment while the kids spent the weekend with my parents. I left him curt phone messages. I cried and cried and cried.

I pleaded with him to give up the girlfriend, to come back, but he was happier than ever, he said. I was sure it was an early midlife crisis. I spent another month or two planning suicide before I realized that no matter what, by intentionally dying after their dad intentionally left, I would totally screw up my children's lives. And that, to be sure, was the last thing I wanted. It was time to suck it up and be a grownup.

Out came the yellow pad of paper. As a writer, I had several stashed around, by this time half-filled with morose scrawling and angry, never-sent letters, but I needed one for a higher purpose now. I needed to figure out just what the hell I was going to do with my life.

Come on, girl: Think. What have you always wanted to do and never done?

I stared at the paper. My right hand and its Paper Mate hovered above the blank sheet for minute after minute until I gave up and went to bed.

The next day: same activity, but with small squares of Post-it notes instead. Bright yellow with more lines than I could possibly fill, the legal pad had stifled me. Now I had only a three-inch-square piece of pink paper with a narrow strip of tacky glue.

Think of something. Anything.

In the past, I'd asked my husband about taking community college classes, but money was always tight and he was adamant that education wasn't the key to happiness or success. "Yeah, someday," he'd assure me. That someday wasn't up to him anymore and damn it, I wanted a bachelor's degree. Majoring in what? Who knows. I'd figure that out later.

On the pink square I wrote: *Go to college.*

Getting something down broke the small dam, and the ideas started flowing, big and bold (Be a millionaire!), then tempered by reality (I make $8.50 an hour!). Finally I settled on three:

> *Go to college.*
> *Live in a house again.*
> *Travel somewhere.*

I stuck the post-it to my index finger and then read it aloud. Yep, that's good enough to start with. Not too restrictive, but not too easy. Absolutely do-able. Retrieving my journal from the bookshelf above my bed, I opened it to the next blank page, dated it, and pressed the pink Post-it below. Forget New Year's resolutions, these are my new life's resolutions.

Six months later, I found a house in the Brooklyn neighborhood of Portland. Rent was almost affordable, with a fair amount of penny-pinching. After I got a full-time job with a wood stain manufacturing company, income was steady enough to justify the splurge on a two-bedroom house. We had a back yard, complete with a worn hammock hung across branches of the magnolia tree that covered much of the yard in cool shade. I'd lie crosswise, swinging, watching two-year-old Audrey play in the wading pool I set up in the sunlit area of grass while Stuart, then seven, played Zorro nearby. For the first time in thirteen years, that fall I'd sit in a classroom again.

The first few terms were an exercise in fortitude and motivation. Older than 90 percent of my fellow students, I didn't quite fit in, but I had more life experience, so more appreciation for what I was learning. Two years in, I took my first Women's Studies class. In Professor Hummer's class, I learned how the intersection of my gender, religious upbringing, age, and class had created a filter that influenced the decisions I'd made. I began retrieving the independent streak that had been buried during my marriage. I took another class from her and another, then ventured out to other teachers and slowly emerged as a fiercely independent woman devoted to her children. For the first time in my life, I had a small hold on that mantra I'd long heard proclaimed: I can do anything I set my mind to.

My four-year degree was turning into six years, but I could finally see a light at the end of the college tunnel. There, in the too-near future, full-time work and after-school care awaited me. Was that what I'd been working for all this time? In a way it was, but not quite yet. What better time to take a break in life's course? None; I'd spent seven years as a stay-at-home mom and another six as a student. Now, I had the freedom. I'd take a Gap Year, like so many other university graduates do, and spend some time "discovering myself." And my children would get to do the same alongside me. So without looking back, in my last year of school, I decided that we should go to Vietnam. Why not? I had a friend living in Hanoi; we could volunteer at some orphanages and see a bit of the world. No matter that I was an international travel virgin. *Travel somewhere,* I'd written, and Southeast Asia seemed as good a place as any other.

The plan was basic: My last quarter ended in December. We'd leave a week later and end up in Tam Ky a week after that. Best laid plans and all, but life gets in the way sometimes. I managed to fail my online class and wouldn't be graduating after all. It was three days before we left, two days until Christmas, and one day until we had to be out of our house—my plans seemed shot to hell.

I registered for the next term, taking the same online course once again, and packed my textbooks into the suitcases. I'd just pray there was Internet access in central Vietnam. Without it I'd have to fail again and wait to graduate until I returned to the States, at an unknown date in the future.

The night sky was still pitch black as we boarded the plane with one-way tickets and $13 in cash. I'd spent the months before reassuring my overwrought mother and my still-angry-about-the-war father that we'd be fine, but as the plane took off, engines whirring, I couldn't help but wonder if I should have started with something easier, like a trip to Orlando.

This sultry June day in Thanh Hoa, Vietnam, is the zenith of my divorced-mother life, and we're celebrating. I finished my second try at the anthropology class two months ago, earning a mere B-, which means I have finally, after more quarters of three-credit classes than I care to count, *finally* satisfied the university's requirements for a bachelor's degree. Tonight, over seven thousand miles away, my name will be called in the graduation ceremony. I won't be walking across the stage. Instead, I'm walking hand-in-hand with my children, across the busy street to the open-air market where they sell the best coconut ice cream on earth. Audrey and I grab an empty table while Stuart buys three bowls of ice cream. I pull the sweet pineapple out of my bag, specially chopped earlier for the occasion. Audrey requested Milo for her bring-your-own-toppings sundae. The locals who surround us aren't sure what to make of our concoctions, watching carefully as we spoon fruit and chocolate powder over our ice cream.

Sweat beads on my nose; the night air is still humid. Stuart catches my eye and I smile, sincerely. I love it here in this warmth and simplicity. The stars fill the sky and the crescent moon looks tilted. My whole life looks different from here—nothing like I'd expected all those years ago as a young bride—and I'm elated.

*

Yanking Tulips
h. k. brown

even good girls get divorced. i'm proof. i am an episcopal minister's daughter, the elder child of two, a lifetime straight-A student. I took flute lessons, for goodness' sake. Baby-sat. Graduated second in my high school class. Double-majored in college. Fell in love with my second boyfriend, dated him exclusively for five years, and then married him a month before graduating from law school. My father walked me down the aisle and then turned around and performed our ceremony.

Six years later, my little suburban world—perfect on the outside—exploded into moondust as I careened out of the driveway, abandoning my husband, my two precious beagles, my four-story house on a rocky hill in Virginia, my rock star law firm job, my circle of friends, and our wine-tasting parties. My heart felt like it was crushed in a mammogram machine.

I so easily could have raced back home, made it all better, swallowed my wanderlust, had babies, and continued smiling for an audience that couldn't see the angst in my eyes for my Cover Girl makeup. But I didn't.

i married my husband at twenty-four because, in addition to believing I needed him like oxygen, I craved acceptance and security, and what I believed then to be the pot-of-gold reward for being a good girl for so long. I wanted the booty: the good-looking husband, the marquise diamond ring, the law firm paycheck, the white picket fence, the Jeep Grand Cherokee, the Jamaica vacations. And I got it.

We had fun playing house at first, using our new cappuccino maker and make-your-own pizza kit, and sliding into bed together every night between our Crate & Barrel sheets. But after six months of the reality of marriage (after five years of the surreality of long-distance dating), I grew conscious of, or actually paid attention to, our differences. I loved to read, study, go running, lie in the sun on summer Saturdays, work hard, make money, travel. He didn't. He liked to play sports and watch TV and hang out with his family. Then an event ripped a jagged tear in my young heart, leaving me wondering whether this boy was really my perfect mate after all.

A few months into my new law firm job, I traveled to San Francisco for my very first business trip. One evening, my father called to say that my eighty-four-year-old grandfather had passed away. I called my husband on the East Coast and—new to the whole zany East Coast/West Coast time zone thing—woke him up. We argued about something inane and he hung up on me. I stayed awake all night staring at the phone and willing it to ring so we could patch things up, and so he could make me feel better about the fact that my grandfather had just died of a heart attack—the first of my four grandparents to perish. But he didn't call. I flew to the funeral in Ohio alone. My father performed his own father's interment service. I got home three days later and my husband bought me flowers, and we pretended like everything was fine.

Fifteen years later, that burn still stings. But at the time, I couldn't communicate why. I couldn't pick up the phone and, in a rational manner, explain what I needed from him. I also wasn't strong enough to simply console myself, give my soul the room to get upset and then mourn, and then pick up and carry on. So I just let it fester.

We played our roles well for five years of marriage. I bopped along to his various sports events and he donned a tux for my law firm black tie affairs. We looked fabulous and filled our photo albums with gummy grins.

Yet, I know I disappointed him. I never fit the typical domestic role. Making my law firm seventy-hour workweek my priority, I avoided most household chores. I never put my clothes in the dresser; I simply washed and rewashed them, pulling clean underwear out of the wrinkled pile on the laundry room floor. The extent of my cooking repertoire was red beans and rice and Hamburger Helper. He couldn't understand my lack of effort. He also grew tired of my emotional sine curves. While he was "sunny and seventy-two" at all times, I was like a tropical rain forest, hot and humid with intermittent torrential downpours.

Distracting myself from not-quite wedded bliss, I filled my free time with setting and achieving goals. I ran three miles a day so I could stay skinny and try to win his attention, and if that failed, win the attention of his softball teammates. I didn't know how to be alone without always trying to accomplish something. At one point, I decided to redirect my energy toward cultivating my inner homemaker. One weekend I painted our guest room (and most of the carpet) yellow. The next weekend, after a flopped attempt at making key lime pie, I turned to gardening. It was a September Saturday and my husband was ankle deep in a sandtrap somewhere, trying out his new golf clubs. I—bored and lonely as usual—drove to Home Depot and bought a sack of tulip bulbs and a trowel. A green thumb I do not possess. In fact, I have managed to kill every plant I ever owned, even cacti and bonsai. But I have always loved tulips. You can plant them one lazy weekend in the fall and then be surprised in the spring when they just pop up unannounced, resilient little buggers surviving a cold starving winter with no nurturing whatsoever. Give me tulips over roses any day. They are so low-maintenance and charismatic compared to fragile roses that you have to prune and coddle, but just prick you with their thorns anyway. Long smooth green stalks, no thorns, bright colored petals. No real odor except freshness and moisture. And they always sprout each year around my March birthday.

My September Tulip Planting Extravaganza started off well. I toiled in the rocky dirt, injecting tulip bulbs into sporadic holes around the yard. No plan or design. I felt like an artist. A haphazard bulb-wielding Pollock. Predictably, my desire to be Martha Stewart waned after about forty-eight minutes, when my back started to hurt and my trowel broke apart in three pathetic pieces. By the end, I was grubbing out a bunch of holes and dumping five or six bulbs in each one. I completed my project, went inside, and plopped down on the couch next to the dogs, my hands and arms satisfactorily covered in dirt and Virginia clay.

The next Spring, around my birthday, tulips started popping up in random locations all over the yard. Explosions of color: red, pink, yellow, white. It was fabulous. It put a smile on my face every morning for a month. Each day another one popped up at random. It was so natural and free and a little nutty . . . like I aspired to be, I suppose.

My husband failed to note the charm. "Why didn't you make neat tailored flower beds like a landscaper would? This haphazardness looks ridiculous. It's embarrassing."

Whatever. I liked it. Those crazy helter-skelter tulips came up year after year around my spring birthday and our wedding anniversary and consistently made me smile.

Because of my parents' role in the church community, my family was routinely on display and had to project an image of wholesomeness. We rarely spoke freely about real, or unpretty, topics. In fact, growing up, I had little practice in voicing my truth, without adding a shiny veneer to it. But as I entered adulthood and began developing opinions that differed from my family's, or experiencing not-so-pretty feelings such as jealousy or resentment,

I started trying to assert my true self. But it didn't go so well. Whenever my mom asked how my marriage was and I started to reveal snippets of malaise, she cautioned me against being too "self-absorbed." As proud as my mother was of "my daughter, the lawyer" and my liberated, independent, working–woman role, she advised me to care for my husband first. That's what women in my family did: took care of the men. My mom and grandmother baked chocolate cakes and cut the crusts off cucumber sandwiches. They washed the laundry, starched the shirts, and hemmed the trousers— all while holding down jobs outside the home. So whenever my voice cracked on the phone, she counseled, "Sweetie, I hope you don't always burden him with all your problems. You need to be positive and happy when he comes home and not complain." But it reminded me of that 1950s guide to wifedom, like I should make sure to put a ribbon in my hair and be kneading a pie crust upon his return to the homestead.

As I segued into my mid-to-late twenties, restlessness began to stir inside, a baby tornado gathering strength. Luckily, my job allowed me to travel to places like San Francisco, New Orleans, Puerto Rico. But I wanted to see more of the world. My husband did not. He didn't want to go to Europe with me because he'd already been there. He described himself as "Mr. Content." He liked his life and didn't see the need to add to it. "Just be happy," he'd request. I wished it was as easy as slapping on Clinique Happy perfume. But I constantly wanted more. A lot more. Our interests and dreams subtly began to drift in two directions. Or maybe he stood the course we had chosen together, and I drifted away. I grew bored. Unchallenged. I felt misunderstood. Unappreciated. Maybe he did, too. We never talked about it.

Instead, we coexisted. He worked and played sports. I worked and drank red wine. Our friends started having kids. He began getting paternal urges. Childbearing was the last thing on my mind. But I obliged. I got pregnant but had an early, albeit traumatic, miscarriage and felt it was a sign. How could I be a mother? I was struggling to even be a wife. My husband insisted I do some "soul-searching" and get my priorities in line so that we could try again. My brain whirred along. What else is out there? Is this it?

A few months after the miscarriage, my body and brain still recovering, I was invited to New York City for a holiday party thrown by my most important client, a Manhattan-based international company. My husband and I had only been to New York together once, and I had visited the city only a few times for client meetings, so it still seemed as foreign as Cairo. Nixing the party, he opted to play in an amateur football tournament. I was relieved. I needed to get away, alone.

I arrived in Manhattan the day before the party and spent a brisk December afternoon visiting the sky-high Christmas tree in Rockefeller Center, gift-shopping in Soho, and treating myself to an eight-dollar pedicure in Chinatown. That night, I settled into my hotel suite on the Upper East Side. I ordered a large cheese pizza from Joe's Pizzeria, picked up a bottle of cabernet from a corner liquor store, along with a four-dollar bouquet of yellow tulips, and ate and drank alone, sitting on the floor Indian-style in my flannel pajamas, pizza grease dribbling down my chin. I opened the sliding glass door to the balcony to let the cold winter air dance into the room. I called my husband and halfheartedly said I wished he were there. Over the din of his football teammates ordering barbequed ribs and chicken wings, he said, "New York's loud, smells bad, and there's no light." I hung up. *Loud, smells, and no light?* Even with my sliding door open thirty stories up, it was quiet, smelled like pizza, and the city lights twinkled as far as I could see.

Maybe I could live here?

that trip to new york shifted the tectonic plates of my life.
Only three months later.

Twenty-five days before my thirtieth birthday and thirty-nine days before our sixth wedding anniversary.

I stayed home from work. I packed all my clothes into the car trunk and hid them beneath a blanket. I called my husband at work in the afternoon and asked him to come home early.

"Should I be worried?" he asked.

"Just please come home."

After chugging two lukewarm goblets of a bad chardonnay to repress a migraine headache, I sat on our white couch with its preppy pink and green pillows. Then I looked into my husband's eyes and said that I had done what he asked. I had soul-searched. And concluded that I was not ready to have kids. I needed some time alone to think. Just a little bit of time apart.

"I have rented a short-term apartment." My heart kaboomed inside my chest.

He was wrecked. "No, no, no. I knew it. I knew something was wrong with you. Oh man, what are we going to tell people?" I thought I was going to die right there of guilt and grief, but instead I tried to console him—my strong, athletic husband who had cried only once in our eleven years together.

Three hours later, I managed to walk out of our home, the beagles giving me panicked silent looks. I thought my heart was going to implode, and yet this conscious decision and affirmative act was completely within my own control. *I can't believe I am doing this. I can't believe I am choosing this. Go home. Turn around. Take the easy way out.*

I drove away, clutching my belly. I knew my husband was at home, panic-stricken and desperate, wanting me to return before any of our friends found out. There was nothing I could do to rescue him, or myself.

Those first few months, I felt like I was hacking off my right arm with a dull pickax. Why was I leaving the person I had spent the last eleven years with, when it was causing both of us such guttural pain? But I kept going. Events unfolded at warp speed. Ultimatums flew. He listed our house on the market. We hired lawyers. I tried to show up to work but could barely string a sentence together.

Though I planned to let my husband have most of our material possessions in exchange for some of our more portable assets, I begged my dad to accompany me home to cram what few belongings I could fit in his minivan. Looking around my home, at the cutesy balloon valances and Pottery Barn accent pieces, I had no idea what to salvage. Dad encouraged me just to leave it all. "You'll have an even better house someday." I didn't believe him. A wafer-thin sliver of my heart left behind with each discarded item, I climbed into my father's gray minivan, clutching my glum assortment of photographs, books, and college sweatshirts. As Dad backed the car out of the driveway, I took a last glimpse at my house, my home. Grief pinched at me, until . . . anger slapped me upside the head.

"I am NOT leaving without my tulips," I announced.

I assaulted the car door handle, threw open the passenger side door, and leapt from the van. I zigzagged through the yard like a madwoman, yanking up as many tulips as I could. Red. Yellow. White. Pink. My yanks were violent. Roots, bulbs, dirt, broken stalks. Divots scarring my immaculately groomed yard. I returned to the van swaddling my sad bouquet, bulbs still clinging to clumps of dirt.

I slid back into the passenger seat. Dirt sprinkled onto the floormat. My father shifted into reverse. I kept my gaze on the floor.

new york city is likely one of the toughest places i could have chosen to start over. The city kicked me hard with a pointy boot while I was down. Everything was a struggle: finding housing without rodents, sleeping without a few glasses of shiraz, landing a new job despite the skepticism of the few headhunters I called— especially because each morning I awoke inside a mushroom cloud of grief and guilt. Initially, if a cab driver dropped me off at East 22nd Street instead of West 22nd Street, I sat on the street corner and cried like my dog had just been run over. However, once the city decided I had wallowed enough, it simply picked me up, plopped me back on my feet, gave me a smack on my behind, and said, "Enough, sister. Time to get over it, and on with it." My very own urban tough love program.

And so, after a year of grieving, I slowly began to recover, and discover.

I started off by visiting a different museum every day just to drag myself out of the apartment. Then I vowed to try one new thing every day. Sea urchin sushi, Brazilian bikini waxes, and electrified acupuncture needles went on my "Not Necessary to Repeat Anytime Soon" list. I stopped pretending, or aspiring, to be perfect. I let my hair grow long and wild and started dressing like a beatnik poet rather than an uptight attorney. I embraced my flaws and began to like them. I landed a new job in the World Trade Center, took writing and oil painting classes, went to therapy, did yoga, tried waterskiing, dated and broke up with several exotic men with accents. I quit my job in the World Trade Center a few weeks before 9/11, survived 9/11 at a NATO airbase in Canada after my flight back from a spontaneous trip to Greece got diverted there, and returned to New York to mourn our giant loss and stop feeling sorry for myself.

In the eight years of my divorce recovery, I have totally lived. I have resided in New York City, Connecticut, and California, visited Europe six times, traveled to Central and South America three times, Canada once, and the Caribbean four times, driven cross-country, written and published five editions of a legal textbook, written a screenplay about love and women's infidelity, met my second husband—a wild-and-crazy Brit—on a blind date, dated him for four years, and got remarried on a gondola in Vegas. Elvis was not involved.

If I had stayed in Virginia, I would still be driving my same commute to work every day and would have experienced none of these things. For many women, that life would be more than enough. But I'm glad I took this unpaved path. My life is now richer, fuller, and completely unpredictable.

My second husband and I joke that I spent the first three years of our relationship trying to get him to break up with me. I was petrified that he, like my first husband, would conclude I'm not really all that great. I didn't feel like going through that again, and I decided I'd rather be alone than have to do backflips to justify my worthiness. It took me forever to trust and believe him when he said that he unconditionally loved me—because of my idiosyncrasies, not in spite of them.

I always groan when people say "things happen for a reason," but I now know I was meant to go through my divorce, however agonizing. Whatever seed sprouted inside me back in Virginia— maybe my lost pregnancy—germinated anyway, took hold, and prodded me to discover that there was indeed something more in store. Every year on the anniversary of the day I left my first husband, I stop and take stock of what I have learned, and what I have yet to learn. I make lists and goals and assess who I am and still yearn to be.

In living through my ordeal, I unearthed my demons—my insecurity, my codependency, my tendency to drink too much red wine, my fear of not having money, my need to be loved—faced them head on, and learned to like myself anyway. I no longer apologize for being me.

My advice to women and men who are going through something similar: Keep Going. Tolerate the Discomfort (to quote my fantastic first therapist). It will be worth it. And there is someone waiting for you out there who will love you back the way you want, once you figure out who YOU are. And maybe that person is simply you.

*

✳ Safe
sabrina porterfield

the day arrived for their wedding. it was a delightful wedding. People still talk about it; the perfect weather, the sing-along to "When I'm 64," the children batting beach balls about, laughing. The bride and groom were well-suited—both had theater degrees, enjoyed science fiction and foreign films, and were compatible in all of the ways that matter. He was her first boyfriend; she was the woman who really mattered to him. They had gone out for a year and then moved in together, waiting another four years before getting married. She proposed to him over a bowl of guacamole at her grandmother's house and bought her own engagement ring. When her father died unexpectedly three months before the wedding they went on with it anyway, supported by family and friends. She stepped firmly down the aisle alone, her heels only slightly sinking into the grass underfoot.

There were no obvious blemishes. He never laid a finger on her. He was not verbally abusive; in fact, he rarely raised his voice at all. Granted, he had a tendency to use her as the punch line for his jokes, but the jokes were all in fun, right? They were both doing well in their respective jobs—nothing to write home about, but certainly enough to ensure them a nice townhouse and two cars in the suburbs of San Francisco, enough money to buy quality furniture and pay for a housekeeper once a week. They attended concerts, the theater, ate dinner at nice restaurants for their anniversaries, spent Thanksgiving with his family and Christmas with hers. He was a fanatic over baseball, and she attended games with him occasionally. He left town for three summers in a row to do theater, and she stayed home alone, attending his opening nights and making small talk with the other actors. No kids yet, but they were both still young, and anyhow, lots of people nowadays waited until their mid to late thirties to start a family. She had a group of girlfriends that she enjoyed time with, and he liked to occasionally hang out at the comic book shop and talk superheroes. He cooked and cleaned, even ironed his own shirts. She never orgasmed when they were making love, but she learned to fake it to soothe his ego. If he always strode a little bit ahead of her it was written off to his much longer legs.

Everyone congratulated themselves on a match well made.

The day gradually came when she couldn't find herself in the mirror anymore. The ten-year-old who devoured *The Lord of the Rings* and wrote her own stories late at night when she was supposed to be sleeping. The passionate sixteen-year-old who stood in front of the entire school board and a sizable portion of the town's citizens, arguing that the school needed to teach proper and comprehensive sex ed. The college freshman who lay outside on the grass at midnight, discussing Akhmatova and quantum physics, who went to discos to dance until she couldn't move her feet anymore. This vibrant and promising girl had been buried under a chubby woman who wore Land's End polos and took the train into the city to sit at a desk for nine hours a day.

When they agreed it was time to try for a baby she stopped taking birth control pills, and he stopped touching her. She lay in bed at night while he turned away and faked sleep, the pregnancy test collecting dust in the bathroom drawer. *I thought you wanted a baby,* she said, and he told her he did, but on second thought maybe it would be better to wait a few more years. For what, she wasn't sure, but she agreed with him, telling herself that they'd try again later. She brought up the idea of a puppy, but he dismissed the idea, only accepting the cat she became heir to upon the death of her grandmother.

She tried the usual things to spice up their lives. Suggestions of vacations invariably turned down for one excuse or another. A few carefully selected toys from the local sex shop cooperative buried in a box under the bed. A disastrous girlfriend meant to provide a threesome. Marriage therapy abandoned in a huff when the therapist gently suggested that he might need some therapy of his own.

What do you want? she asked, again and again. He assured her that she was what he wanted, that this life was what he wanted. Sure, he wanted more material possessions, who didn't? But he was essentially content.

She wasn't certain that contentment was enough for her, but she bought another pair of shoes and tried not to think about it.

The day it changed was the day she stopped asking him and instead asked herself what it was she wanted. *Not this,* was her answer, and that was a start. She found she no longer had the faintest idea what she wanted, and that frightened her. She was twenty-nine years old and had spent the past decade being safe. Safely attending a good university, safely dating and then marrying a good guy, safely living in a nice part of town, safely driving a Honda Accord, safely commuting to a secure job.

Fuck safe.

She took a deep breath and left him. She turned her back and marched away, sleeping on a friend's sofa, living out of the trunk of her car. She didn't plan ahead, didn't pick a safe exit, just went without thinking too much, fearing that if she thought too much she'd end up staying. *The only person you can change is yourself,* the therapist said, and she knew no one else was going to save her from a life of moneyed monotony.

She let it be her fault. She let him say what he would, blame it on her, nudge the truth over to his side, keep all of their mutual friends. She listened to the shocked exhortations of both families, not understanding why she would leave a good man and a good marriage, knowing that she was being talked about behind her back. She spent money she didn't have, didn't argue when he stole her grandparents' beautiful maple side table, or several of her books. She kept it polite, let him keep the washer and dryer, the car (that she'd paid for out of her salary) because it was his parents who sold it to them. She gritted her teeth and made no comment when he whined to her that it was hard for him, too, as he continued to live in the nice townhouse and she struggled to make the payments on the new car she was forced to buy.

She sat silently when she was told that maybe it wasn't that he didn't want kids; maybe he just didn't want them with her. Stared into the distance when it was predicted that she'd never find anyone else and would end up living the rest of her life alone.

Months of living hand to mouth. She refused to cry, simply put her head down and one foot in front of the other. There wasn't a light at the end of the tunnel, but that was the risk of not being safe. She spent her thirtieth birthday on the beach with her best friends, fighting off the loneliness, refusing to consider whether she had made a mistake or not. She was not someone who believed in recrossing bridges. Moving forward was what she did best, even when she stumbled.

She was not expecting to find someone else. She was not looking, and love found her from across the world, broadcast across the Internet, full of uncertainties. She moved into her own flat and waited for her new lover to walk toward her through customs, fidgeting with the new skirt she'd bought for the occasion. She filled her refrigerator with fruits and vegetables, bought American chocolates, scrubbed her floors, and painted her fingernails a deep crimson in tense anticipation. Her best friend warned her of the dangers of lovers unseen; she didn't tell her own mother for fear of censure. It was unsafe and unpredictable, and the night of her lover's arrival she orgasmed twice, speechless in her surprise. A trip to the local animal shelter meant another dog, joining her own cat and her lover's cat and dog that had been brought over. They took a month off together, driving across the desert, camping in tents, and buying cheap tchotchkes, boiling endless cups of coffee on the camp stove, naming the constellations in two different languages. She got bit by red ants and banged her thumb painfully with a mallet, and they listened to Harry Potter books on tape as they drove countless miles, the dogs panting in the back seat. She laughed more than she had laughed in years, took silly photographs with rubber duck sunglasses and Germans in spandex. They came home and watched Jane Austen movies and drank Slurpees, went to the movies and rescued a kitten from the side of the freeway.

The day she boarded a plane for Finland and a new life was the most terrifying day of her life. She was going there sight unseen; two dogs in the hold, the kitten in a carrier under the seat in front of her, her belongings in boxes slowly making their way across the ocean. Once there, she sat on a borrowed bed and watched the Olympics being announced in a language she could not make head nor tails of. She couldn't tell the difference between cottage cheese and sour cream at the market and only knew how to say *thank you, yes,* and *no.* Her new partner told her in accented English to close her eyes when she surprised her with chanterelle mushrooms freshly picked from the forest.

She struggled through the first Scandinavian winter and came out the other side. Summer came, and she floated in a blood-warm lake under the midnight sun and knew it was safe to rest for a little while. Soon after that she felt the babies swimming inside her, squirming jabs that caused most of what she ate to make its way back up. They got married when Finland legalized it and the twins were born and the years ran past her and the flat was too small, and the car they bought was old, and her partner had back surgery and couldn't work anymore, and they told her that both her children would need special education and the dogs both died, and the winters were long and cold and dark and hard. It wasn't safe.

The day is here, now. The children are squabbling over a toy, the new dog is barking, the books are causing the overloaded bookshelves to sag, there's no room in the flat for the spinning wheel they inherited, her wife has the flu and is calling down the hall in irritation at the children, the locks in the back seat of the car don't work in the cold anymore. She looks in the mirror and sees the gray hair she hasn't gotten around to dyeing again and the mounds of unwashed laundry and the sink that has flecks of old dried toothpaste and "content" is not the word she'd use. Safe is not the word she uses to describe her life now. Her life is painful and chaotic, complicated and glorious. She skips forward, tripping over toys and sleeping cats, her children and wife tumbling along with her.

Breakup Buddies

marrit ingman

the first was my friend jonas, who called up to offer advice because he knew I was miserable. Jonas has himself divorced twice. (I hate the phrasing "has been divorced," as if it's not possible to be an agent in the process.) Jonas's divorces are among the messiest I have seen, mitigated only by the fact that there are no children. There have been property disputes and lingering resentments in which I stoutly have refused to take sides.

I have known Jonas for twenty years, since we sat across from each other in eleventh-grade English. In that time, relationships have come and gone for each of us, but we have remained steady.

"Your marriage is already ending," Jonas said. "You know that, right?" His bluntness is one of the things that bonded us as friends years ago. He knew about the arguing and the couples' therapy. He knew we were having trouble breaking the cycle.

"It can't be happening," I said. If I said that, would it stop happening?

"It might take you years. It takes however long it takes."

We were quiet for a while.

Another day, it was my friend Allison. She told me to get out while I was still young. Allison is an alumna of acrimonious custody litigation, and she does not tell people to leave their marriages idly. I once swore in an affidavit that Allison, who was first in line after the grandparents to baby-sit my infant, was a fit mother. I could hardly write the statement for all my spluttering with confusion and incredulity.

"Get out while you're still young," she said firmly. "I know how this sounds, but God, don't be like my mother." Allison's mother attained foxy-grandma status before she ended her miserable marriage to Allison's father. I wasn't going to last that long. My son was five.

"You'll have more of your life to enjoy. *More of your life,*" she added.

How much did I value the rest of my life? A Unitarian Universalist, I wasn't sure of anything beyond the rest of my life. A hypochondriac, I wasn't sure how many years I had left. A depression survivor, I had resolved to value my life, to live it out honestly and self-respectfully. Much the same way, my husband and I had pledged to love and honor each other, but we no longer did. We both admitted it. Though we were not cheating on each other, we certainly were not upholding our vows. The only question was how much we valued the rest of our lives.

"Anyhow, you're still young," she said.

These were my Breakup Buddies. More than a shoulder to cry on, they are the wind beneath my wings. The sun through the clouds. The foot in my ass. The truck that moves my couch.

"You have to let people take care of you as if you were a little baby," said another writer, whose husband walked out on her rather abruptly. "Let them cook for you, even."

You need them. Divorce is painful like a spray of buckshot. There is a sudden profusion of pointy things that cause emotional wounds. Some of your injuries are big chunks of hot metal right in your gut. And some of your injuries are tiny pinpricks on your elbow. They are annoying, perhaps: transient petty feelings, a spell of "catastrophizing" (a so-called word I learned during the required training for change management related to corporate layoffs) that you scoff at because even at the time you know it's kind of silly. Surely, you think at these times, it's not so bad. You're not that hurt. You are coping well. Then you shift positions just a bit, and the bigger lacerations reopen:

* You are a failure.
* You will continue to fail.
* You are hurting your children.
  - They'll blame themselves.
  - They'll feel hurt and betrayed by you.
  - They will hate having two households.
  - It will be difficult to co-parent effectively.
* You are headed for financial ruin.
* You should have done something different, or something differently.
* You are damaged goods.
* Actually, you've always been unworthy of love. (This reopened cut is already, at least once, opened by something else.)
* Unless you are a physically abused spouse (and perhaps not even then), people will feel empowered to spout off about how stupid you are and how people like you are ruining the world.
  - Especially if you're a woman. My family physician tried to convince me that husbands cannot be kept from straying, but wives should pray to appreciate their marriages and be grateful for what they have. I don't know where that shit came from all of a sudden (previously, he had saved me from an episode of liver failure), but I fired him.

And then it's back to the little nuisances. You wipe spills and take out the trash and change your insurance policies and deal with everything yourself, and if after that the dog shits on the floor, you're cleaning that up, too. There is no reasonable hope of any delegation in a single-parent household with very young children, and henceforth children will do chores as often as children do chores in your household, but that's it. Your ass will be tired. Stuff will stack up around you. It is not life-or-death, but it makes you wince.

But as you crawl from the battlefield that is your emotional landscape, you get a buddy to lean on for a while. Someone who is willing to tie a tourniquet on your arm or radio for help by meeting you for coffee or IMing with you or helping you unclog your drain. Someone who listens to you and helps you schlep your burden for a little while. They're doing you a solid. Of course you'll pay it backward and forward when you're back on your feet—but you're not there yet, not just yet.

I met a friend I hadn't seen in a while at a school function last month, when my decree was complete but not final, and she told me she's become like a Harriet Tubman for slaves escaping marriage. Not all marriages are like slavery, but some are, and she makes herself available to help these people. She is a Breakup Buddy by avocation.

You've probably been a Breakup Buddy to someone, sometime, too. Breakup Buddies are everywhere, but we seldom take time to celebrate their contributions to the fabric of our global human well-being. As rectification, I offer these further reminiscences of Breakup Buddies I have known.

Consider the unlikeliest: those not themselves divorced.

"Marrit, you did everything you could," twanged my dad from behind his can of Tecate. He and my mother have been married since 1965, and their current adventure is surviving her three cancers. They are as cofunctional as Torville and Dean skating to "Bolero." "You did the best you could, and now it's time to give him the gate." (Cowboy metaphors are his conversational baseline.)

My friend Ingrid, a newlywed, came over to play Scrabble one day. I didn't mean to talk about my divorce, but here was my house with half the stuff in it compared to when she saw me last, so the topic came up. And in some way she wanted to talk about it, or so I gathered from the way she squirmed in her seat and pursed her lips but said nothing.

"I just have to admit," she said finally, "that I'm really uncomfortable."

I nodded. She was not disapproving, but she was uncomfortable. It made sense.

And I knew what she meant. It made me uncomfortable when I was still married and other women said to me that a couple I knew and regarded highly was calling it quits. I tried to never take it personally, but you can't hear about someone else's divorce without imagining it happening to you. It is proof of the mortality of marriage. You watch a woman you know strike out on her own after a period of partnership, and you wonder if *you* could do that.

I couldn't do that, you think automatically, especially if you have misplaced your self-reliance in the dysfunction of your marriage, like the playgroup mommy some girlfriends and I literally tried to rescue from her abusive marriage—to the point at which we had packed her suitcase and gotten her on the phone with a domestic-violence shelter whose volunteers were going to send over a cab, but still she said, "I can't do it."

You can be solidly convinced that another couple's relationship is simply not working, to their obvious mutual detriment, and still be terrified to hear about the divorce when it happens. Because the thought lurks, more and more often as your relationship dies: What if you have to do it—you can't live with the marriage, and neither can the other person, your children, and your animals—and you still can't leave?

"I remember feeling that way when people told me they were divorcing," I told Ingrid. "It's okay."

"I still believe in marriage," I added. "Mine just didn't work."

She relaxed visibly.

Sometimes people I didn't even know personally turned out to be my Breakup Buddies. Anthony Swofford, the author of *Jarhead*, wrote an essay in *Glamour*, of all places, about the breakup of his marriage. It was reflective and open, but also measured and well-considered. I read it in my therapist's waiting room, of all places, and it helped. The essay was presented in a cloying Guy's Eye View context by the editors, but the experiences it described seemed ironically universal. We had similar injuries. I nodded as I read it.

Other buddies I observed directly. Mostly I knew other women who were also mothers.

* Kathy got pretty quickly into roller derby and BDSM, and I'd never seen her look happier;
* Marcia moved into my neighborhood, got a day job in a call center, and took her photography to the next level;
* Courtney cohoused with Marcia and sold pleasure products while she went back to school;
* Heather got only a tiny amount of support from her ex and traded childcare with me during the week so each of us could work;
* Jessica was divorcing an addict and had an autistic son;
* Randa got her daughter back from visitation with uncombed hair and (once) a broken arm; and
* Sadie, with two daughters and a husband who had emotional affairs, got a minivan, a peaceable kitchen-table settlement, and a dachshund puppy, and she started teaching preschool.

no one's life was made easier and simpler by divorce. we sweated our decisions and juggled our obligations. Our fortunes declined. But at the same time, our struggles had a reason, at last. Bad odds were better than no chance at all.

"Did I really do everything I could?" I asked Jonas. He laughed.

"Honey, you did everything you could. And then you did it again. And a third time."

Not Otherwise Specified
laura andré

i was stubbornly opposed to online dating. it had been a harrowing year and a half since my breakup with Ann, my partner of ten years, and somehow I had lived through an agonizing three years before that, while we watched "us" disintegrate before our incredulous eyes. I had been suffering from a series of major depressive episodes for fifteen years, and I had steadily dragged friends and family with me into what we all snarkily liked to call my "black hole of morosity," which at that time was in full sucking mode. When my close friend suggested that it might do me good to expand my social life, which consisted solely of her, I vehemently argued that putting myself "out there" would only confirm my craziness. I was never going to make myself vulnerable again. The last thing I wanted was to exasperate another poor soul, from whom I would extract every shred of emotional reserve, just like I had with my friend, my parents, a dozen old friends I had lost, and most importantly, with Ann. I tried to harden my heart.

About six months earlier, I had been diagnosed with an illness that had a rhyming, well-metered name: "bipolar disorder not otherwise specified." According to the *Diagnostic and Statistical Manual of Mental Disorders,* there are several types of bipolar disorder, and for those of us who don't quite fit any of them, there is a paradoxical "category" called "not otherwise specified." In other words, a category that refuses categorization, a diagnosis without gnosis. *How apropos,* I thought. *While I'm floundering around in the purgatory of this post-breakup period, trying to move on from the past, yet still unable to imagine a future, I'm officially labeled as not otherwise specified.*

My illness—whatever it is—also led to my resignation from a tenure-track position in the year following our breakup. I had spent eight years in graduate school, earned a PhD, and miraculously landed a dream job at a major university with my first application. I loved teaching and was good at it. But as my illness and crumbling relationship took their toll, I was not doing the research that was expected of me. I had to get out or I'd be given the dreaded terminal contract. Four years into what I thought would be a lifelong career, I was finished; my relationship was finished; I was finished.

It was a fine time to craft a personal profile that prospective dates would scrutinize and judge. I was in no position to sum up my personality, history, and future desires—unless it would be attractive to say, "Hi, I'm a barely employed, depressed, worthless failure with a poor body image. But I'm not otherwise specified. Let's get coffee!"

My one friend had been experimenting with Match.com, going on a few dates and generally injecting a dose of fresh experiences to her own stagnant social life. She kept saying to me, "Just try it. You might meet somebody interesting. You might not. At the very least it will give us something to talk about beyond our numbing analysis of Perez Hilton's blog or 'Must-See TV.' There's no risk in just looking."

For a month I, voyeur, trolled the profiles, relieved that I wasn't investigating seriously, because the pickings—at least those that appealed to me—were, um, slim. I did come to a screeching halt

when I came across one stunningly elegant and beautiful woman—
or at least the photo of her disembodied head—whose intense brown
eyes peered from behind kick-ass, smarty-pants glasses, while wavy
chestnut tendrils escaped from her long pulled-back hair. She looked
like a writer, and as it turned out, she was an exquisite and alluring
writer. Anyone who has read even a few online dating profiles knows
that they are often understandably awkward at best, and, at worst,
rife with misspellings and cringeworthy illiteracy. Claire's profile
was miles above anything I had read on Match. "Wow," I thought,
but "wow" became "whoa" when I learned that she lived an hour
away, and shared custody of two young kids with her ex-husband.
I was already shaky, and these obstacles might as well have been
prison walls. I would absolutely not contact her anyway, since I was
sure I would never work up the courage to reach out to someone, no
matter how great she seemed to be.

Yet still I lurked online. The social insularity I had nurtured
in the two years since Ann and I broke up made it seem perfectly
natural for me to increasingly constrict the parameters of my survey
so tightly that I was soon "searching" only for all the highly educated,
liberal, dark-haired, feminine women aged forty to forty-two who
lived within a mile of me. When I was "surprised" to come up empty,
time after time, I turned into a spoiled brat. "There's nobody out
there for me! And I don't want anybody anyway!" Charming.

I honestly don't know how or when it happened, but my
friend's urging somehow inspired a caprice. Or maybe that day I
was slightly manic, and defenseless against impetuosity. Whatever
the catalyst, I tentatively posted my profile after my friend wrote a
glowing profile of "me." There were no lies, just a serious polishing
job; I sounded great—the real me, finally exhumed from under
years of depression! Nervous, alone, a few glasses of wine later, I
paid my dues and hit the upload button. And so the wait began. It
was late at night and, mercifully, time to go to bed. I felt painfully
alone in the immediate aftermath. Briefly, I thought of Ann, who
was happily living with a new partner, and I felt a twinge of guilt,

as if I were somehow cheating on her. And the long-held resistance that evaporated when I inexplicably decided to join Match came rushing back. I instantly regretted going online and decided I would ignore any replies. Since I narrowed my search so impractically I hadn't seen anyone in whom I was remotely interested, except one not-even-my-type woman who was a professor, and I ruled her out for being intellectually intimidating. Oh right, I remembered, I was a professor, too.

Whatever was to come of it, in retrospect I think my stab at online dating was an effort to "divorce" Ann once and for all. Prohibited from marriage, we were prohibited from divorce. Our relationship was not otherwise specified, too. Although we decided to dissolve our partnership years ago, no formal rite sealed the deal; both of us were unclear about how and when it was final. Was it when we stopped sharing a bed? Or before then, when I got my own checking account? Was it when I moved out, or when I signed over the deed to the house? How about when we stopped wearing the rings we had bought together? When I assumed full custody of the dogs? Or maybe it was as recent as a few nights ago—a full two years since our split—when I cried as she gave back the last of my belongings: some Christmas decorations that had been packed away for years.

Ann is moving to San Diego this week, and she brought those decorations to give to me at her going-away party. Although we have always remained amicable, we hadn't really spoken or seen each other for almost a year, and the impending goodbye coaxed out unexpected waves of grief for both of us. The night was heavy with finality. Promises to the contrary, I think both of us feared the unutterable possibility that we would never again see the person with whom we each spent a quarter of our lives. We both worked hard, but I in vain, to choke back tears, neither of us wanting to make the situation more awkward than it already was. And so, on a quiet Albuquerque street, we hugged and garrulously said, "Drive carefully." "Take care." "Send me emails." "Say hi to your parents."

"Come visit!" And with that final "Goodbye," we came as close as we ever will to finalizing our divorce.

I've read many stories and case studies and seen movies and performances about the anguish mental illness can exert on a relationship. Usually the parties either come together, growing and adapting to the challenge, or, in the most untenable situations, they part ways. These narratives are often told from the perspective of the healthy person. In my account I'm the one who caused the ultimate, damaging blow. I'm the one who got sick, and, although that's not my fault, Ann is not the one who did "take-backs" on who she was. She did everything she could to help me, but neither of us understood what was happening, what was wrong, until my illness progressed to the point where our relationship became unsalvageable.

Once, after I had been diagnosed, Ann was visiting my house and saw a pile of books about bipolar disorder (few of which, I might add, even mention the not otherwise specified flavor). Gesturing casually to them, she half-jokingly asked, "So, is that what's wrong with you?"

"Yeah, bipolar!" I said, a bit overenthusiastically, as if I had just hit BINGO. "Problem solved!"

She replied with a flat "Oh."

I knew Ann cared deeply, but I also understood that she couldn't and wouldn't venture into a discussion about the territory that both of us had tried to negotiate blindly. It was as if we, in trying to deal with my illness, had been lost in a hostile, labyrinthine city. We escaped separately, by chance, only to discover a map of the place later. Ann didn't want to look at the map; she was never going back.

When we met, I was just starting graduate school, an endeavor that I believed finally legitimized me after a severe depression a few years earlier. Now I would become the productive person I should be. I was intensely focused on my work, optimistic, in the best shape of my life, outgoing, and fully committed to forging a life with Ann. I didn't know it, but I was in a state of hypomania—

the "up" mood that stops short of full-blown mania. Ann fell in love with hypomanic me.

About four years into our relationship, I experienced a recurrence of the major depression. I hoped it would go away. It didn't. *This is not me,* I thought, *All I need is a little Prozac.* It had worked wonders for me the first time. I went to the university's student psychological services, where a nervous counselor refused to refer me to a psychiatrist, instead directing me to join a dissertation support group and—I'm not kidding—do jigsaw puzzles. I saw three doctors before I got a prescription. The Prozac helped, but not for long. The depression was firmly entrenched, and not going away. Ann supported me and helped me find the doctors, but I sensed that my desperation and unrelenting foul mood was eroding her commitment to us.

She became more and more frustrated and skeptical. She recognized that I needed help but hadn't the slightest idea why I wasn't improving with the help I did get. Our sex life was nonexistent, due in part to the medication, and in larger measure to the widening fissures in our relationship. Once, the psychiatrist asked me how my libido was—I think more out of prurience than genuine medical interest. I replied that I had not one inkling of desire. And he unsympathetically pronounced, "Well, you can either have a sex life or relief from depression." I was getting neither.

More—much more—Prozac later, things began to turn around. My depression lifted; I successfully defended my dissertation; I got a great job. Again, as it had years ago when I started grad school, this turn of events seemed like a permanent shield against the crippling depression. I had finally "arrived," Ann was proud of me, and I was elated. Our sex life was rejuvenated, and it seemed like our difficulties were over. I now understand that shift as evidence of another mood swing, back to the up side.

Like before, the pendulum swung back down—this time only a year later. And in the next years it swung up and down, less a pendulum than a misfiring jackhammer that erratically and mercilessly broke us into too many fragments to piece together. Our relationship had become the jigsaw puzzle I never solved in grad school.

When I think about our time together in Albuquerque, I hold close many fond memories of things we enjoyed until the very end. I miss having dinner on the patio, marveling at the impossibly pink light on the mountains; I miss playing with the dogs together in a living room more spacious than we ever dreamed of; I miss hiking to the top of Sandia Peak and peering down at our house below. I miss our companionship. I do not hold close the other things: the raging anger, the stunned catatonia both of us felt, the simmering resentment, her anger at my uncontrolled drinking and my bouts with self-injury, my anger that she couldn't save me.

Our last trip together was to California, where we often went to stay at my parents' house. We visited wineries in Santa Ynez and hiked the mountains in Santa Barbara. We had already broken up by then, but we went anyway because we both love California. I'm happy that she's going back there to live. I know a part of us is there.

Overall, since last year's diagnosis and proper treatment, I'm better. But bipolar is an evasive illness with no cure. It's an endless trial of "best guess" medications, doses, therapies, and lifestyle management. I still alternate between episodes of wrenching depression and more balanced moods. I'm frightened of the unknown, indeterminate nature of the condition. The etymology of "diagnosis" is "to learn," "to know apart from," "to find out the solution to a problem," even, as it were, to solve a puzzle. I'm frustrated that my so-called diagnosis neither pinpoints an exact problem (much less a cause), nor offers a lasting solution. But I'm starting to come to terms with the idea that not knowing in what direction things are headed has its own rewards.

The morning after I posted my Match.com profile, I woke up early to check my email. Despite my reluctance, I was disappointed that nobody had responded. *Ouch.* I reprimanded myself: *You fucking idiot! I told you not to do this!* My impulse was to take my profile offline right then and there, less than a day after posting it. I was late for work, though, and decided to do it that evening. Two hours later, my inbox lit up: "Match.com Message: wow." Oh my god, it was the drop-dead gorgeous Claire, the one who made me say "wow" a month earlier, when I was browsing in spite of myself. The one who lives an hour away with two kids and is a really great writer and smart and whose disembodied head gave me an undeniable rush. I had forgotten what it's like to have sweaty palms.

"Wow." That was her first word to me: a pleasantly cheeky, but uncharacteristically clipped response from someone whom I have come to love for—among other delicious things—her verbal prowess. Bashful, and with racing heart, I read on. She said all the right things, keying into the obvious and subtle interests and experiences we had in common (i.e., how our—as she adorably and incisively put it—"nascent lesbian yearnings" were fashioned in part by early J. Crew catalogs), honestly sharing just enough about herself to negate any creepiness factor (you can't be too careful), dropping the little flirtatious hint that she thought I was "darn cute," and something about how "all cylinders are firing" (again, a bit saucy, but endearing; I liked it). She even gave me an out: "But if the chemistry isn't there, or whatnot," (she had me at "whatnot") "I still think we would have a gangbusters conversation, or seventy."

"Way more than seventy, silly," I fired back.

And the next day I took my profile offline. I wasn't interested in anyone else. I had met someone, despite my (mostly) best efforts, and I could at least have the integrity not to complicate what had been so far, and promised to be, rewarding contact with a human being outside my bubble. I hadn't counted on someone like Claire. I was intrigued and, as I said to her on our first date, "I'm in this thing, whatever *this* is." Indeed, we struck up email conversations that we soon took to the telephone, and soon after that to dinner, and then nine months of lots more than just dinners—and counting.

We fell precipitously in love and landed hard, kissing the first of way more than seventy kisses while snow fell gently through the cold air of a late-winter night. A few weeks later, I remember feeling giddy about identifying us as "We." And I am so overjoyed to have found someone who passionately loves me and calls me on my shit and takes my breath away. Sometimes I say, "I don't deserve you," to which she replies, "I love your humanity." She is radiant. She has taught me to show up emotionally. She reminds me to be present and live fully, whether that means impetuously running off to Mexico a month after we met (thus astounding my imperturbable hair stylist), or unblinkingly confronting our worst demons (there will always be some). Last night at dinner, those deep brown eyes peering intently at me over her signature kick-ass glasses, she affirmed, "We do life well together."

We do, in part by learning about ourselves as much as us. In the past few years I've learned to exercise a little more self-diagnosis and a lot less complacency. I've learned to know myself apart from Ann, and she from me. I'm in the process of understanding myself apart from my illness, however annoyingly unspecified it is. And, funnily enough, I'm learning that the unknown is both less predictable and less evasive than I assumed it to be.

We almost didn't find each other. Astonishingly, Claire managed to climb through the impossibly narrow opening in my twelve-hour online dating window. She found me. If she hadn't, I would have retreated to live the life—such as it was—that I was resigned to live. I may not have gone on living at all.

Had we never met, she wouldn't just forever be the one who lives an hour away with two kids and is a really great writer and smart and whose disembodied head gave me an undeniable rush; she would be "the one who would forever elude me." Rilke's achingly poignant verse, "You Who Never Arrived," tragically evokes the implied loss:

You, Beloved, who are all
the gardens I have ever gazed at,
longing. An open window
in a country house—, and you almost
stepped out, pensive, to meet me. Streets that I
chanced upon,—
you had just walked down them and vanished.
And sometimes, in a shop, the mirrors
were still dizzy with your presence and, startled,
gave back my too-sudden image. Who knows?
perhaps the same bird echoed through both of us
yesterday, separate, in the evening. . . .

In sending me these lines, Claire, an infinitely more eloquent romantic than I, understood that her discovery was more providential than lucky. She wrote, "I did find you. But you wanted to be found, even if it was just for the span of one day . . . and you are still wanting to be found, and I am still finding you, more and more, every time we connect. And you are finding me."

And together, we are finding us.

✳

The Badge on My Biceps
elaine soloway

✳

"right here?" john asked, as he pointed to a spot on my left bicep. I turned my head sideways to check the area where John's finger was touching. "Perfect," I said, then quickly faced forward, just like I do when a doctor draws my blood. But unlike that queasy scene when I'm loath to watch what happens next, the tattoo needle about to touch my flesh was one I had giddily anticipated.

It was August of 1998, and I was celebrating my birthday by adding art to my sixty-year-old body. It was not only a milestone birthday but also six months after I married husband number two in a Las Vegas ceremony, and eight years after number one left me for another woman.

Today, as I am about to start my seventieth year, the tattoo's colors remain bright and stare-provoking, the second marriage continues strong and contented, and my ex-husband's phone number is comfortably listed on my telephone's speed dial.

Not surprisingly, I'm often asked about my arm's three-square-inch yellow, blue, and red design of a banner with two names scripted across its width, a chubby heart, musical notes, rays of sun, and roses emanating from all sides. After all, I'm a grandmother, not a tough broad, I drive an eighteen-year-old Honda Civic rather than a Harley, and I curse only when I step on the scale each morning.

Some observers of my tattoo are only interested in the names I selected to stencil, while others are more curious about its impetus.

The first query is easy. "Faith and Jill," I answer, "my two daughters, a musician and a writer. I want my tattoo to celebrate their creativity and talent." (What I omit, but is true, is I didn't want to jinx my baby chick marriage by permanently inking in my new husband's name.)

The second question is tougher. When I elected to join the ranks of shore leave sailors, scary bikers, carnival workers, and young hipsters, I believed the reason was tied to my age. In my mind, achieving sixty seemed a chance to stray from conformity, and thumb my nose at a society preferring I wear pearls, comfortable shoes, and a frock that covers my knees.

While that bit of age rebellion still holds true, I now understand there was more at work back then, and much of it tied to my divorce and second marriage. For if I was an admirer of body art, why not do it to mark an earlier decade, like when I hit thirty, forty, or fifty? Why wait until the possibility of showing off a bare arm and its trailing pinchable fat might lead to disgust rather than admiration? And why *after* my second trip down the aisle, and not during the eight years in between marriages when I was a free-and-easy single gal?

Like an archaeologist "who studies human history through the excavation of sites and the analysis of artifacts and other physical remains," I've explored these three eras of my life and unearthed several theories—some linked to the guys I wed, and some to the gal I became.

Let's begin our dig on a sun-kissed day in June of 1960 where we find a 4'10", dark-haired, twenty-two-year-old bride staring up adoringly at her 6' tall, skinny, black-haired groom. The girl caught in this wedding album photo appears dreamy-eyed; but in truth, she is trying to focus because her mother has snatched off her face the black-rimmed eyeglasses with Coke-bottle lenses before the photographer could snap his shutter.

As we flip through more plastic pages of that long-ago album, we imagine we are witnessing a match every Jewish girl, and her image-conscious mother, dream about. We have our tall, dark, and handsome (flattering pounds will be added later) premed student; and our short, slightly pudgy (she has vowed to lose hers), cute-without-her-glasses schoolteacher. Surely bliss awaits this happy pair who share the same religion and Russian *shtetl* ancestry, and similar goals of happy anniversaries, two kids, and a house in the suburbs.

Back up. Let's examine that photo a bit longer. Perhaps there were missed clues that hinted at trouble ahead. No, remember the year was 1960 and it would be three years before Betty Friedan would publish her book *The Feminine Mystique*—a polemic that ignited a women's movement and stirred discontent in households across the United States. There was no way you could've predicted our young wife would come to feel the same constriction and unhappiness Friedan outlined.

And the young husband? In that outdoor scene, when he is gazing downward at his small wife, his smile is wide and his stance confident. There's nothing in that black-and-white photo to suggest the dark moods that will hover throughout his married life, like thunderclouds that threaten and disappear, or, at times, drench the picnickers down below.

During my thirty-year marriage, there were, of course, warm-hearted scenes of the honeymoon years, parenthood, summer vacations at the shore, European trips, and other delights that made the unhappy years tolerable and encouraged both my husband and me to stick around.

And I can't blame husband number one for the absence of a tattoo, because the thought of its application never entered my mind. Although we did make a few detours from our original plan—like shucking the suburbs for the city and my career switch from schoolteacher to public relations—we led a pretty conventional upwardly mobile life, one where tattoos and other in-your-face signage would be shocking.

Our breakup was unusual, though, with its absence of flinging crockery, recriminations, and mutual hatred. Ours was a sad divorce, enacted by two people who still cared for one another, but admitted that although the other woman was the plot device, the marriage had been in trouble from Chapter 3.

In truth, I was happy when my husband had made his awkward confession about his affair, for I had long wanted out of our dispirited union but never had the courage to leave. Whenever those unpredictable dark clouds lasted longer than I thought bearable, or when they erupted into thunderstorms, I sought refuge in a variety of ways. Some retreats were healthy and sensible, like my gym and therapist. Others were secretive and risky and included J&B and water on a hotel nightstand, Carmen McRae on the stereo, and a man who found me both sexy and adorable.

But it was my husband who walked out, an overnight bag in hand. Now, I had been given a gift: freedom from a marriage that had become joyless, plus a husband who was the fall guy.

All that was required of me was to hang tough; to recognize the tears that flowed during phone calls between us were tied to the loss of a long relationship, rather than a desire to win him back.

After he left, to move in with the woman he had fallen in love with (fifteen years younger than I), I felt like a kid let out of school. I ate pizza on the living room couch, went to bed as early as I wished, rose at the crack of dawn, traveled to visit our daughters in Boston and Los Angeles every few months, treated those same girls to a trip to France, and engaged in other activities that my separated spouse would have vetoed.

And, I bought a dog. Owning a dog was something I had wanted since childhood, but back then, my mother nixed a pet. My husband had also been against the idea, and since all our residences were sleek city condos or narrow townhouses *sans* yard, I didn't press the issue. But at the time of his departure, we were living in a single-family home with a fenced-in back yard. Husband out, yard ready, enter dog.

My golden retriever, Sasha, turned out to be more than the furry companion I had longed for. She also became my shield and my judge. I'll explain: As often happens in a banal breakup like ours, my husband had second thoughts. He'd phone from his office to learn how I was holding up and then timidly suggest a reunion. "You'd have to get rid of the dog first," he'd say.

I'd remain silent on my end. On the one hand, my finances were a mess and getting back together would return me to the cushy life his generous income provided. Although our separation agreement awarded me with a monthly support check, it was nowhere near the amount I was used to. Credit cards made up the difference until I was $10,000 in debt. But in the beat before responding to his offer, I told myself, "Elaine, you have a window of opportunity here. Don't blow it."

And besides, I had grown attached to my pet, so much so that I often had nightmares where my lost child turned into a missing golden retriever. I felt as relieved when the red-haired dog, with red collar, big grin, flopping ears, and wildly circling tail, came running toward me.

"I can't get rid of the dog," I'd say, grateful for the shield, as protective as a Roman soldier's escutcheon in blocking my husband's return.

Along with that role, Sasha served another key function during my long marital separation: She was my litmus test for the lineup of men who came to call. Before opening the door to a potential replacement for the male in my life, I put myself through a makeover. Contact lenses replaced eyeglasses, henna gave my gray hair a disguise, adherence to Weight Watchers and regular exercise zapped ten pounds from my fifty-four-year-old body, and Victoria's Secret changed underwear to lingerie.

You might wonder at my willingness to make myself date-worthy considering how I exalted and protected my newfound freedom. But soon enough, I detested being the third wheel in evenings out with sympathetic friends. And when bar mitzvahs, weddings, and other celebrations with an orchestra leader bellowing "Everybody onto the dance floor!" found me at the circular table for ten watching the dancers' purses, I wanted a partner, too.

While waiting for friends to fix me up with every man under 5'8" and twenty years older (not my criteria, but that was the crew that came a-knocking), I placed an ad in the Personals of the *Chicago Reader*. It read: "DJF [I fudged on this part as I had been warned the word *separated* would turn men off as though I had described myself as *man-hating shrew*] seeks widowed or divorced JM, 55-65, health-oriented, gray hair [a personal preference], with grown children. Should be financially secure, college educated, a city dweller, and early riser. Reads NYT, listens to NPR, and watches Masterpiece Theater. Loves dogs, jazz, Stephen Sondheim, and ethnic restaurants."

As you may note, this description was pretty vanilla, no RFPs to rebels, hippies, ex-military, or others who might sport a tattoo. Again, body art was not top of mind, neither on a potential swain nor me. After all, I was attempting seduction, and any deviance from the norm of a DJF would certainly lower my chances.

The ad did produce results—none of them matching my requirements, of course—but I was willing to try them out. First Sasha had to do her part. As is the case with goldens, she fell for anyone who walked in the door, so I had to rely on the gentlemen callers' reactions to the dog.

If the guy said "Down, boy!" the moment he entered the room, not only did he lose points for incorrectly guessing the dog's sex, but immediately got eliminated for his anti-pet reaction.

A pat on the head and "nice dog" might've gotten the guy a first date, but if he brushed off the fur from his pants leg and headed straight to the sink to wash his hands, he struck out. Fortunately, Sasha and I did find a few dog lovers among the lot, which led to some sweet romances, but no one who inspired a phone call to my lawyer to speed divorce proceedings. (Evidently my husband felt the same inertia, for he wasn't pushing for a quick end to our lengthy separation either.)

Other than trying to find a suitable companion during my separation, my primary goal was to get my financial house in order. Eventually, sanity returned: We sold the house, split the profits, and I moved into a rental apartment that accepted large dogs. I canceled my health club membership, magazine subscriptions, maid service, and dog walker. I curbed eating out in favor of dining in, checked out books from the library instead of buying them online or at bookstores, and stopped buying new clothing.

Also, I visited elderly mothers of friends as *tzedakah* instead of making charity contributions, and told my showbiz daughters I was shutting down my donations to their health and car insurance bills.

If my financial recovery plan sounds draconian, think again. I was so proud of my fortitude that I felt my 4'10" stretching to the height of a Chicago Bull. I not only paid down my debt but started a nest egg that within a year hatched into a down payment on a brand-new townhouse, with my name on the title papers.

And it was in this townhouse, while sitting on the long staircase that led from front door to sidewalk, that I met the man who finally stirred me to call my lawyer and suggest it was time to talk divorce.

Sasha, of course, made the introduction. Every predawn morning when I took her for the first walk of the day, we met Tommy on his morning run. Out of breath, he stopped midstep to wish me greetings and pet my delighted pup. On his way home from work, as Sasha and I sat on the stairs enjoying an early evening Amstel Lite (me), and the sights, sounds, and smells of the outdoors (her), Tommy's approach caused Sasha to race headlong down the stairs and greet him as if he were her long-lost owner.

As it turned out, Tommy possessed only half the features I carefully outlined in my Personals ad: he was not Jewish, never went to college, was childless, lived on a very limited income, and his hair—what remained—was brown. But he *was* a mere three years older, was obviously a health-oriented, dog-loving city dweller, did listen to NPR and watch Masterpiece Theater, and was indeed a fan of jazz and Stephen Sondheim. *The New York Times* came later.

After one date (instigated by me) we learned the things we had in common trumped those we didn't, and we became a couple. Little by little, the number of his sleepovers increased, as did the articles of clothing carried down the street from his closet to mine, until we made it official in a Las Vegas ceremony.

As you may note, there's nothing in Tommy's bio to hint at a man who would encourage a tattoo on his sixty-year-old mate. But since he didn't raise an eyebrow when I let my hair return to its natural gray, deposited my contact lenses into their watery graves, gave up wearing bras in the house, and selected his T-shirts and gym shorts as my favorite getup, I knew he wouldn't object.

No, the tattoo was solely my idea. But if he had protested, I would've either talked him into it or ignored his dissent. After all, I had survived the loss of a thirty-year marriage, waved goodbye to beloved daughters who settled on either coast, gotten deep into debt and dug my way out, lived through a puppy's puddles and chewed-up furniture, and traded in public relations and its behind-the-scenes invisibility to become a writer whose personal life is online and in books. That's not the type of gal a husband orders around.

On that day in 1998 when I returned home from the tattoo studio, my left bicep was covered in Saran Wrap and had to remain protected overnight. "Can't I see?" Tommy pleaded, but I told him he'd have to wait until morning.

I couldn't sleep at all that night. Visions of regret, onlookers' gasps, and lifelong pain prohibited repose. Finally, morning came and I raced to the bathroom sink to unwrap the plastic and wash the area well with Ivory soap and warm water as directed.

Carefully, I peeled off the covering, performed the cleanup, and then stared in delight at my tattoo. It was gorgeous—bright, fun, and, well, tough. I shook Tommy awake. "Look, look!" I demanded.

"Sexy," he said.

Today, Tommy and I, and Buddy, the golden retriever who we rescued after Sasha died in her ninth year, live together in a house in an old Chicago neighborhood. We have a front porch (another satisfied long-held desire) and a back yard big enough for my dog and my husband's vegetable garden.

Husband number one and I remain great friends. He and the other woman didn't last, and as of this writing, he's never remarried. He now lives happily single (by choice, I imagine, as he's still a catch) in a high-rise apartment near the opera and film houses he enjoys.

Tommy thinks my ex is a great guy and welcomes him to our home with a handshake and back slap when he arrives for our daughters' visits, holiday dinners, or other occasions. In between these events, number one and I chat on the phone, or lunch together near his office. It's a relationship I treasure, Tommy supports, and my daughters are grateful for.

Now that I think of it, my ex never reacted to my sixtieth-birthday tattoo. If he had said anything noteworthy, I'm sure I would've remembered. It's not as if he couldn't notice it. As you'll recall, my emblem is large, colorful, and easily seen whenever I am sleeveless. Perhaps his reticence is due to disgust at the garish display, or his belief that since I'm no longer attached to him, it's none of his business. I'd certainly be interested in his opinion; but that wouldn't change my pleasure in the tattoo's presence.

Every morning, when I look in the bathroom mirror and see the badge of courage in my reflection, a smile erupts on my still groggy face. The tattoo jars me awake—a sunny reminder of the journey traveled, and the happy destination where I landed. Only one question remains for me: What shall I get inked for my seventieth, and where will it go?

Why I Got This Tattoo

nine

I

THE FIRST MONTH AFTER

when you move in somewhere new and the space isn't quite your own yet, you have to sit around awkwardly a lot, wondering what to do. It's best to read a book, one you haven't read before. Of course, if you're fragile due to just having broken up with someone, you have to be sure it's not the sort of book that will set you off in floods of tears, reminding you on every page of the damage you've suffered. Luckily, I seemed to have kept plenty of books for just such an occasion, picked up cheaply at a few years' worth of Meadows Festivals and kept aside until I needed the distraction.

You also have to go out and buy groceries, first thing on Sunday morning so you can actually eat some breakfast, and if you go via the cash machine you can summon up enough money to get things like badly needed laundry detergent. Be sure not to get carried away with the urge to stock your new kitchen with unfeasible amounts of healthy food with a rapidly approaching expiration date; be calm, and be realistic.

I thought my new home looked like how my ex would want his to be like, if only he could break free from his parents' hold. They paid most of the mortgage on the flat we shared, and consequently our flat was done up according to their tastes: alternately old-fashioned with china dogs on the mantelpiece and heraldry on the walls, or tidy and bland, no decoration, no personality. I wanted something more, wanted a space I could call mine, for so long. The flat felt so formal and it didn't even look like I lived there. I'm sure that environment was part of what was killing me. The décor of my new home reflected the years that my new flatmate, the Hip Hop Lawyer, had spent living in Japan. It felt like I was allowed to breathe at last.

I moved in on a Saturday and I drove the Hip Hop Lawyer and his friends to a dance that night because I wanted something to do. I thought it would do me good to go for a drive on a Saturday night, listening to Jawbreaker. My friend Rick and I used to do that all the time, back when I was about seventeen. He'd come round and pick me up at my parents' house and we'd just take off, driving around the dark countryside of North Down, listening to a succession of obscure punk bands that he introduced to me oh-so-casually. "Chesterfield King" was the first Jawbreaker song I heard; it was his favorite. I could relate to the song. I'd look out the window at the artificial lights passing us by in the darkness, and imagine a perfect Jawbreaker-song relationship, intense and romantic and beautiful and fragile.

Driving the car with the Hip Hop Lawyer beside me, I made unexpected mistakes. First I tried to start it in gear and couldn't understand why it kept going dead; he had to explain it to me. Then I didn't notice a light changing from green to red and he had to tell me. Then, after picking up his friends, I went straight through a red light. The Hip Hop Lawyer looked at me and asked if I was sure I was okay. There are only so many times you can use "I'm tired" as an excuse. I couldn't work out what was wrong with me. When the car was stopped at the lights, I realized my leg was shaking uncontrollably. I guess it had just been a stressful day.

In my previous relationships, whenever anything got serious, when the other person said something special to me, I would think *All this will come back to haunt me.* In my early teens, when I was new to having someone to kiss, I'd fall for it, expecting to live happily ever after, only to be dumped a few days later. After that, I graciously accepted the compliments, the affection, the love, but the moments would be rendered bittersweet by the certainty that someday I would look back at this beautiful time and weep. I would wonder what had happened to that person's feelings for me, how the person could be so callous or so casual, how the person could justify holding me at arm's length now like a stranger.

All this will come back to haunt me.

I stopped pausing to think that with Mike. Because it was perfect, it was a sure thing.

my realtor returned my call. "so how much are you bidding for this one?"

"112."

"112?" She checked her records. "That's your usual, isn't it? 112,112."

My usual? I'd only placed one bid before. "I was thinking this time I'd go for a palindrome. 112, 211."

"Good," she said approvingly, giving me a shred of optimism.

superchunk is still underrated in my own head. i can't name more than a couple of songs, but I have a whole bunch of albums now, and when I remember to play them they continue to blow my mind, in an uplifting kind of way. Stuff like Red House Painters is not appropriate breakup music because it will cause you to collapse sobbing on your bed. Superchunk, however, will do just fine, because the songs will invigorate you, give you fresh hope that there's something worth getting up for in the morning. Take note.

How do you ensure luck when you're bidding on a flat? The first time, I told everyone I encountered to think positive thoughts for me, including some drunken strangers in a club (not as drunk as me) and my taxi driver on the way home. This time, I chose the subtle approach: mellow, contained. Apart from deciding to wear my favorite boxer shorts, I did nothing special. I lay on a beanbag in front of the fire and read a novel. I listened to Superchunk again and again.

And I decided what to do if I didn't get the flat. I would take the schedule straight to the paperbank with all my other recycling, and let it go. Then I would buy shower gel, pine nuts, and pumpkin seeds at the health food shop, and go to work.

I dozed off, waking after 2:00 P.M., my mouth nasty and dry as it always is when I fall asleep in my clothes. I remembered then that the flat was being sold by a brother and sister, and the brother was in Australia, so it might take longer for the sale to be sorted out. I gradually got up and went to switch the kettle on, and my phone started ringing. I went to it thinking, *If I don't get the flat, that's okay,* and I didn't get the flat. Second in line again. It went for 115k.

Of course, it wasn't *really* okay. But at least I had more of a sense of what my living situation was going to be for the next few months. Stability is good. Life with the Hip Hop Lawyer was working out well.

i was not really sure what to do with my time, not yet used to this space as my own. I looked out over the Meadows and wondered where Mike was and if he was with Christine. I wondered if they'd kissed yet. I wondered if he held her the way he held me. I wondered if she told him he was beautiful, like I did. I didn't want to know the answers. All I wanted was for him to feel wracked with guilt. Fuck the natural course of things, maybe it was always in the cards, but the fact that I didn't hate Christine for it didn't make it hurt any less.

I put a few decorations up in my room. A framed painting of poppies, done by my mother with her left hand after the chemo messed up her right arm. The Mirnyi diamond mine. A small, kitsch, framed picture of Ganesha, given to me by my sister, which I hoped didn't trivialize the Hip Hop Lawyer's Hindu background; an Adbusters postcard of a man sitting on a rock in a lake, worshipping a TV; a few dozen divers, an eerie congregation underwater. And I decided to hang my Peters world map upside down this time, challenging the accepted notion that north always means up. The world looked completely different like this, more so than I'd expected; it took some getting used to, but it felt somehow good to look at it from a new angle. It was only on further reflection that I considered it could be read as my own world turned upside down.

Having all this free time by myself was weird. Living with Mike, I would frequently spend all weekend indoors. I had become estranged from my friends, isolated. I found my only support from strangers online. We smoked too much dope. He'd watch films, and I'd sit at the computer in the same room and hope he wouldn't start reciting our problems to me again, hope he wouldn't want sex, hope we could just stay in this cocoon of relative silence and never address the mess we were in. Now that I was living with a stranger, I had to find healthier things to do. If I was sitting at the computer when the Hip Hop Lawyer went out, I couldn't still be there when he returned hours later. I didn't want anyone to learn my secret: that the gregarious, creative person people knew me as no longer existed. And so I had to turn into that person again.

II
AFTER THAT

edinburgh is a good city in which to be newly single in spring. It started with the boy with the funny accent. I noticed him in the pub because he had a punk rock vibe, in contrast to the overwhelmingly goth clientele. Later, he came over and asked me about my T-shirt, which had been given to me by someone it turned out we both knew. We drank together, went for chips together, talked about race and politics, and I invited him in for tea ("I mean, really tea") before he gave me a hug and a peck on the cheek goodbye at 3:15 A.M.

The city was fucking freezing but all of a sudden I felt good. There were so many people and things out there and I wanted a part of all of it.

After that, I developed a crush on him that made me feel like I was twelve years old, but that's what it's like when you're getting started again. I used to consider myself practically a master of seduction. Now I was wondering if this was truly what it was like to be twenty-six. Given my idiotic behavior, the boy with the funny accent was surely going to think I could only speak when I was drunk.

We wound up going out to dinner at a fancy French restaurant, and I was too nervous to eat. I couldn't figure out if it was supposed to be a date or not. I picked at the food while trying to pretend I wasn't picking at it. "You seem tense," he said, and I tried to say I was fine, but I knew I wasn't fooling anyone and that he would just keep wondering what the deal was, so I had to 'fess up.

"Okay, so I'm a bit nervous."

"Why are you nervous?"

"UmbecauseIkindoflikeyou."

If this made me twelve, at least it came across as sweet or something. After the meal we drank cider in an alcove at a bar. And now I had loosened up and I was telling fabulous stories and he knew that I was wild like him, despite my earlier shyness, and it all felt so easy now. And then he made reference to my having just come out of a relationship and being in the resultant headspace. I said, "Do you want to know about my headspace?" and I told him. I told him that I was coping okay, fine even, and I knew that I did need to take it easy but that I was in control of it. Something like that. And he was looking at me and hearing me, and then, "I'd really like to kiss you, would that be okay?"

I'd said things like that so many times but always when I had a lot more confidence than I did now. Back in the day, it was a Line, officially, guaranteed to get me where I wanted to go. Right now though, I was saying it because I totally fucking had to say it, and that was a big difference. It put me in a kind of vulnerable space that I wasn't used to being in, and that's got to be something to meditate on. But I guess that's what made it all the better when he obliged.

Things didn't really go anywhere with the boy with the funny accent after that night, but that was okay. Once I'd shaken off feeling like a twelve-year-old with a crush, I knew I was back where I used to be and that there were plenty of adventures around the corner.

the forest is a large building comprising a cheap vegetarian café, free shop, art gallery, and event space. There are always things going on, like workshops, gigs, film screenings, and parties. If it were in Belfast, it would be run by punks, but it's in Edinburgh, so it's run by hippies. Much as I like to complain about hippies—too goddamn cosmic for me—the Forest helped me out when I was still trying to figure out what to do with my time. It was one of the few places where I felt comfortable turning up alone, to sit at a table and drink tea and read books or write train-of-thought letters for hours without feeling like I had to spend a fortune or vacate the premises. It was a hub for people I'd started to meet elsewhere, and a place where new connections could easily be made.

My first meeting with Lea took place at the Forest as well. She was one of the people who had given me support online and by phone during the relationship of doom. We met in person during the Forest's week of artistic space rearrangement. We sat in an indoor tent and left presents in it in an effort to interact with the art. Lea was gorgeous; her photos hadn't lied.

III
TRIP KIDS 2004

speaking of people you meet on the internet: then there was David. David moved to Dublin from the States, and he stopped off in Scotland for a weekend on the way. We were both kind of giddy about each other's company from the beginning: queer feminist punks in a city where we felt like an endangered species. Our first weekend was spent at a pagan festival (mocking where appropriate), gate-crashing parties, bonding over crushes and politics, and dyeing my hair on the Meadows. He missed his flight, which was to become something of a theme throughout the course of our friendship. Since Lea lived in Dublin, I put them in touch with each other.

Meanwhile, my life in Edinburgh was turning into a whirlwind of socializing and scandal. Clubs and parties almost invariably ended with action; I was unstoppable. I'd scuff home through the cherry blossoms at 6:00 A.M., enjoying the freedom I never had with Mike—the Hip Hop Lawyer wasn't about to give me grief for drinking or staying out late. Occasionally, it occurred to me that maybe I was suffering from low-level heartbreak, but when I focused on the present instead of the past, I was having fun and I felt in control. I hung out with Mike a few times, but it was too complicated for me to be in his company, so I started asserting my need for space and distanced myself from him.

When the bizarre love triangle kicked in, it felt like a roller coaster that lasted several months. David and Lea. Lea and me. Me and David. It evolved unexpectedly, of course. David and Lea's fling had already commenced, and then suddenly Lea was kissing me in a queer club in Dublin, and she was the most beautiful woman I had ever gotten off with and I couldn't believe she thought I was cool enough to qualify. As an encore, David and I made out on his balcony at the end of the night. He was just a platonic friend, I wasn't attracted to him, we were only making out because it was fun, but then every time we saw each other we were making out, having fun, and things went further. Sandwiched in between all my other scandals, and our respective relationships with Lea, it took quite a while for me to figure out there was something crucial happening here. "You're always going on about David," said my friends. "David David David. You're in LOVE with David." "Shut up," I would say. "I am always going on about David because we are having epic adventures together and he is fabulous. Now let me enthuse about Lea."

How do you make sense of these things when you're in the middle of them? It was nonstop. Every time I saw David, something big would happen, like we'd spend all night bluffing someone that I was a born-again Christian, or we'd make a suicide pact involving giant African land snails, or we'd decide to get married because we were both antimarriage and thought it'd be funny, or we'd make out with the same boys, or I'd draw a star at breakfast and then we'd head straight to the tattoo parlor so he could get it transferred onto his arm. When we were apart, he'd phone me up at 2:00 A.M. so we could sing Guns N' Roses to each other. Even Lea found it hard to infiltrate our private jokes.

But then, oh, when I moved into my new flat, the one-bedroom flat I bought just for me, twenty thousand cheaper than I expected to shell out, and David helped me move, and we built my bed together in between glasses of wine, and the next night Lea flew in for my flatwarming party, and the three of us sat in our own private-joke world and wrote on each other in marker pen while the other invitees drank and tried to pretend they weren't being shut out of our tiny elite circle, and Lea and I inaugurated my bed while David slept in the living room. . . . It was July and it was another new phase of my life. I'd never lived on my own before and I had desperately wanted to, much as I enjoyed life with the Hip Hop Lawyer. After they returned to Dublin, I set off to the Forest to use the free Internet, wondering again what to do with my time, needing to get into the right headspace for living alone and not getting lonely. It was another challenge, but this time it was one I'd set myself.

Maybe my relationship with David was just too epic to be sustainable. After a few weeks traveling together, after more adventures and more private jokes and more action and yet, ultimately, too long in each other's company, I knew it was over. I didn't want it to be. By now, we'd both been using the L-word, but already things were different, strange, and strained. I knew I wouldn't see him again when he left Edinburgh this time, but I just wished he would acknowledge it. I never liked leaving things unspoken. Eventually, after months of silence, he emailed me to tell me he'd figured out that we were never really friends.

It must have felt weird for Lea, being kind of shut out of our world even though she was the only one with any real access to it. But ultimately, our bond endured even though David fell away. Maybe it was better to cultivate friendships and relationships without quite so much hi-speed intensity. All the same, though, despite the confusion and the hurt at the end of it, I was grateful for the times David and I had shared. I'd been picking up the pieces after my relationship with Mike, and David had shown up at just the right time. When I was with him, suddenly I was the best version of myself. Nothing was ordinary. After he left, nothing could be ordinary again.

IV
ALL THIS WILL COME BACK TO HAUNT ME

here is what came back to haunt me: our unhealthy codependence. All the times Mike recited the chronology of our problems at great length while my stoned brain struggled to unpack what was wrong with his take on things. How I lost track of the frequency with which I cried. And most of all, the countless times I'd have sex with him in the hope that it would keep him happy for a few days and give us some peace. This was two and a half years of my life, and it was set to go on indefinitely. I missed none of it. After moving out, I cried maybe once, twice, for the end of our relationship, the love—or we called it love, it's hard to look back on it and feel that way—that couldn't save us, the security, and the sprinkling of good times that keep you in a bad situation. And then I moved on. The negative aspects of our relationship still haunt me, but as a warning signal: I will not be in that place again.

Sinking. I realized that that was the best word to describe what had been happening to me. And now it was over. I was waking up to the freedom now available to me, going out, taking trips away, meeting new people, having new experiences. Some of my experiences would cause me heartache, some of the new people would hurt me, but my freedom was not going to leave me again, and that meant I could cope with whatever came my way. I got "sinking" tattooed on me, upside down, with a strike through it. Over. Never again.

Redeemed

kristin tennant

when you've been raised by two parents in a loving, Christian home, then you go to a Christian college and meet a Good Boy you want to marry, it's easy to imagine the arc of your life's story. It's like an architect's model, unveiled to great fanfare for all to see and admire. There it is: a neat, pristine, compliant, happily-ever-after representation of something that hasn't even been built. Yet.

That was my story. My husband got a tenure-track job at that Christian college where we met. We bought a brick house on a tree-lined street in the alternative, artsy neighborhood. I got pregnant, as planned; we went to Europe before becoming parents, as planned. We were involved in a church filled with talented artists and musicians, and people who signed Amnesty International petitions. About six months after our second daughter was born, I secured the perfect part-time job at one of the best design firms in the city. This is what a life smiled down upon by God looks like, I thought. Every aspect fit my romanticized, preconceived notions perfectly. It seemed like a done deal.

But, it wasn't. My marriage and my sense of self were loosely modeled on structures I had always admired and subscribed to, but they were only facades, their foundations crumbling below the surface. The stress of having two very young children, followed by a move away from friends and family to a place known by local farmers as "East Central Illinois," brought an end to our floundering marriage. We invested time and money in all the recommended therapies—counseling and marriage rescue seminars, self-help books and scheduled date nights—but we couldn't seem to hit on the right fix.

As we sorted through the necessary logistics surrounding separation and divorce, a barrage of questions kept me up at night: How will I handle two small children on my own? How will I pay the bills? How will my extroverted self survive long evenings and weekends alone? After my life began to settle down, I was left with more real questions and fears—the kind I couldn't problem solve or reason my way out from under: Did I really know anything about myself? Was my entire vision for life based on false premises? And, perhaps most troubling, had God tricked me, luring me into a miserable trap? On the surface, at least, I had done everything I could imagine the God of Sunday School might want me to do. And this was my reward?

People at the church we had been attending since moving to town two years earlier weren't helping matters. They weren't cold, exactly, but they were uncomfortable and possibly suspicious. They didn't know what to do with us, or with the D-word. They didn't understand it, nor did they seem to want to. So they chose to handle the situation with the classic Elephant-in-the-Room approach.

I, on the other hand, was done with facades. I was determined to be as transparent as possible. This approach backfired when I began dating someone—after my husband and I separated, but before our divorce was legally finalized. It wasn't the best time for me to get into a relationship; that's just how it happened. As it turns out, legal matters have a way of dragging on, especially when children are involved. And apparently some people believe God sees things through the eyes of the legal system, because one of the church leaders asked me to kindly stop taking communion.

so much of the world sees things as black or white, good or bad. Church: good. Divorce: bad. Commitment: good. Change: bad. What's funny is that I can easily think of people I know who see things just as starkly, but in a completely flipped universe. Commitment: bad. Change: good. Church: bad. Divorce: good. Mostly, people want fodder for what they already believe. They want to hear the divorce horror stories in terms of the victim and the oppressor. They like knowing about a church that tells one of its members to not take communion, because it points to the judgmental absurdity of the institution, and, in all probability, of God.

I was right there. I could see—clearly—that the institutions of marriage and church were all wrong. In My Life (Take Two), I would get it right. But stories, like lives, take unpredictable turns. And although I desperately wanted to demonize both the church and the idea of marriage, this, it turns out, is not that story.

It was a nagging guilt, strangely enough, that began to turn me around. Eventually I'll probably learn to call it something else, but at the time it felt like guilt. And it kind of saved me. Just to be clear, though, I'm not pro-guilt. Divorce is riddled with blame and remorse, and it can eat you alive. Every time you examine your post-divorce life, there are more leaky holes—holes you know you'll never be able to plug. Guilt has a way of turning a thirsty soul into a sieve.

If you have children, most of your worries seem to leak out on them, those little people you love so much that it hurts. It's like they're magnets, pulling and guiding all of your thoughts toward the cores of their beings. So there I was, faced with my daughters, and my guilt. I wasn't so much wondering things like "Are they okay?" and "Do they feel loved?" My guilt was stemming from the legacy I was leaving for them. The two questions pulling at me most persistently were "What am I teaching my girls about marriage?" and "What are they learning from me about God?" I was pretty sure it wasn't good, on either account.

Being a good mom demands skill at both offense and defense. The defensive stance comes out in what I call Mama Bear mode: wanting to protect my children from harm. This impulse, I found, is exaggerated in the months surrounding a divorce. I was a mama on the edge, my eyes open, my ears alert, and my fists always partially clenched. Not only was I intent on protecting my girls from physical and emotional harm, I wanted to defend them from harmful ideas, like the concept of a marriage devoid of love, respect, and kindness. I wasn't going to let *that* idea work its way under their tender skin. Another concept I wasn't comfortable with was the idea of a church (and, therefore, a God) void of forgiveness and hope. And so, it was in Mama Bear mode that I gathered up the willpower to end my marriage, and eventually to leave that church.

But it wasn't immediate. When I look back on that time in my life, the one aspect I still can't get my mind around is my choice to *stay* at that church as long as I did. I kept going, my girls in tow, for months after I was asked to not take communion. I know I was confused, hurt, and tired. I know the guilt monster was haunting me about the many traumatic changes my daughters had gone through the past few years. Everything in their lives had changed—the least I could do was provide some stability on Sunday mornings. If I squint my mind up really hard, so everything's blurry, I can sort of get the confused logic and rationale behind why I kept going. But then, I stop squinting and I think, they told me to stop taking *communion*—something I had been raised to understand was between me and God. And they asked me because of some societal legality I really didn't believe mattered to God at all. And still, I kept dutifully going, Sunday after Sunday.

Until the Sunday, months later, when a member of the church's council came up to me after the service and said something like this: "Perhaps it's time to talk about reinstating your communion privileges." My response, equal parts pride and principle, was "No thanks. I'm here only as a chaperone for my children."

As soon as it was articulated, I knew without a doubt it was time to leave. I certainly didn't want any residue from the judgmental, controlling, hurtful side of the church to rub off on my kids. But even more importantly, I didn't want them to witness my own detached, lifeless, going-through-the-motions (minus the communion motions) take on organized religion. There were two things I knew for certain: If being a part of God's community doesn't provide measures of care and grace in our lowest moments, I couldn't imagine the point of being there. And if I didn't see any point in being there, my kids would certainly see that in me. So I left.

i was free. for the first time in years, i felt a certain lightness. It came from my enlightened understanding as much as from my trimly edited circumstances. I didn't need marriage. I didn't need church. I probably didn't even need God. I was beginning again, with a fresh determination to be *real*—to not depend on the social constructs and institutions I had previously trusted that had clearly failed me. While at first glance this stance looks like freedom, it's also fertile ground for rebellion. And that is, essentially, what I did next. I decided it was perfectly okay to get more inextricably involved with a man who was as far from my belief system as possible, and I determined it was perfectly acceptable to dig myself ever deeper into the relationship, even though I knew I would never marry him or want him to be a stepfather for my children.

Not surprisingly, soon after I found my so-called peace with this arrangement, the relationship began to implode. Through the debris of yet another example of love in shambles, I saw, of course, my children. And although I trusted my parental defensive moves, I began to seriously question my lack of offensive tactics. I knew what I wanted to protect them from, but what did I want to teach them?

This new take on love certainly wasn't it. My cynical approach to the church wasn't it. What would I give them, to help them win? After all, leaving your children with a zero score isn't the ultimate parenting goal.

And in that moment, I understood something for the first time. I thought I had been freed from the confines of marriage and church. But the freeing process didn't simply involve cutting ties and walking away from the institutions that confined me. The freeing process, as it turned out, would demand embracing those institutions again, in different forms and new ways. It required a whole new paradigm—one I would be able to explain to my children with confidence and pride.

i tentatively stepped into that new paradigm first by finding a new church. Thankfully, I didn't have to embark on a church-shopping spree. The church basically found me, in the form of a Mercy and Justice pastor named Jeff, who had spoken at my former church about a year earlier. Right when I was coming to the conclusion "I have to find a new church," I ran into Jeff, who was just an acquaintance, at a café. I was there working on some writing; he was there for a meeting. He asked how I was doing, we chatted for a while, and when we said goodbye, I knew which church I would visit first.

As it turned out, I didn't even bother visiting other ones. The first time I sat in that space, I spent half of the time blinking back tears. It wasn't The Voices of Angels, or The Warmth of God's Love, or anything directly religious like that filling me with emotion. It was the people. The very ordinary people. A group of hippie-looking teenagers sitting together in the front row. Families of every size, shape, and color. Couples that looked like they belonged together, and couples that looked like they didn't. A grandmother with her grandchildren. Middle-aged single people sitting all together, not alone. And lots of children, everywhere, roaming so much from lap to lap that I couldn't tell which kids belonged to which adults. It was a room full of humanity. They were people who weren't perfect. And they knew it. That's what brought tears to my eyes.

I found a home in that place, which was good. And I was beginning to straighten out a lot of past misunderstandings with God, which was also good. I was happy, but at the same time I was worried. Mostly I worried that figuring out church and God wasn't going to make finding true love any easier. I was actually pretty sure it would make it harder. I was in my mid-thirties, divorced, with two young children. I was a Christian, and my faith was becoming more important to me than ever, but I also thrived on being a bit of a bad girl (in other words, I wasn't looking for a full-fledged "good boy"). I wanted to go out and drink a martini. I wanted to hear my favorite band play too loudly and wanted to go dancing with friends after midnight. Not every Christian wants that. Not every Christian wants to talk politics with me, either. I'm one of those rare pro-choice Christian Democrats, which rules out a large percentage of potential Christian partners. And I was pretty much rooted in this small Midwestern town so that my daughters could be near their dad. I had to meet someone who was okay with being stuck here, too.

If you mix all those factors together and give them a good shake (squeezing in a few extra hopes along the way), you get a singles ad that reads something like this: "Thirty-something woman with two young children seeks tall, dark, handsome, thirty-something man who loves kids, dreams of having an instant family, goes to church, is serious about his faith, didn't vote for George Bush, knows how to have fun on a Saturday night, and is generally a social, successful, hip, big-city type who is perfectly happy to remain in a small Midwestern town for the next 10+ years."

Now you begin to get my sense of hopelessness. And being alone didn't seem like a good alternative. Sure, after my husband moved out, I learned that being alone is far less lonely than being in the wrong relationship. I had even come to a place where I managed life alone, with and without the kids, somewhat effortlessly. But I'm a true extrovert and knew I wasn't cut out to be single for the long haul. I also knew I would never feel secure in a relationship with someone I couldn't see myself marrying. The problem was no longer the idea of marriage, the problem was my clear lack of prospects. I began to systematically think through which dream-man requirements I could do without. Maybe a Christian guy who's not a whole-heck-of-a-lot-of-fun? Someone who's smart and fun, but agnostic? Or smart and successful, but scared to death of kids? Handsome and great with kids, but not too bright? I didn't want to sacrifice anything, but I just knew I'd be forced to, in light of my limiting circumstances.

God really likes irony, though. Because right there, in the crazy mix of people at my new church, was Jason: the perfect answer to my hypothetical singles ad. To be more specific, sitting right there, in that church, was Jason, his daughter, his ex-wife, and her lesbian partner. All there in that space, singing songs together on Sunday mornings.

Not surprisingly, it took me a while to figure out what was up with Jason. I had a crush on him from a distance for a few months before he invited me to join him and a group of friends for their regular burgers-and-beer lunch after church. I was thrilled. At least until his daughter came up, asking "Where's Mom? And when are we going to lunch?" My heart sank. I had a crush on a married man. But not five minutes later, as we were walking down the sidewalk to the bar, Jason indicated that the two women walking a block ahead of us were his *ex*-wife and her partner. I struggled to wrap my brain around this information: So I *don't* have a crush on a married man, but I *am* going to lunch with his ex-wife. Right. I was still digesting this concept long after the cheeseburger.

That's how it all began and essentially continued. Jason and I were just friends over the next few months, and I became friends as well with his ex and her partner. About six months later, when Jason and I had officially been together for about a month, a group of us gathered to celebrate the birthday of Jason's ex-wife's partner. Jason, a fabulous cook, prepared a delicious meal. After we finished eating, as the adults lingered over wine and conversation, my heart was comprehending and then leaping. It was so natural, yet so impossible: *My boyfriend had just cooked up a beautiful gift of love for his ex-wife's partner.* I was awestruck the rest of the evening. It still hasn't worn off.

less than two years after we met, jason and i got married— in the very sanctuary where we first laid eyes on each other, surrounded by the people we work and worship with, eat and dance with, and attempt to sort out the world's problems with. There's no question that my day-to-day life looks different because I am someone who was married and then divorced . . . and then married again.

I see my own daughters only two-thirds of their days. When they're not here, I simultaneously miss them terribly and treasure the couple's time Jason and I have together. I now have a third daughter—my stepdaughter—to nurture and worry about, to take joy in and love. That means there are more sibling relationships to monitor, too. (Incidentally, my stepdaughter and my eldest daughter look so much alike that people sometimes confuse them. Explain *that* to me.) I have not one parenting partner to communicate and make decisions with, but five: Jason, our two exes, and their spouses. People who think it's challenging for a typical family to sort out schedules should pause and imagine the process we go through. And because of our children, all six parents are pretty much stuck in this town we rather randomly ended up in. No one is willing to be apart from the kids, so if one of the three couples wanted to move somewhere, we'd all have to move together.

It isn't as crazy as it sounds, seeing as how we genuinely like one another. We don't share a community with my ex-husband

and his new wife, the way we do with Jason's, but we have a really good relationship considering the anger that was churned up in the divorce. We all go out to celebrate the girls' birthdays together, and we share special times like the first day of school, classroom picnics, and trick-or-treating excursions. My kids are just kids with four parents, and they seem miraculously okay with that.

Recently, for the first day of school, Jason and I gathered with my two girls and my ex and his wife. It's an annual co-parenting event in our lives. After the photos, we traipse down the sidewalk to the elementary school, the girls with their usual load: backpacks, lunches, bulging bags of school supplies, and four parents. We walk, and I watch my daughters closely as they interact effortlessly with the four most important adults in their lives. My worries recede further into a corner as the girls spread their sweet affection around—not in careful, measured ways, but in ways that follow their whims and the natural impulses of each relationship. Then they see friends on the sidewalk ahead, and the little one runs to catch up while the big sister maintains her fifth-grade composure. I wonder what she's thinking. Isn't it just a little embarrassing to be walked to school by four parents? But the girls appear to feel extra loved and celebrated on this special day. I choose to leave it at that, for once, rather than resort to doubt.

Which brings me back to guilt and legacies and hope. More than anything, those words are touchstones for how I've changed since my divorce. I've learned an important truth I can't imagine struggling through life without: Guilt and resentment have the capacity to kill all hope for a future. I'm not done making mistakes and screwing up, but I'm done with guilt. I lived too much of my life struggling with it in all the wrong ways over all the wrong things. Then I connected that guilt to God and resented God even more than I resented my ex-husband and the painful decade we spent together.

One Sunday morning, just as this was all beginning to crystallize, our pastor shared with us something Desmond Tutu said. It has embedded itself into my being. "Without forgiveness, there is no future."

My post-divorce life has a lot of forgiveness in it. I've forgiven God, he's forgiven me. Jason and I have forgiven our exes, and they've forgiven us. Jason and I have to forgive each other, too. We're trying to live out that forgiveness every day. It's important, because we'll never get it completely right.

And in the end, I think it's that paradigm of forgiveness that will be the greatest legacy we can give our children. Maybe some people can learn lessons like this in the midst of happy, successful first marriages. But I needed to journey down a more roundabout road to reach this place. And I'm very glad I did.

In My Universe
kathleen wiebe

"yeah, when we got home they were sleeping like angels," my ex told me the other night. "And they didn't wake up until 7:30 the next morning."

He'd been to dinner with his girlfriend to celebrate their first anniversary as a couple. Friends of his, who are also friends of mine, baby-sat our two sons, aged three and six, while I was at home without my children. As is often the case, the boys slept through the night at their father's house. At mine, they stir and wake and cry and call for me in the wee hours. I often spend some or all of the night with them, depending on what's going on in their dreams.

I have to admit that while I would have killed for a good night's sleep a couple of years ago, I feel honored to be tuned in to the deepest, darkest secrets of the children and their psyches—even if it means that I stumble about the house groggily in the dark and often spend half the night collapsed on a mattress on their bedroom floor.

From the beginning, I found it easy to give myself wholly to the children. In fact, as many women do, I lost myself in them. Giving so much without refueling either myself or the relationship with their father contributed to the demise of our eleven-year "marriagelike" common-law relationship. While I tuned in to them, believing that parenting is something you do 24/7, I tuned out many of my own needs, not to mention the needs of the other adult living with me. A child's arrival changes the dynamics of a marriage. You go from being a couple to being a family. Not everyone makes that adjustment smoothly; obviously many couples don't. I certainly don't think that becoming parents created our problems—it just illuminated them, magnified them, and, finally, ended them.

Now, six and a half years in, I see the mothering portion of my life as nothing less than sacred. It is the most meaningful work I have ever done, and the most satisfying. Every moment with the children is precious. Every moment with them is a moment of reality, a hit of pure now, that highest place of spiritual attainment where all my focus is awake and my energies are unified.

"You're bigger than a flower," says Primo to his little brother.

"I am?"

"But a sunflower can be bigger than you."

"I just saw a daisy what was tall and tall and tall."

They are always engaged. Always interested. Curious.

"Are we just puppets?" Primo asked me last summer. I didn't say yes or no and asked him what he thought. He nodded. "And how about the hand?" I asked him. "Are we the hand behind the puppet, too?" He considered this. "Maybe someone is just reading a book," he said. "And when he closes the book, we go to sleep."

I love to see the world through their eyes.

I explained conception to Primo: "There's one egg," I said, "and a million sperm. And the sperm race each other to see which one can get to the egg first. And when it touches the egg, the baby begins." He absorbed this, was quiet for a while, and then he said triumphantly, "So I won!"

Not every utterance is profound, of course, sometimes it's nonsense, or just plain scatology. "Die-a-rhee-a," Secundo chants, as I wash my hands after a particularly messy bout. "Die-a-ree-ah!" Primo chimes in. And then the chorus: "Poo poo bum bum, die-a-ree-ah!" I roll my eyes. And smile because this is the earliest form of humor.

We live near Swan Lake, a nature sanctuary. Now that Primo can ride a bicycle, we regularly bike to a favorite spot where willows shade a little stream that runs beneath a bridge. The other day we encountered two teenage girls there and Secundo asked matter-of-factly, "Does she have eggs?" This was his way of checking that she's female. "Does she have a 'gina?"

"Yes," I say, hoping the girl is not horrified. She isn't, luckily.

"And you, mumma? You have a 'gina?"

I nod.

"Do you have a penis?"

"No, I don't," I say. "Do you?"

He nods. "And I have a 'gina, right here." He points. I don't dispute him. He will sort it all out in time, in his own way.

They are so unformed in many ways, not imprinted yet with the beliefs and opinions of others, not yet brainwashed with all that we so unconsciously accept as truth. They teach me all the time how to be creative, how to trust in the unfolding of life, how to participate in the evolution of consciousness that happens when we allow ourselves to continue to grow and grow and grow. I constantly assess and reassess my values, my assumptions, my patterns—in relationship to the children. I am very interested in cocreating a new way of being, healthier ways of behaving, of contributing to a shared future that comes out of our remarkably complex and dynamic relationship.

And nowhere is this reevaluation and evolutionary consciousness more tested than now, now that their father and I have uncoupled, that we no longer live as a nuclear family under one roof, that my boys spend chunks of time away from me.

In this new configuration of family life, with this adjusted description of mother, I have to be okay with being separated from my children. I must confidently and happily (ha!—that took some time, you'd better believe it) let them go into the care of a man whom *I* don't want to live with any longer.

"Why?" asks Secundo when I explain that it will soon be time to go to his father's house. "Because it's his turn to love you and take care of you," I say.

"I'm gonna miss you, mumma," he says in my arms, dropping his head onto my chest when it's time to go.

"I'm gonna miss you too, honey," I whisper, sniffing his hair, which smells of summer and little boy. I am happy to notice that I have become strong here. "And I love you so much."

"I love you, too, mumma. As big as the moon."

"I love you when I'm with you," I tell him. "And I love you when I'm not. I want you to have fun when you're gone. You know I'll always be here when you get back."

And then, he lifts his bright face and zooms in for a kiss and goes happily to his father. He learns, at such an early age, that life includes these separations, that it's okay to feel sad and to express his feelings, that longing is part of life, that he can feel all of this and still be fine.

And I go into another part of my life in which I am not their minute-by-minute caregiver, their referee, their leader and cheerleader, their observer, their constant companion, their plaything, their servant, their disciplinarian, their harpy.

This separation from them, as they are still so young, ironically completes the circle of my personal surrender. I gave myself to them so fully when they were babies, and let go of so much of who I was and what I thought I wanted. And now—quite miraculously—I have the opportunity to once again redefine myself, to reexamine who I am now, to learn what *I* want and what *I* need, and recommit myself *to myself.*

Strangely enough, this is a most difficult piece. I find that I'm not quite sure what to make of the part of my life that doesn't include the boys—two- and three-day stretches, usually, every week. At first

I felt absolutely lost, bereft, alone. I would find myself at a beautiful beach thinking only that they should be here with me. I couldn't find the simple joy I once took from nature because they weren't there to share it. I couldn't sleep at night because I was so accustomed to the warm press of their bodies. It was a most painful withdrawal.

When they're with me, it's *Sturm und Drang*, a tsunami of noise, a whirlwind of activity. Without them, it's quiet, static. Peaceful. Adult. I have stretches of time to ponder and think, to file my bills, to make a to-do list and actually tick off some items. I have time to work, to write, to practice yoga, to create my own agenda. It is a bit of a double life. The various bits and pieces do balance each other out in the big picture, though not entirely with ease.

When they're away, I worry. Will they remember me? When they come back, will they know me? Will I know them? Will I miss out on something vital? Will they? Is it okay for them to grow up in two households? Is it too jarring for them to move back and forth between homes like that? Is it okay for children to spend so much time apart from their mom? How can I meet their needs when I'm not with them? How can I *know* their needs when I'm not with them?

Grief begins to rise like a tide then, seeking that deep groove to flow into. I miss them. I miss how good I feel when I'm with them. I miss how uncomplicated and clear my role is when they're with me, how life is so creative and fun with them, how meaningful life is. Suddenly I have a hard time swallowing, and I recall Secundo pointing to the sky and shouting, *"La luna! La luna!"* at the top of his lungs when we were leaving the park the other evening.

I cry because I don't want to miss out on anything: how Secundo says *reptile* for riptide, and *sea lemony* for sea anemone. What if I miss the moment when that changes? I cry because I want to be the one Primo shouts for when he sees a snake or a skunk or a salamander.

In my more rational moments, I see how this grief is really only about me feeling sorry for myself. When Primo's not with me, he will share his joy with his brother, his dad, his dad's girlfriend, a teacher, caregivers, friends.

And I can enumerate all the benefits of two households and a variety of caregivers: A child's resilience is built when he has several or many people who love him passionately; his confidence increases as he learns to make his way through the world; he receives a diversity of influences, models, and supports within his two homes. In short, I realize that I can never be everything my children need, or give them everything that they need to grow, even though, as all mothers do, I wish to.

At this point in the carefully supported evolution that transitioned our nuclear family into two households, the children are all right.

We've come a long way. When I couldn't bear to say goodbye in the early days of our separation, neither could they. Secundo, especially, aged two, used to act up on the days before leaving; he cried and clung to me when he saw his dad. It didn't help when I was fighting tears.

My new partner, a patient, openhearted man who never wanted children of his own and loves mine, has been a tower of power for me. He observes patterns, does not react, but responds. He asks me questions, probing, pointed, purposeful questions whose answers eventually bring me around to this understanding: I have to model the behavior I want the children to exhibit. We all need to be all right with our separation, because it is a fact of our life. If we want to get on with life—and we do!—then I have to get my emotions in check. If I want the children to be whole, independent, and individuated humans, then I have to want the same for myself.

Now, eighteen months after the separation from my children began, I can finally appreciate the time when the children are not with me. It is simply a pause. It is as though our lives together go on hold, and we start again when they return, exactly where we left off. Except that we've all had a break from each other, and time, perhaps to rest, refuel, reflect, certainly to anticipate reunion.

Our times apart create breathing spaces that don't occur in the hectic lives of most other families. Many people say they envy the breaks I get, the opportunity for spontaneous sex that many couples lack, the space to have a moment's peace. The time spent apart from the children is respite, a deep crevasse that accepts the broken bits that must fall away to leave the surface smooth again. Our times apart, I find, actually lengthen and strengthen our times together.

I could easily let guilt get in the way of these gifts. But I'd be a fool to look this gift horse in the mouth. When I was that full-time stay-at-home mother with a partner who worked and traveled and stressed, I felt close to losing my mind.

Happily, the children always come back, full of hugs and kisses, stories, new words, experiences, curious to see what has changed while they were away. Primo charges directly to the garden, examines his peas for new growth. "Mom, Mom!" he shrieks. "Come here." He shows me the plump pods. "Are they ready to pick?"

Secundo looks bigger every time he returns. His vocabulary increases. He has had Chicken McNuggets or gone to the zoo and seen hippos—without me—and, truthfully, I am happy for him, finally. I now know what healthy attachment is all about.

The other day the subject of conception came up. "An egg and a sperm," I told Secundo. "That's how you started. Then I carried you in my uterus until you were ready to be born."

At dinner the next day, we discuss the Easter display at our local recreation center. The kids are curious about when and how the chickens will hatch.

Secundo climbs down from his chair and opens the refrigerator door. He pulls out the egg carton and points. "What's in here?" he asks.

We go over it again. "Those are just eggs; to make a baby chicken the rooster has to supply sperm."

He looks at my partner. "You're a big man," he says.

Yes.

"You have sperm."

Yes.

"Can you make a chicken?"

We laugh and explain that chickens make baby chickens, and humans make baby humans.

Secundo looks at me. "Before I was born, mumma," he says, "you carried me in your universe?"

We laugh again. "I carried you in my uterus," I say, sobered at the aptness of his words.

I do carry them in my universe. Wherever I go, they are with me, they are part of me. They formed inside me, from my genetic material. I birthed them, nursed them, and gave myself to them. I love them and care for them so selflessly that I am ready to let them go—that I have let them go—into their own lives. And in so doing, I come more fully into my own life, into my own universe, which I have only just started to explore.

*

Phantom Condo
julie hutchison geen

divorce starts long before the first phone call to the lawyer.
I am still married, but with each sad night spent sleeping beside
my husband, each fight that fleshes out my story that we can never
make a good life together, an apparition grows.

I have a Phantom Condo. I live there in my mind with the
children, the cats, the frog, and the hermit crab. My husband and I
once had a fight about the frog, when he was still a tadpole. He had
been a tadpole for an unreasonable amount of time. My husband
decided he needed a bigger tank, and I, after our endless bickering
over money, decided to take a mean little stand. Let him live out
his life of tadpole purgatory in his little plastic habitat. He certainly
wasn't going to change into a frog at this point, and we did not need
to waste money on a new tank for him. Like most money battles,
I lost this one. The tadpole got, for ten whole dollars, a gorgeous
setup and, after some daily nurturing from my husband, promptly
turned into a frog.

Maybe he should have custody of the frog. The story of how
he saved it will make a heartwarming and attractive story to tell his

new, younger girlfriend. I will be happy to take my son to the pet store to pick out the replacement reptile or amphibian of his choice. I'm that kind of single mom: ready to take on a new pet or have an adventure at whim. I'm sure that's who I really am. It's this marriage that makes me an anxiety-ridden, irritable killjoy. Right?

So, that's settled. He gets the frog. Like the tadpole, I am in some kind of purgatory. I am married and going to couples counseling, but I inventory our belongings mentally as I clean the house. I will be sorry to lose the massive and, more important, adjustable book-shelves he made. They really are ingenious. But, after all the hours he spent in the garage laboring over them, it's only fair. Alas, the stereo equipment came with him when I got him, so that's his. That means the big-screen TV is mine, I reason. Think of the children, and their DVDs. This leads me to the thought of all the nights ahead where I will be the overlord of movie choice. Night after night of tortured, sensitive beefcake wading through intense drama will be up on my great big television screen. Sometimes I will take a break and put some old school beefcake up there: macho, sweaty, and shooting at each other.

I can't think of anything without my mind grabbing the thought and superimposing it on my new life. It's very *If You Give a Pig a Pancake* around here. "If you give a woman contemplating divorce a dust rag, she'll probably start dividing up the furniture. As she's dividing up the furniture, she'll realize she needs a sassy new haircut. When she makes the appointment for the haircut, she will suddenly think about her underwear. As she's going through her underwear drawer, she will realize she needs new lacy boy shorts right away. When she's combing the Internet, she'll. . . . " No wonder I can't get anything done.

At first, I imagine a small house. Perhaps a cute cottage with a picket fence. A picket fence while still married offends my rebellious nature, but I can have one after I am divorced. How in the hell I will fit all the kid's toys into the cottage is beyond me. I'll bet it doesn't have good closets. Unfortunately, my inherent practicality, or, as some may label it, my anxiety, is with me every minute and even intrudes on my fantasy life. I imagine coming home from work and having to mow the grass. I see myself red-faced and near tears, struggling with the lawn mower. I try to make it quaint by envisioning a push mower, and myself in a really cute straw hat and maybe some overalls. I attempt a garden, visualizing the kids scampering around with baskets of fresh vegetables. I keep seeing my red face.

So, condo it is. It's in our current school district and has a pool for the kids. What a relief. I'm so glad I'm being reasonable. Now, my husband will live in a sexy loft in the city. Magnanimously, I give him an artsy coffee shop within walking distance. I can do this because I do love him and want him to be happy. I can do this because I will be rid of him and can paint the walls any color I want.

Of course, there are moments of terror and pain. Our wedding picture is in the hallway. In black and white, my arms clasped around his neck, my eyes closed and a blissful smile on my face. He holds me, looking straight at the camera. He looks surprised and pleased, like he just caught a big fish. As I labored with our daughter, he leaned into my lower back with the perfect amount of pressure. His hands were warm and gentle and kept me sane. My labor was twenty-eight hours, and he never flagged. Our cries of joy were simultaneous in the quiet summer dawn as our son was born at home, the tree blooming outside the window scenting our bedroom. How do you reconcile that joy with this ending? I work on the idea that those good years were as right and meant to be as this pending dissolution. Everything changes, everything ends. One way or the other.

What I really do is find solace in my new, perfect, Phantom Boyfriend. I do a bad, bad thing. I get on eHarmony and start filling out the personality test. "I've heard it's a really informative test," I bullshit myself. Like I don't know my own personality after forty-some years of living with it. I get accepted and receive a report. Except for being a goddamned married liar, I am absolutely lovely. Oh, and I get some matches. Because I cast my net wide, I get a diverse lot. There is a NASCAR-loving truck driver in North Carolina. Two matches are with artistic types in Santa Fe. Some of them sound pretty good. There are no pictures, because I don't pay. But that's just as well. This way, I can be in charge of what they look like. The only problem is that this triggers the addict in me. I get that Internet shopping feeling, and I want to see more, more, more matches. Not to mention that I am still married. And going to couples counseling. Ashamed, I immediately close my account.

I play a game. When catalogs come in the mail, I get to magically have whatever I want for the Phantom Condo. I only get to pick one item from each page, though. Sometimes the perfect leather couch sits on the perfect wool rug. Tough choices have to be made. I always choose rustic dishes in spicy earth tones. My mix is eclectic, bohemian, but sophisticated. Nothing like the mishmash of hand-me-downs that inhabit my reality. You have no idea how happy I am as I whip through the pages. Sometimes I am imperious and fussy, and sometimes I am meek and grateful and I don't pick from every page to discourage gluttony. That makes me feel good about myself. When I get to the last page, or a little hand knocks urgently on the bathroom door, I come down to reality with a hollow feeling. It was good while it lasted.

I tell my friend Sarah that my next man will be a long-haired, tattooed biker in recovery.

"No," she says flatly.

"Why not?" I am disappointed. I had it all worked out.

"You need someone emotionally stable, who can take care of you."

Sarah is in no way an advocate for traditional gender roles. She is icily pragmatic and simply feels this is what I need based on my sorry track record.

"His name is Luis," she continues.

"Luis," I repeat, trying it out.

"He is a policeman," she says, firmly. "He likes to barbeque on the weekends."

."Can't he at least have a motorcycle?" I whine.

She considers this. I adjust to Luis. I can see, if I'm honest, that maybe someone other than myself should pick my male companions from here on out.

"All right. He can have a motorcycle."

Because I am a fair person (I wish you could read my eHarmony report—I am lovely!), my husband gets a Phantom Girlfriend. And yes, she is younger. With a slim, toned body that has never been stretched out while harboring a fetus. She has a job of some importance, with an excellent salary. Being somewhat sporty with lots of energy, she doesn't look at him balefully, from the couch, when he suggests a wholesome outdoor activity. The children really like her, but not too much. Let's face it: She's a great girl, but next to my complexity, she's a touch dull.

They met on Match.com (he got rejected by eHarmony) and on their first date, they went to the movies, just like he and I did. She didn't appreciate the indie flick he picked, like I would have, but she is accommodating. Maybe too accommodating. Hey, that's her business. Who am I to judge? She doesn't mind the way he chews his food, and she thinks his moodiness is part of his artistic nature. She already has a great deal put away for retirement.

I know that Luis and I don't make nearly the attractive pair that my husband and the Phantom Girlfriend do. But you know what? Luis and I have something that can't be seen. Luis and I have the kind of serenity that people have when they love each other for who they are, in a spiritual sense. Or something like that. We also have that glow that comes when people stay up all night long having sex. So, I can smile indulgently at the slender, classic silhouette those two make. The sight of them getting into their new luxurious but environmentally conscious car with their dog (I think they should have a dog, don't you?) doesn't make me jealous. Luis and I don't even make fun of them. We are just too evolved.

I play the catalog game with clothing, too. Again, I can have one item from each page. If the item is a basic, I may have it in three colors. I'm just not sure what my new style is going to be. I hope this isn't like college, where I morph into the opposite of my previous incarnation every three months. One thing I'm pretty sure about is that I'd like to have some attractive pajamas. And a superb pair of boots. Comfortable, but commanding. I must use the opportunities for revision that divorce offers. There won't be anyone to tamp me down with a look that implies my new boots are wearing me. No eyes that see from the past through a filter of all my shortcomings, real and imagined. I may even dye my hair that shade of bitter wine red that women love and men fear.

I know my single life won't just be watching as many Daniel Day Lewis movies as I like on my new couch in my new pajamas with a carton of Ben and Jerry's. The adjustments will be huge. I will likely lurch around out there in my new haircut, dating long-haired tattooed bikers in recovery, like some kind of Frankenstein, pieced together and newly risen from the dead. My needs will be vast and largely incoherent. I won't have the language for what it is I want. I may not know how to walk in my new boots. Mistakes will be made. That's okay. That's to be expected. I'll figure it out. I will date the bikers before I find Luis, you know. Sarah can't stop me. If you are a serial monogamist like me, you have to make the most of the in-between times.

But what I need more than bikers, or even my dear Luis, are the times when I will wake up at dawn, a few minutes before the kids, and breathe and think without so much as a molecule of anyone else's breath vapor in my space. No one else's agenda interrupting my thoughts, no one's expectations pressing me into places I don't fit. In those few minutes, I can stretch farther into myself, dream wild, healing dreams, and be happier than many think a middle-aged divorced woman with young children should ever be.

Lost Mind, Found Self

sue sanders

i checked my reflection in the subway window yet again and tried to smooth a strand of flyaway hair as the 4 train shook and shimmied toward Union Square. I glanced at my watch, swallowed another nervous lump in my throat, and nibbled on a fingernail—my breakfast. I was on my way to meet the man I'd been flirting with through email and phone calls—my first date in nineteen years—and I was scared. As I raced toward Barnes and Noble, excitement began to knock fear out of the way. He was already standing on the steps, tall and thin, in jeans and a black sweater, with gray curly hair. He looked exactly like I expected, like how he wrote. Studying his handsome face for the first time, I knew he'd be as smart and funny in person as he was in his letters to me. I wanted to dive into his pale blue eyes. "Hi," I said as I stood on my toes to give him a kiss on the cheek. The way he smiled at me, I knew it would go well. At thirty-eight, I was about to begin my new life.

When you're in an eighteen-year relationship, you get used to using "we" when talking about your life and future—"We'll go backpacking in Laos," "We'll move to Brooklyn and watch our child grow," "When we're old and wrinkled, we'll take walks, hand in hand." It never occurs, even in nightmares, that mental illness might make you conjugate verbs differently: "I'll tuck my daughter in," or "I'm eating dinner alone."

John and I met second semester of our sophomore year of college. We spent our young adulthood growing older together but tried our best to actually avoid growing up. We thrived on adventure, harnessing ourselves to oversize backpacks and bumming around an atlas of countries—from Australia, Bulgaria, and the Cook Islands to Indonesia, Latvia, and Turkey. We took underpaid jobs and lived in a tiny New York apartment, saving and dreaming of the next trip. We finished each other's sentences. We read poetry to each other without embarrassment. I just assumed we'd always do so.

But after thirteen years together, he developed bipolar disorder, triggered by an antimalarial drug we took for a trip to Vietnam. It came on suddenly and strongly. Five years of hospitalizations and denial followed, by him (that he was sick) and by me (that I could make him take his meds and he would get better). Still, there were good and bad periods. During one prolonged "good" period, I got pregnant. As my daughter grew inside me, I managed to convince myself that a baby would solve all our problems, that he would stay better and stay on his medications this time. I was pregnant with my daughter, and with denial.

I'd study John while he was sleeping, searching desperately for a glimmer of the person he used to be. If during the day I'd occasionally see something of the old him, I'd cling to that thinning thread of hope that he was finally getting better. But he wasn't. Despite my continued pleading, he refused to take his medications, and in his prolonged manic phase he would stay out most of the night, drinking—a lot—to self-medicate. He spent money we didn't have on clothes he didn't need. Then, right after my daughter turned three, my parents decided to come visit. A week or so before they were due to arrive, he turned his psychosis toward them. "I know your uncle is with the CIA. What about your dad?" He raised an eyebrow as if he'd just uncovered a vast conspiracy. "I think your parents should sleep outside." He pointed to our weed-strewn back yard, and suggested they pitch a tent. The next morning I woke up to find that he'd turned all the pictures of my parents, grandparents, and great-grandparents upside down. That was the end. I'd had it with my fantasy; I couldn't pretend that he was getting better or would stay better. I packed a bag, picked up my daughter, and fled.

Even though our life together had not been normal for years, it was still as if my universe exploded—my own private big bang. For a week, until we got John hospitalized, I curled myself into a ball on my in-laws' sofa and sobbed. I didn't think I'd ever be happy again. When we finally went back home, more than the apartment felt empty; part of me did, too. I realized I needed help. So every Tuesday for the next year, after walking my daughter to her preschool and kissing her three-year-old cheek goodbye, I'd head to the Land of Therapists on the Upper West Side. There, sunk into the stuffed armchair of Dr. Orr with a box of Kleenex on my lap, I slowly began to sift through the debris of my relationship until I realized that maybe the idyllic years with John weren't as idyllic as they had seemed. I'd had relationship myopia, and it took separating to put it in focus.

"What if he didn't get sick . . . do you think you would have stayed together?" Dr. Orr asked one morning, looking across the table at me as I clenched a damp tissue. It was a question I'd been wondering about myself. It brought to mind an incident from a half-dozen years before. John was a talented writer who had stories and articles published in a slew of magazines. One day, I'd scraped up my courage and showed him the beginning of a story I was attempting to write. He read it, chuckled, and actually said, "I think it's cute that you tried to write." I laughed along but inside was ashamed for thinking I could actually write anything, and I never tried again.

Dr. Orr also tried to get me to think about why John was "The Decider" in our relationship. He was the one who usually chose the restaurants, the movies, and where we went on our trips. Why didn't

I push to do what I wanted? Dabbing my eyes, I said I was afraid. John was so brainy and clever, and I was completely insecure. I thought if I asserted myself, he might leave. I didn't feel that I was all that smart, and when I met John, who took center stage wherever he went, I felt lucky that he'd chosen me. If our marriage was a movie, I was an extra. Finally articulating the thoughts that had been lurking unsaid in my mind shocked me. The more I thought about it, the more I realized big parts of our relationship weren't healthy, even before John got sick. It was only by John losing his mind that I was able to find myself.

I mulled all this over on the train back to Brooklyn, rushing to be on time for preschool pickup and a playdate. The good news was that my daughter had no apparent problems when her father vanished. "My daddy's sick," she told her friend Eva, matter-of-factly, as they skipped to the playground. "My daddy's Jewish," Eva replied, the discussion over as they galloped to the swings.

Evenings, I would sit on the closed toilet and watch my daughter carefully in the tub for any signs of sadness, but as she splashed happily there weren't any. Afterward, we snuggled together under her blue kitty bedspread, reading *The Stinky Cheese Man* and *Jamberry*. *Dinosaurs Divorce*, which I'd bought weeks earlier, sat untouched on the bookshelf. It turned out that a house without a mentally unstable dad is a far easier place to live. Still, I took her to a child psychologist for a checkup.

Dr. Barton's office was on a winding Village street that looked like it belonged in one of my daughter's picture books, with its gas lamps and brownstones. My daughter loved the squeaky sound of the old wooden steps and the wonderland of toys in his office. In a small wicker basket, she discovered a checkered cloth. She took it out and smoothed it on the floor, then carefully set three plates, cups, and silverware. "Who's this for?" said the doctor, with a smile, pointing to the third setting. My daughter looked at him like he was crazy (as if she expected this from all the men in her life) and said, "You, silly." Dr. Barton noisily slurped invisible tea and told me when the session was over, "She's fine. When she's ready, just talk with her honestly, in a way she understands, about what's going on."

We did talk, but I also made sure we got out of our apartment and out of ourselves. On sticky summer nights, she jumped and bobbed to music at Prospect Park's free concerts. We caught the train to Manhattan to go to friends' art openings. At first I was certain there was a neon sign over my head, blinking wildly: "ALONE=LOSER." But after a while I stopped caring about what others thought and started to do exactly what I wanted. I invited friends and their children over for barbeques. The children splashed in the kiddie pool while adults splashed wine into their glasses.

Brooklyn was a great place to be a single mom, and our neighborhood was filled with them, although I didn't know any and wasn't sure how to meet them. But since leaving John, there'd been an internal seismic shift—and a subtle fault line had opened. I realized that my tendency was to wait for things to happen to me—that's how I ended up waiting five years for John to get better. Now, after getting a second chance with my life, I decided to live it in the active, rather than the passive, tense. I would make things happen in my life: I'd meet some single moms. In the childcare room of the local food co-op, I taped a note on the wall: "Newly single mom of preschooler would like to meet other families like ours." I quickly heard from eight other women. A group of four of us began meeting regularly for dinner, companionship, and support. We talked about schools, pediatric dentists, and dating—the latter as real to us as the fairytales we read our children each night. But one night, as the hummus congealed and babaganoush darkened in blue Moroccan bowls, one woman let drop that she was thinking of trying online dating. We looked at each other, and in a split second, we dashed out of the kitchen and into the bedroom, flipping on the Mac. On one dating website, we scrolled through page after page of single men smiling invitingly at us. I grinned back at all those faces and thought, *Why not take them up on it?* I resolved right then I'd become a swinging single mom.

The next day I cobbled together a profile, found a digital picture of myself, posted it, and then waited anxiously for what I hoped would be an avalanche of email from cool and interesting single New York City guys. As it turned out, that didn't quite happen— thank goodness.

Within an hour, I received my first note—an angry diatribe written solely in capital letters. I hit delete. But then, a few hours later a more promising email appeared in my inbox:

> *I live about a zillion miles away from you up in Westchester, so maybe this is silly, but I enjoyed your listing so much I thought I'd write and say hello. I still have a "love conquers all" theory about romance, so who knows, maybe it even conquers Metro North and the F train.*

He continued for several more paragraphs, saying he was a writer (uh, oh) who'd had a few books published. He said he lived in the city for twenty years and sometimes missed it, but he also liked the fact that the longest line at the post office was usually two and that he could have a conversation with the guy behind the counter about his beloved Mets when he picked up his stamps. I laughed. I reread his note, carefully examining it for any signs of insanity. When I didn't see any, I bit my lip and tentatively started typing my reply. Then I hit the "send" button and waited.

A few hours later came his answer. From that and subsequent emails, I learned that he was separated, that he was passionate about his writing and cared deeply about the world around him. Each one of his notes made me smile at least once, and he was not only funny but he also asked questions about me and seemed genuinely interested in learning what I was about. He also used proper grammar, spelling, and punctuation in his emails, which mattered to me.

I felt like a giddy teenager, and that was in fact the last time I had dated. Every few hours, I'd rush to the computer, dial up, and hope there'd be something in my inbox. There usually was. With each email, the conversation seemed far more than casual flirting. Behind the safety of our monitors' screens, we were getting to know each other.

After a week or so, he suggested that maybe it was time to actually speak to each other. I wasn't so sure. I liked our email flirtation and was afraid that he'd see me for the nervous person I wasn't electronically, and with awkward silences the flirtation would dissolve. On the other hand, how long could we keep this going? Reluctantly, I typed my phone number and hit the send button. The phone rang as soon as I disconnected from the 'net. It turned out that the words came as easily from our mouths as they did from our fingertips. During that first phone call I told him all about John and made him swear he'd stay sane.

Feeling confident, I asked him, "So, when are we going to get together?"

"How about tomorrow?" he suggested.

I hadn't expected that response. I thought I'd have a few days to prepare emotionally for my first date. I was just getting used to the *idea* of dating—not actual dating. But I agreed. After I hung up the phone, though, the self-assuredness that I'd felt moments earlier instantly transformed into insecurity. That day and night passed in a jittery haze and I was jolted awake from a fitful night's sleep by the alarm clock's beeping.

But the next morning, after we greeted each other on the bookstore's steps and decided to take a stroll, our fingers naturally found each other. It felt strange to hold a different hand from the one I'd held for the last eighteen years, but somehow it also felt like I'd been holding Jeff's forever—and I wanted to.

"How long did it take you to write your profile?" he asked. I told him I didn't take it seriously and churned it out in a few minutes. He seemed surprised and very impressed. "You're a natural writer," he said, with pride. Suddenly I felt smart and pretty, feelings that had been hibernating for a long time.

We'd been walking and talking for almost an hour, which seemed like both minutes and years, when we passed a diner. "Want to get some breakfast? Is this place okay?" He wanted to know. I nodded and, as he held the door open for me, I couldn't help but notice he was asking me to help make the decision, rather than making it for me. Inside, we scooted onto the red vinyl benches across from each other, studied the plastic menu, and ordered. The diner's air was thick with the scent of sizzling bacon. Jeff ordered pancakes. I asked for a cup of coffee, still too nervous to eat, and worried that my hands were quaking so much that anything I tried to put into my mouth would end up dangling from my chin. My hand was still trembling when Jeff reached across the table and held it. His warm eyes' focus on me made me feel like I was the only person in the crowded diner. He rubbed my fingers, bitten nails and all. My hands stopped shaking. My first date since I was a teenager was going very well.

We left the diner and didn't want to leave each other, but I had to get back to Brooklyn to pick up my daughter. We rode the subway downtown (the opposite direction for Jeff, but he wanted to make the date last as long as possible), and I couldn't help noticing that our legs were touching. In my mind, I was already envisioning a new life around the bend, like the next stop on the subway line. As I grew dizzy from excitement (and all the coffee), I did something the old me would never have done: I squeezed his hand, looked into his eyes, and asked him to kiss me. It just felt natural. He did. Two hours after we met we shared our first kiss on the 2 train. It seemed like we'd already begun a relationship, not just finished a date. Years later, Jeff told me that he knew that morning that we'd eventually get married. I did, too.

The differences in my relationship with Jeff and with my first husband quickly became apparent. After we got to know each other well, I handed Jeff the first draft of the second story I'd ever tried to write. It really wasn't very good, but his reaction was the opposite of John's. He encouraged me, helping me dig up the better parts, and didn't complain as I handed him revision after revision.

"You choose, sweetie pie," Jeff said one day as we were trying to decide which movie to see that night. As I studied the *Times,* I realized that he and I constantly and naturally took turns and shared. My grown-up relationship was a bit like my daughter's preschool. We also discussed everything, from choosing restaurants to solving disagreements. Neither of us had a bit role; we were both supporting players. It felt good.

He was far more giving than John in other ways, too. Until Jeff, I'd never heard four little words in the bedroom: "How does this feel?"

Early on, I did go out with a few other men, just to reassure myself that what we had was as real as we both thought it was. Philanthropy Guy reserved a table in a downtown bistro. I put on a black dress, tights, shoes with heels, and someone else's personality—it felt a bit like I was playing dress-up. When I told the maitre d' that I was meeting someone, he unfurled his arm, pointing to five tables, each with a balding, well-dressed man. Could I choose whichever one I wanted? I wondered. I quickly found the right man, but instead of pinpricks of excitement this date was more jabs of indifference. As the waiter pulled my chair out, I put my manners on and felt like a stage version of myself. Instead of the braised monkfish and wine in crystal glasses, I wanted pancakes and coffee with Jeff. I just wanted to go home, peel off my costume, and call him.

Violin/Writer Guy was smart and cute. I met him in his workshop and, as he leaned toward me for a kiss, I took a step back. He confessed that he had cheated on his wife before they'd divorced. I craved Jeff.

The big test, though, was what would happen when Jeff met my daughter. I wasn't nervous. I had no doubt that they would get along, but I was scared that they would, and then the relationship would end and someone else would vanish from my daughter's life. Their meeting: a gold seal indicating that our relationship was Official and Real. I was scared of hypothetical loss—if it ended, what might happen to her? To me? Part of me wanted to stay with our gals-in-Brooklyn existence, a land without men, a magical place where we couldn't get hurt.

But, just as hurt is a possible side effect from living, so, too, is happiness. And I wanted it—for me and for my daughter. We decided to keep the meeting very casual. "My new friend Jeff is coming over tonight—then we'll go out for pizza," I told her, clipping a butterfly barrette into a clump of blond curls. When the bell chimed, she raced to the door as fast as a four-year-old could, then promptly retreated to the safety behind my skirt. The stuffed white rabbit in Jeff's hands drew her out of hiding. She grinned, slapped her hand over her mouth, and grabbed the toy. Apparently the bunny gave her an idea—she ran into her bedroom with it and, a minute later, emerged wearing a pink tulle tutu and performed an interpretive dance to Tchaikovsky. Jeff applauded with genuine delight. I watched, enraptured with the scene.

Over the next year, we took our time, fell in love, and made a family. At times it was messy, but it kept moving forward and growing stronger. While my daughter slept, one hand flung over her head and the other clutching Fluffy the Rabbit, Jeff and I held each other under the down comforter in my bedroom, laughing and whispering about his past, my past, our future.

By the next summer, moving in together didn't feel like a big deal—it felt right and natural. Brooklyn started to close in, so we moved to the openness of the countryside to raise our free-range child, choosing a green town in a blue state as our new home. Our daughter wore a pouffy white dress and sneakers to our wedding. When Jeff told me, during his vows, that when you are in love, the air smells sweeter, the colors are brighter, and even the Mets play better, his eyes were the most brilliant blue I'd ever seen.

Sometimes, my old life intrudes, and that aspect of it can't possibly end well. John is on and off his meds, in and out of hospitals—the prepositions of his life. After a hospitalization, he'll decide he wants to get to know our daughter. He'll call a few times, and if he's doing well, we'll schedule a meeting. My daughter says she "feels weird" when we visit the stranger who is her biological father. She doesn't seem to care if she sees him or not. I'm not sure if that makes me happy or sad.

But at night, when it's Jeff's turn to read her stories, I'll peek in the door and watch her snuggling into him. I hear her laughing when he strays, as he inevitably does, from the book's text into a silliness that sends her into fits of giggles. This is what I want: a happy ending to a tale that began with our journey through loss.

On the Run

michele peterson

it was christmas eve, the stars were shining brightly above the cactus silhouetted in the valley, and I had a .45 Magnum in my hand.

"Don't worry, the safety is on," said a burly guy in a cowboy hat, who noticed how gingerly I held it. The gun was still warm. He'd just finished firing it several times into the air—a common celebratory practice in these parts. In certain bars, you don't want to be on the second floor when a party gets started.

This is San Vicente, Guatemala, an area so far off the tourist trail that it doesn't rate even a mention in *Lonely Planet*. Unlike the Mayan highlands, where colorful markets draw busloads of tourists, this stretch of the lowlands, an arid patch between two mountain ranges that border Honduras and the Caribbean, doesn't see many visitors.

That's no surprise. With a population of only four hundred people (and 60 percent of those children), there are no hotels and no restaurants. So if you can't speak Spanish or don't have family in town, you'll go hungry. But I'm family—guaranteed a meal.

I was here with my partner of seventeen years. Although we'd visited Guatemala several times, his family had always come to the capital city to meet us. But last year, his father suffered a massive hemorrhagic stroke and, although Papa had recovered sufficiently to be discharged from the hospital, the doctors advised that he could relapse at any time. So, this time, we headed to his family's *finca,* or ranch, for Christmas.

The last time I was this close to a gun: eighteen years earlier in the middle of my divorce. My ex-husband and I had met on a scenic train across Canada. I was eighteen, leaving my hometown on the prairie and looking for adventure on the Pacific coast. He was six years older, played the harmonica, and lived on the Gulf Islands. Two years later we married. He worked as a truck mechanic and I had a job at a bank. The relationship was good and bad, but with two small kids, I was grateful for the help.

That is, until things took a turn for the worse. One night I came downstairs and found him seated at the kitchen table with a tape recorder, a box of cassette tapes, and several parcels in brown wrapping paper.

"What are you doing?" I asked.

"Mailing these to the head office," he said, slowly stacking the parcels in a tidy row like dominos. "They need to know about what my boss has been doing."

"How many have you sent?" I asked, as a chill rose up my spine.

"Maybe half a dozen."

He'd been secretly following his boss, collecting evidence, and sending it to upper management. After the damning tapes were received (his boss had been shopping for groceries on company time), my husband was the one who got fired.

With a growing sense of dread, I began to notice other strange behavior. He forgot the directions to my parents' home and spent hours in bed. Finally, when he called from a pay phone crying that he couldn't remember where we lived, I drove him to the ER. The diagnosis was acute schizophrenia, and the conditions of his release included medication and group therapy. He did neither. Instead, he took up target practice at the local rifle range.

He didn't bother to hide his growing preoccupation with guns, and pinned addresses of shooting ranges ripped from the Yellow Pages onto the kitchen bulletin board. Believing I was having an affair with my boss, he began to tail me.

"Look out your office window," he told me on the phone.

There he stood, waving a large piece of plastic.

"This sign says you suck your boss's dick," he shouted.

He was finally sent to jail. Once released, he was back like a magnet. In a warped version of a daily newscast, he held a throw mike, just beyond restraining order distance, so he could listen and record conversations in our home.

Our daughters alternated between sympathy and terror. The oldest got picked up for shoplifting, and the youngest started lighting fires at daycare. I worried about our safety and began to lock our bedroom doors at night.

During each incident, I felt as though I was immersed in a macabre dunk tank, alternately doused by icy cold water and then brought up for air. Terrified he would kill us and then reassured when his former self briefly reemerged, I also worried that I'd lose my job.

Strangely, as my marriage deteriorated, my career took off. I'd started a new job as an analyst in a financial services company, received several promotions, and was now a senior manager. And I was on the brink of really having an affair.

Not with my boss, but with a Guatemalan guy I met at a political function. A political refugee with a degree in agriculture and several pairs of cowboy boots, he could read the prairie sky, predicting rain, wind, and clouds like a road map. Even now, I recall how strongly I was drawn to him when I first saw him across the room.

Despite my initial attraction, things got off to a bumpy start. On our first date, we made plans to meet for coffee at a downtown shopping mall. Javier waited on the second floor and I on the first (a misunderstanding due to the language barrier), until so much time passed that we only had a few minutes to chat before I had to rush to pick up my daughter at daycare. For our next outing, he invited me to a friend's house for a bowl of *sopa de pata de res,* a ceremonial dish comprised of meaty beef hooves and large chunks of a gummy substance I later discovered was tripe, scraped from the honey-combed insides of a cow's stomach. While he slurped up the liquid with gusto and recounted his mother's advice that the wiry tendons were full of protein, I did my best to look enthusiastic. Although the thought of eating it made me shudder and I managed to stash most of my bowlful in the kitchen, I did enjoy the after-meal dancing.

By date three, some of my earlier enthusiasm was beginning to wane. In addition to our language barriers, he was rich in land (back home), but poor in cash. All he owned was a bicycle—which wasn't much of an asset in a city where it snowed for six months of the year.

Then, one hot summer day, we met up at a nearby beach where a long stretch of dusty sand led to a big cold lake. Thousands of people jockeyed for space as far as the eye could see. Within ten minutes of arrival, my eight-year-old daughter went missing.

Lifeguards, neighbors, and friends combed the murky waters. I was hyperventilating in panic by the time I saw Javier leading her by the hand back toward me from across a pile of rocks on the other side of the bay.

Even today, he has an unerring ability to find us no matter where we are. To test out this theory, I once ducked into the crowd at a busy jazz festival just to see if he could find me. He did. In less than five minutes. He claims it's from years of experience looking for cows lost while grazing the hills in Guatemala.

After our first series of half-dates, he began spending more time with the girls and me. Soon, he had planted a garden in our tiny scrap of yard. Tendrils of squash, peas, and tomatoes wrapped their way up the stairs and into our home. I breathed in his essence like an asthmatic seeking relief.

After my divorce, the girls and I moved to the furthest edge of town. My ex took his divorce payout, packed up his Dodge Valiant, and disappeared. The years passed in peace. I became a vice president and was rumored to be in line to replace my boss once he retired. I had a company car, stock options, and enough money to send the girls to summer camp and dance lessons. We spent hours swimming in the pool and, after Javier moved in, even more time cooking with his friends, fellow political refugees fleeing the bitter civil war in Guatemala. Medical doctors, schoolteachers, and scientists—our kitchen was filled with people chopping shrimp and grilling tortillas.

The girls drew comfort from the positive activity in our home and developed insatiable appetites for refried black beans and fresh tomato salsa. The youngest learned a few select words of Spanish (all the bad ones she could manage to overhear) and, in turn, took pride in helping Javier expand his English vocabulary.

"Did you know you just washed your hair with flea shampoo?" she once said, pointing to the tiny label on the cat's shampoo bottle.

We all relaxed and grew closer. Even my father took up the habit of hugging people when entering or leaving a room.

As for Javier, he launched a landscaping business and learned to live in a house filled with teen and preteen girls. Between mysteriously disappearing hairbrushes, thongs that got tangled in our toes while navigating the laundry room, and the conga line of teenage boys winding their way through the back door, life was full—and happy.

Then, the peace was shattered.

Turns out, money wasn't what my ex-husband wanted. He wanted me. He'd emerge from behind a tree, form his fingers into the shape of a gun, point it at me, and pull the imaginary trigger.

"Do you want us to take care of the problem?" one of Javier's friends with silver teeth asked when they spotted my ex sleeping beside the wheels of my car.

Instead, I wangled a job transfer and we left town, providing no forwarding address. Later, I realized we were running for our lives.

Toronto is a city of close to five million. While pantyhose and a suit were enough to make the corporate grade on the prairies, they weren't enough to cut it in my new role as VP of sales in the big city.

"I can take you from forgettable to unforgettable," promised the company image consultant. Suddenly, I had a jewelry buyer, a golf instructor, a maid, a clothing consultant who wheeled in new suits each month, a public speaking video coach, and thousands of freeway miles on my odometer. It was exhausting.

Our home was no safe haven either. What had initially seemed so idyllic, wasn't. Hidden behind the park bordering our neighborhood was a nuclear power station that hummed silently from its squat position on the waterfront. Nearby was a string of chemical plants that sounded sirens when spills occurred. The sky was often yellow with smog and humidity.

In response, I began to take refuge in nature and escaped into the virtual world of writing about the outdoors and community activism: feeding squirrels, flying kites, walking, and the value of volunteerism. I submitted a couple of stories to our community newsletter and was given a column. For one story, I interviewed a volunteer who had just come back from an assignment in Azerbaijan with the Canadian Executive Service Organization (CESO), a development organization that sends experienced executives overseas on short-term assignments.

"I could do this," I thought. My name was added to the roster as a sales and marketing expert.

Meanwhile, Javier was discovering that what had been an obstacle in a small city was actually an advantage in a large, ethnically diverse city. His easygoing personality, combined with his training in agricultural engineering, positioned him well in the booming housing construction business. Although he wasn't much of a handyman, he could read blueprints and understood soil, topography, and, most of all, conciliatory relationships—he was the bridge that cemented the numerous construction trades together. Starting out as a landscaper, he was soon lead supervisor at one of the city's largest home builders.

During those years, we made it to Guatemala a few times. On our first trip, I served as a human shield in case of problems. Some of Javier's former university colleagues had been killed or disappeared. As instructed by Project Accompaniment, a solidarity program where returning Guatemalans are accompanied by Westerners who serve as human rights observers, we avoided public events and I kept myself highly visible to ward off army attention.

It wasn't too difficult to stand out. If Javier was considered an unusual choice for me in Canada's corporate world, I definitely wasn't what his family had been anticipating either.

The eldest son in the family and the first to get a university degree, Javier was the catch of his village and Catholic. I was divorced, had two kids, and barely spoke Spanish. Plus, with my studious-looking glasses and a propensity to wear black, I was more likely to be mistaken for a nun than a spicy Latina or vestal virgin. Traditional gender responsibilities also ran deep. Upon arrival, his sister and aunts would rush to open his suitcase, and begin ironing all his clothes.

"Don't tell my family I wash dishes," he reminded me as he headed out to the corral to brand some steers.

If his family had serious reservations about his choice of a partner, they didn't show them. I was overwhelmed by the crowds of family kissing, hugging, and touching me and would often retreat to a bedroom to read a paperback.

"¿Qué pasa?" they'd worry, leaving platters of peeled mangoes and papayas outside my door in case I felt faint. When they discovered I was prone to heatstroke, terrified of insects, and slept with ear plugs, I became even more of a mystery.

"She's like Zorro," said Javier when someone commented on my sleeping mask.

Despite their reservations, the family chased cockroaches out of my room, gave me instructions on hiding money in my shoes when shopping, and did their best to understand me.

I seemed to fit in best with one of two groups in his family, the beer-drinking uncles or the women in the kitchen. The former found my Spanish funny and the latter could always use a spare hand.

Half-inebriated, I learned how to make *pepian,* a fragrant mole of smoky wood-fired toasted seeds and chiles; chiles rellenos (stuffed peppers); and tamales. Although everyone could recognize my handmade tortillas in a stack of hundreds, nobody refused them.

Even Papa, who said they looked like *pata rajada,* or the "cracked heel of a foot," ate them with only a moment's hesitation.

Back home, engulfed in corporate stress, I was sliding downward fast. En route to appointments, I'd pull over on the side of the highway, vomit, and keep driving. My heart pounded so hard that I was getting EKGs monthly. The doctor prescribed pills to help me sleep. More than exhaustion, I was feeling increasingly disconnected from what the company considered success factors.

One evening, I attended a sales launch at a swanky private club. Somewhere in between the cocktails and the awards ceremony, a Brinks truck rolled up and armed guards wheeled several shiny display cases filled with sparkling diamonds up the red carpet. The jewels were motivational tools intended to incite enough longing in the sales representatives to catapult us to higher targets.

It was a pivotal moment for me. While I'd never been particularly motivated by money, I did love the competition, strategy, and creative opportunities of corporate life. I viewed it as a well-paid chess game. Coming face-to-face with the materialistic heart of it sickened me. I felt set adrift from the corporate mandate, and the distance grew with each passing month. But shackled by golden handcuffs, I hung on.

One morning, the news showed an airplane hitting the towers in New York. At the office, we all stood and watched it happen over and over. Then, another plane hit the second tower. I closed the office, sent everyone home, and spent the rest of the day hugging my daughter on the couch while watching the horror unfold on the TV.

Several months later, when the company decided to centralize operations, I had a choice. I could take a severance package or transfer back to the head office. The prairies were out. Someone had let our address slip, and we'd already begun to receive strange letters from my ex, images of demons scribbled with such force there were holes in the paper. I decided to take a month off to think.

By coincidence or fate, my first assignment with CESO materialized. I was to help create a strategic plan and raise funds for a sixteen-thousand-member women's cooperative in Honduras. The country had been extensively damaged by Hurricane Mitch and to survive, the Honduran women needed help starting small businesses. I spent a month visiting women in remote areas where temperatures reached 115 degrees during the day, armed thugs patrolled the streets, and insects bit so voraciously that blood ran down my legs.

Despite the physical discomforts, I was inspired by the women I met. One entrepreneurial group had been making coffins to bury the dead after the hurricane and had developed enough carpentry skills to diversify into making furniture. Another wanted to borrow $100 to make a wedding gown to rent out to villagers for wedding photos. Many of the women faced violence in their home, yet conquered their fears, and took considerable personal risks to begin new lives. My work helped raise three years' worth of funding, meaning that for some, dreams of fish farms and dressmaking shops would become a reality.

The work felt real and it felt right. Changing the lives of others inspired me to make changes in my own life. Additional CESO assignments in Bolivia and Russia gave me the confidence to apply my corporate experience to the nonprofit world. Soon, I had a permanent position at Canada's largest environmental justice organization. We moved into the heart of the city and I sold my car. My work was both challenging and satisfying, but I held on to the belief that it was only temporary. After all, it paid a fraction of my former earnings. Someday I would return to the real world, the corporate world of profits and measurable results.

I began writing more. Several stories were published and one about my daughters was selected for an anthology.

"Did you have to use our real names?" moaned one, as the other snickered.

What I lacked in formal writing training, I made up with sales techniques. Using sales pipeline theory (more prospects in the funnel equates to more sales), I set a goal of sending three pitches a day. It wasn't easy. For every editor who liked my writing there were dozens who didn't.

"You're not going to want to read this one," warned my daughter as she checked my email.

I took writing courses and soaked up terminology about leads and paragraph transitions. Many stories hit national newspapers, others sold internationally. Before long, I was receiving offers from tourism boards to travel as their guest. Malaysia, India, Spain—I wrote about fortune tellers, tiger safaris, and hiking the Camino de Santiago.

At least once a week, I'd scour the map. I was still running and couldn't stop. First, I had been running from my ex-husband and now I was running after success. My travels, which had once been solo forays into the world to challenge myself, overcome fears, and emerge transformed, threatened to become moneymaking enterprises driven more by compensation than passion.

But somehow, things always slowed down in Guatemala. Whether it was the tropical temperature that forced everyone to retreat to shade by midafternoon, the leisurely cooking routine, or gaps in my Spanish, the pace of my thoughts always seemed to be as languorous as the sway of a hammock.

This past Christmas Eve, the evening air was thick with smoke from the outdoor fires that kept the tamales steaming until midnight arrived. A pig ran across the road with a wishbone-shaped tree branch lashed to its head. Although it looked like a medieval instrument of torture, it was intended to stop the pig from running into people's homes. Everyone was in outdoor kitchens, tending big, black pots of steaming tamales.

Unlike Canada, where Christmas festivities all led up to the big event on the morning of December 25, here the big day was Christmas Eve and the sharing of tamales. In San Vicente, every household had prepared its own version—beef, chicken, and pork—each tamale wrapped snugly in a banana leaf that had been charred and softened over charcoal earlier in the week.

"Not much shooting this year," said Javier, sounding disappointed as he eyed the gun in my hand. The guy in the cowboy hat, who turned out to be a distant relative, offered to take me into the field to practice my aim.

We can use papayas as target practice," he said. I imagined the fruit splattering their tangerine-colored juice in a burst of gunfire and quickly handed it back, worried about invoking bad memories.

Instead, an image of a gun at the starting line of a race emerged. I reflected on the distance we'd covered during the past eighteen years—Javier, who had forged a new career in a new country, my daughters, one a successful entrepreneur and the other a keen college student, and my own career change that combined a passion for writing and social justice.

I could stop running. It was time to celebrate living.

✳ Birth
amé solomon

i attended my first birth in new mexico when i was twenty-five years old. My sister-in-law Karen was eight months pregnant, and I traveled from Oregon to help her.

Her deadbeat partner, my husband's brother, had taken a job as a river raft guide up in Montana that summer, rather than stick around Santa Fe and pretend to be interested in her growing belly. My husband had been sleeping with other women and lying to me, and I'd finally reached my breaking point and left him.

In Santa Fe, she and I were both somewhat homeless, and so we stayed with our mother-in-law. Neither of us had any money, and neither of our men offered to pay our rent. The night Karen went into labor, I was sleeping beside her. She woke me in the middle of the night, whispering, "It's time." It was autumn, and my first thought was that it was time for me to drive out to my mom's farm to help harvest her cornfield, as I'd promised that week. Slowly it dawned on me that even though Karen was a month early, it was her *birthing* time. That October night, I watched as she let her body do its hard work of bringing a beautiful little boy into the world. The midwives placed him on her chest. It all seemed perfectly normal and matter-of-fact that she would have him right there in that bedroom. He was tiny, and perfect. This birth was the most beautiful thing I had ever witnessed.

The next day, sleep-deprived and high on the energy of the birth, I called my friend Sue in California to share the story. During our conversation, I realized that something was going on in me—something pivotal, life-altering, and essential to my life's path. Within a year, Sue called and asked me to attend her own baby's birth. By then I was working at the Kushi Institute, a macrobiotics center out in the Berkshires of Massachusetts, and she was in San Diego. As I was still separated (though not yet divorced), I was free to choose where I was going, when, and how. So I packed up the dog, my shotgun, and my sleeping bag and drove solo back across the country to witness another mind-blowing birth.

I was beginning to realize that all births are totally out of this dimension. There is an element of mystery and a reverence for the unknown, and yet a searing clarity during the moment of birth that does not compare to any other moment in life, other than at death. These ingredients were pronounced at Sue's birth as well, and it was a great honor that my "sisters" had called me to their sides to bear witness.

After the birth, I stayed on to help Sue, her partner, and baby. Unsure what my next move was, and now unemployed, I found helping a new mother to be deeply meaningful and fulfilling. I cooked healthy meals for the new family, changed some diapers, held the baby when the parents needed to rest, and helped out with other tasks. In return, I experienced the gift of the presence of this new being. I needed that little baby's gentleness and trust just as much as he needed his diaper changed regularly.

At this point, my husband had just filed the divorce papers, and after receiving them, I found it difficult to bounce back from their impact. I had trouble getting out of bed, coming up with a good reason to brush my teeth, wash my hair, or generally take care of myself. In a funny way, nurturing the baby recharged my loving nature toward my own self. Babies have a special gift of being clear mirrors for us, if we look closely. It was a good trade.

Eventually I ended up in the San Francisco Bay Area to study midwifery with one of the leading midwives in the country, Elizabeth Davis. She had written *Heart and Hands,* a training manual for home birth midwives. In her weekly class, I and the other aspiring midwives studied the basics of labor, birth, anatomy, and postpartum. There was something about being called to my friends' births that was compelling like nothing before in my life. Serving women, encouraging that sacred bonding between mother and baby, and empowering women in their choice to have their baby on their own terms felt profoundly meaningful.

In contrast, my relationship with my ex-husband had been humiliating, disempowering, and devastating. I'd trusted him to stand in my corner, and we'd started to build a life together before he pulled the rug out from under my feet. I wondered, "How could I have been so stupid to end up with such a man, how I could ever trust my own judgment to make good choices, and how I could trust another partner again?" I felt defeated. Yet through the work with women and birth, I was finding my strength again, and by witnessing their pain and triumph, I was able to find my own way through the darkness that seemed to surround me.

Suddenly I found analogies to the birthing process everywhere I looked. When I considered how hard it was for me to accept abrupt change in my life—specifically now as the single, divorced person I hadn't intended to be—I thought of pregnancy. It takes nine months of gestation to grow a human baby, a period of time that compels women toward introspection, discovery, and personal growth—it's as if the psyche is getting us ready for the next chapter.

I noticed how women were stunned by how drastically different the world looked when they were pregnant: how it changed the entire landscape of their lives. It was as if they were starting life anew. I took that element and tried to apply it to my predicament, so that when I had no idea what to do next, I made an effort to comfort myself in the open range of possibilities. In the laboring mother, I witnessed how her pain was inescapable and raw and overtook her entire being. I saw her writhe in agony, breathe through tremendous difficulty, somehow make peace with her situation, surrender to the process, and face her deepest truth as she brought forth new life. Most remarkably, I saw women reach deep inside and access a warrior-like internal strength beyond compare. Every birth inspired me to reflect on the power and wisdom women possess, and to have faith in my own inner fortitude. I marveled at the natural process unfolding for women as they let go without self-judgment. I observed how they hurt more if they became scared, and seemed more at peace with their pain when they accepted it. I learned from them that there was *pain with purpose,* and that we *can* make it through the most horrific, mind-numbing, excruciating pain, even though we sometimes think we can't. In the end there is triumph, joy, and empowerment beyond imagination.

After the divorce was finalized, I went back to Santa Fe and found an apprenticeship with a couple of midwives. I allowed the gifts each birth gave me to teach me about pain, suffering, and growth. I listened to mothers' moans and primal screams and whispered "You can do it," and I fully believed it. I said it to myself, too, and eventually the pain lessened, and the joy increased. And when self-judgment and doubt reared its ugly face, I made a conscious choice to believe in my core strength and trust that I was where I needed to be in the present moment. Every day, I worked on refining my intuition and trusting my inner voice. It was imperative that I hone those skills if I intended to walk the path of a midwife. And to do that, I needed to be healed first.

Becoming vigilant about observing laboring women and holding the safe space for them brought awareness to my own process of reclaiming my strength, and just as importantly, my vulnerability. When I became downhearted about the choices I had made in the past, and my heart ached with regret, I nourished myself with affirmations of encouragement and love. I tried to keep trusting that I was on my path, and there was divine guidance at work in the journey. It was through this amazing process of serving women that I found, and continue to find, my way back to my self.

*

Sex after Marriage
amy hudock

*

YEAR ONE

he sits across from me at the bar table, the first man i've found attractive since my divorce. Both writers, we have met here at the Griffin so I can help him through his writer's block. I give him instructions that I try to follow in my own journal.

Think of a moment in time when you felt a strong emotion. His fountain pen hesitates across the page. His muscles are tense, like he is fighting the impulse to bolt. He looks away from the page, back at it, then at me. Challenging.

I write about him.

Make a list of the people who were there. A room filled with strangers drinking from pint glasses ignores us. He doesn't want to do what I have asked. The exercise I have given him forces him into writing by rote, which is not what he does. He's accustomed to writing when it comes, words nicely shaped and moving with grace; now he's learning how to write when it doesn't come, when the words come out choked, half-swallowed, or not at all. He resists the false order I am imposing on his syllables. The baby-step warm-ups. Learning to write yourself into inspiration or despite a lack of it is the most difficult part of being a writer. Nonetheless, he wants to please me, so he scribbles reluctantly when I ask.

What did you hear? His chair scrapes in protest as he pulls it back sharply from the table. Against the backdrop of music, conversation, and the *shuzz*ing of the taps, the noise is hardly noticeable. But I hear it; yet I don't stop. Frustration can be good, a push to new creation.

Make a list of objects that were there. What did you see? I want to give him a toolbox, a set of exercises he can do when words can't make their way out. Building metaphors from random objects, listing, brainstorming, freewriting, clustering, making collages, drawing, cutting, and pasting. Because he wants to go far away, and I won't be there. He needs some things to take with him. Something to remind him of the creator-maker-god within. I want more of our collaboration, not less, not a moving away. But he sits across from me, out of reach.

What did you touch? What did you feel? I watch his hand around the pen, a left slant across the page. In a flash of heat, I remember when those hands touched me, my hips, my belly, my breasts as I stood perfectly still, struggling to breathe. My fingers, caught in his, then placed on him. His chest, his belly. His eyes, oh, god, his eyes keeping me there, rooted. Until I broke the gaze, fear turning me away.

What happened? Tell me what happened that day, that moment. Barriers, walls, stone fortifications. How much older am I? Is this wrong? What about my house, my home? My child? Would this be safe? What does he want from me? What will he take? Can I risk this? His are the first hands to touch me since my divorce. Can I trust him?

Now as I look at him across the table as he writes, warming to the task, I am not afraid anymore. I want him to touch me, for me to touch him—but I can't find the words, nor can I get my hand to move toward him. I doodle on a pad, wondering if I dare speak, touch. I stick to talking about writing; for this I have words. I don't have words for the other. My page remains blank as he fills his.

Reflect on what happened. What did it mean to you? He writes about the power of memory, and the need to let go of the past. Of hope. He tells me a story of fake pearls given, held, and given up . . . and replaced by the real. He writes about maybe falling in love again. Maybe falling. Maybe. Giving up what turned out to be fake for the real. And as I look into his eyes, I feel a "yes," like a sigh, like I did the first time he caught me in his camera lens, looking out to sea.

Go back through what you've written. Find what you can use. Write again. But I am shy, embarrassed. I drew the boundary—friends only. Can it be undrawn? Unmade? Rewritten?

That's enough.

Look, you've written. No block here. Energy flows. He takes me for a motorcycle ride, barreling down narrow Charleston, South Carolina streets, my hands in the pockets of his leather jacket, my body against his. Surely and confidently, he dodges runaway soccer balls, slow-moving pedestrians, and oblivious taxis. I laugh at the sudden feeling of flying, being freed from the gravity that keeps me hovering close to the ground. I turn my face to the side and rest my cheek against his back. I let go—trusting him to keep us safe, even though I don't know what will happen, where we will go, where this will end. I give in to the ambiguity. He slams on the brakes, and I slide forward against him. This allowable touch I don't want to end. I close my eyes and let it just be.

One perfect moment.

For that is all it can be—he's transitory, as beautiful and as solid as champagne bubbles; I'm stationary, firmly planted, raising a child in the earth I have chosen for myself. Responsibility, reliability, dependability, patterns, and schedules define my life. I stand as he rides away, knowing the riding away is what will have to be.

Then, I write. I hold him tight in the syntax of my words. And for now, that is enough.

YEAR TWO

our hostess walks inside, leaving me alone on the patio with the first man I've found attractive since the writer left town. Regardless of how I try to pretend I am ignoring it, I can feel his eyes on me like a touch—not the butterfly wings of flirtation but the grip, almost painful, of taking, of wanting. I look away, trying to find a focal point elsewhere. He tips the beer back, pauses, and says, "Let's go make out on your couch."

I blush; my body feels warm. I was crying earlier, missing the missing—my father two weeks dead. My senses are heightened, my emotions more intense than normal. I breathe him in, and he has the same effect on me as the smell of baking cookies. I want them, like I want him now. Our friend comes back out of the house, so I don't have to attempt an answer. He continues on with general conversation as if he has said nothing of significance.

We sit on the patio, torchlights glowing, friends chatting. And I can think of nothing else but what he said, though he seems to have forgotten it. *Make out? Is he kidding me?* He sits there out of reach, offering what is not possible. His girlfriend's face comes to me, even though he says it is over with her, she still comes to me. So, I know that I can't, that he can't. Nonetheless, when I look back at him, his eyes challenge me.

A game of chicken, I think. He wants to see who will flinch first. He won't go through with it. *I can play this game, too.* I yawn and stretch, "Gotta get some sleep. Thanks for the beer." I look right at him, and I smile. He gets up, "Yeah, I need to go, too. Goodnight, all." We walk across the lawn together, silent. He goes to his porch; I go to mine next door. We pause, looking at each other with the banisters between us, the Southern summer breeze making our rocking chairs move slightly. "Good night," I say. He says nothing.

And, suddenly, I know I am on the wrong porch, walking in the wrong door. I want to walk through his door, lie down where he does, and feel the touch his eyes suggest. Longing is sometimes on

the surface, an itch easy to reach. This is deeper, fuller, stronger—
not so easy to reach. Or to ignore.

He says, "You could leave the back door open," and goes into
his house. Okay. My move. Sigh. As I lie down on my bed, I think,
He is two walls and a small space of a yard away. I can't let it go.
The intellectual, analytical me knows I should ignore it. The holier-
than-thou side of me chastises me for even imagining it. I should go
to sleep, stay safe, stay still.

But I also feel that here is an offering from the universe,
something important, and that I shouldn't let it pass me by. Life
has not been good to me lately, and here is some sweetness, maybe
in recompense, if I'll only take it. I was once a person who took
risks. Who didn't care about what others thought. Who followed my
instincts. Who could take a challenge. What happened to that girl?
Where did she go? A part of me has died, too, it seems, long before
this recent loss. I wonder about resurrection.

Life calls to life.

I can play this game. He'll back down. I grab my cell phone and
type an invitation. And then I wait. Nothing. Oh, no. Not a good
idea. I start typing again, backpedaling, big time: *If this is a game of
chicken, okay, then, you win.* Before I can send the message, I receive
this one:

It's locked.

Oh, my god. He is at my back door. Really. Keep breathing.

I stand there in the silence for almost too long, trying to think
it through. But I can't. Beaten, the intellectual side, for once, steps
aside. I twist the lock and open the door.

Four feet of couch stretches between us, each of us on the edge.
It's one thing to suggest an action; it's another thing to do it.

"Remember, when I first bought the house? You came out
because you were worried about the strange man lurking around,"
he says. "I wanted you even then."

"I hated it when you said you had a girlfriend."

He smiles, is quiet for a moment.

"Do you really think it could work . . . between us?" He reaches across the space, curls my hand up in his own, and kisses it.

"It's possible. Fully possible."

He leans in to kiss me. I feel the touch throughout my body, sparklers in the night. We linger close together, his hands moving to my throat, one on each side. I tilt back my head as he kisses from the hollow of my neck slowly up to the chin. Animals expose their throats to indicate submission. I give him mine now.

He pushes me back on the sofa, and I let him. His hands move through me, my breasts, my belly, my hips, lower. His fingers play lightly, expertly. I shiver. The longing goes deeper, grows stronger. My breathing quickens, and I feel tension building—my back arches—and for a moment, I am stunned into stillness and silence. He presses against me, and all I can think is "yes."

"Invite me upstairs," he whispers into my ear.

The intellectual, moral me comes back from wherever she has gone. Upstairs, *no.* I can't, he can't. No matter how much I wish it weren't so, it is. No matter how much he feels his relationship is over, he has to make that feeling a reality, reconcile his inner and outer worlds. He has to go home. He has unfinished business there. "It's over. The business end of it all will be over soon," he says. Fine. "When you are really free of all of it, then we can have this." Until then, I hold my hands up and push him away. Tell him to go. Even though it hurts. Even though I hate it. Even though this could be our only moment.

I just can't take what isn't mine. This is what I tell myself. But I really know that I am afraid to make him mine.

YEAR THREE

we stand, each on one side of the huge bed, sizing each other up. The wait makes it all the more delicious.

We have flirted around the edges of this moment, me holding him off. We live next door to each other, friends, companions, helpers, but not yet lovers. We know what we have come here to do, but the question is, how? We don't know each other's bodies yet. It's been years since my divorce, years since I have stood like this with a man. We are at the awkward beginning, finding our way to each other. Yet, we have to start somewhere. Our eyes locked, we wait, our breathing loud in the room.

Okay. Long enough wait. Show time.

I tilt my head back and to the side, hands on my hips. "A while back, we were making out on the couch and you asked me 'What if I don't take no for an answer?' Remember?"

He smiles. "Yes, I remember."

"Well, today I don't want you to take no for an answer."

He smiles even more.

"I won't give it up easy, though. But don't stop. If I really want you to stop, I'll say 'red light.' But unless you hear that, you're doing exactly what I want you to do."

I move side to side, the bed still between us, taunting him to come get me.

"Try to catch me."

He starts to come over the bed, and I spin away from his hands, out the door, down the hall. I turn quickly into the guest room and hide behind the door. I hear him coming. I hold my breath as he walks into the room. I can see him as he looks around the room, behind the curtains, under the bed. Then, he turns back toward the door and sees me there.

I laugh as I try to keep my hands free, but he kicks the door shut and pins my hands against the wall. Easily. A little too easily. I wince from the grip.

"You thought you could get away?"

He leans in to kiss me, body pressed against me, but I turn my head—the only part I can move except for a feeble kick. Now it's his turn to laugh. He shrugs and goes for my neck. He runs his lips from under the curve in my jaw to the outer limits of my collarbone and then lingers on the shoulder. Suddenly—teeth. I try to jerk away, but with a wicked smile, he does it again, lightly.

"There has to be some punishment. You just can't keep running away."

Sensation intensifies.

I stop struggling, trying to slow my breath. He pulls my hands together over my head and holds them with one hand. Freed, his other hand begins a slow journey down, feather light.

"That's better. Relax. Now, the reward."

He pops open the button on my jeans and slides his hand inside, pulls down my pants. I inhale his smell, taste the sweat on his skin—I marvel at how much he wants me. He strokes me, and as the tightness in my belly, in my thighs, builds, I can't pull away. The wall behind me keeps me still. As the one who says "no," who moderates and stops the action, who is always the mommy, the leader, the boss, I've learned to keep myself in check, to pull away when the feelings get too intense. Now, however, I am trapped with the sensation. And I don't really want to get away. One, two, three . . . the spasms shake my body. I open my eyes to his eyes watching me—he loves the shiver in my body, my mouth. I feel beautiful in his gaze.

He shoves his pants to the ground and steps out of them. He enters me, slowly, my back still against the wall. The first entrance is the most exquisite of all the strokes. The giving away, the pressing in, the opening. The first few minutes, heaven, then riding on that energy to a new plateau. He feels the pressure of my muscles as they start to contract again, and he quickens his strokes. My desire pushes his, and I feel him start his own shivers, spasms, flowing. He lets me loose in a gasp, and I hold him close as we catch our breath.

"Next time," I say, "you're going to have to fight me off. But I get a handicap. I get to put you in handcuffs. Maybe even a blindfold. That'll make it more even."

He seems okay with that. And now I am, too.

Mad for Love
susan carol stein

i put the lawyer through law school. he put me in the loony bin. We called it even and got divorced. Some philosophers out there might call this a *quid pro quo* since both institutions—law school and an insane asylum—strip off vital layers of your soul. If you are one of the lucky few, however, you uncover your beautiful, truest nature when they let you out.

The Lawyer really isn't to blame. The disintegration of my psyche was irrevocably tied to the horror that was my marriage. But, I knew that the union was a mistake well before my bouquet of rubrum lilies arrived at the church shriveled in its box and a torrential rain made me look like the winner of a wet T-shirt contest. The universe conspired desperately to warn me, sending these portents of doom, but this stubborn Catholic girl was having none of it.

By the mid-1980s, the Roman Catholic Church had hipped things up to try and dissuade impulsive marriages by good kids who just wanted to, uh . . . consummate. They created mandatory Engaged Encounter weekends where a handful of young couples learned about the difficulties of marriage from a priest and two happily married Catholics. I thought this somewhat akin to learning brain surgery from a fedora salesman and two head trauma survivors, but I had no choice. I wanted to marry in the Church.

Due to a blinding blizzard, The Lawyer-to-be and I arrived very late to the abbey campus. We thought the whole thing ridiculous, which set us apart from the other earnest couples in our class. But as the hours and multiple choice tests stacked up, it was clear that we rarely answered a question in harmony. I began to get a prickly feeling in the pit of my stomach. The wedding were a month away. I loved The Lawyer-to-be as if he were heroin and yet, according to the score, we weren't compatible. When I questioned our ability to live together, he hugged me and said that I was silly. I sat up all night looking out at the snowy pines backlit by the most glorious full moon I have ever seen. The moon and I had a talk.

"This is a soul mistake, Susan."

"What do you know? You're all solitary and distant. What do you know about love?"

"I know when a woman thinks she can change what can't be changed."

"You know, up until fifteen years ago, I thought you were made of cheese. Now I know better. We are adaptable; people mature."

"Are you willing to risk everything, bet everything on that conjecture?"

"Yep."

"This is a soul mistake, Susan."

"Maybe. But, I love him too much to back out."

"That is not love."

"It is how I love."

Truer words were never spoken by a codependent. I hate that word. It's too similar to codefendant and so I feel terribly judged by myself every time I say it. I prefer "mad for love." It rings of Shakespearean nymphs, excellent entrances, and flower-strewn graves. I come from a long line of ladies who were mad for love. They stretch back as far as the gravestones can attest. Tresa. Julia. Mary.

Delia. Margaret. Emma. Mildred. Mary Kay. We marry Irish and German men who break our hearts and wear out our rosary beads. Sometimes it works out, sometimes it ends in premature death, but we never, ever divorce. So, I smiled my way through the rest of the Encounter, believing I could love my way through anything. It was in my blood. We passed as wedding-ready. Certificate in hand, I married the man. Not moonlit truth, nor sobbing over a dead bridal bouquet had stopped me.

There is no sense in rehashing everything that led me to crack wide-open like a Cadbury Cream Egg, exposing my messy center for all to see. I'll crystallize it down to the night I finally split, figuratively and literally.

It had taken five years for me to get here. Floating in the tub with my body outstretched and my arms crossed over my heart—a mummy without the protective covering—I had come to the guilty conclusion that I didn't want to hang with my ancestors. I felt the suffocating weight of centuries of blue-collar Irish tradition and religiosity. I had contemplated death, his or mine, but that wasn't my style. Divorce—that ugly, ugly word—was. I was getting out. Narrowing my eyes, I took in a slow, yogic breath, and when I exhaled, my pretend happy life, my ancestral connection, and my sanity floated out my nostrils into the exhaust fan above my head.

I got out of the tub and dressed. My eyes wouldn't focus. My body shook.

He was lying in our bed with the light out. I stretched out next to him and placed my hand on his side. He winced and moved away, his usual reaction to touch.

"I don't know how to do this, so I'm just going to say it."

He moved a little farther away.

"I'm leaving tonight. I called my brother and he is coming to get me. I think that I might shatter, that I am shattering."

He said nothing but got up, headed for the living room.

"I've tried everything I know and nothing reaches you," I stammered, tripping after him down the narrow hall.

He sat down in his recliner, picked up the newspaper, and began to read.

"I cannot be invisible. Not one day more."

The backside of the newspaper revealed a full-page ad featuring a gorgeous woman in her 30-percent-off underwear. She belly danced from the force of his grip, but he remained silent. I wanted to rip her to shreds, to make him look at me.

Instead, I whispered, "I love you," and stumbled to my brother's car.

Over the next few days, I unraveled like a poorly crocheted sweater. I started to see things that weren't there, including, sardonically, The Lawyer's death notice in the morning paper. I became convinced that I was pregnant by the now deceased, a parting bonus gift from God because I was a worthy Catholic. This morbid, crazy spiral soon descended into paranoia and oblivion. My confused, anguished family carted me off to St. Francis of Assisi Medical Center, a Catholic asylum. While I was singing songs from *Les Miserables* and traveling inside a giant vortex through all of time, they quietly committed me.

Mapping your way back from insanity is often impossible. Luckily, I came into myself over a period of a few weeks. Proving yourself competent to walk among the sane is not easy once you've become a ward of the state. You have to pass a battery of humiliating tests given by men in literal white coats. Standing before a court, you must convince someone that you are not a threat to yourself or others. My mother described my psychosis as "the worst thing that ever happened to our family." While that was instantly tattooed on my heart, I knew what she meant. No one could relax around me. Hell, even I couldn't relax around me.

For two years, I lived in that limbo. I wasn't who I used to be but I didn't know who I was. I couldn't pull off the divorce. But one morning, I saw an ad for a theater job in Seattle, Washington. It was the impetus I needed to cut the last, sad cords that bound me to The Lawyer. He was in therapy but admitted he was "no more capable of being a husband than flying a space shuttle." As I stood in the post office parking lot, looking up at the full moon, I hugged my resume package and talked to my old friend.

"Beautiful Moon, protector of we earthbound lunatics, you were absolutely right. I should never have married him. I was blinded by pride, by love. My life sucks and it's entirely my fault. But, everyone deserves a second chance, don't you think? If it is meant to be, I will get this job and a fresh start. If not, I'll stay here and find the courage to dig out from under the crushing pile of poop that is my life." The moon held her tongue, but I felt at peace with myself for the first time in a decade.

The moon smiled on me. Soon, I was loading my hatchback to drive cross-country to my new job in the Pacific Northwest. My long-suffering, loving family did not restrain me, even though they worried. I spent one last night with The Lawyer, a somber confirmation that one person's inability to change does not limit another's capacity to transform.

seattle. even after sixteen years, the sheer joy i felt driving through the city the first time bubbles up and makes me giggle. Water sparkled everywhere. It cut streets in half and half again. I was constantly lost, but it never mattered. With each turn of my head, I saw snowy mountaintops, towering cedar trees, and that ever-changing, endless water. If a clean slate was possible, this was the place for it. I was thirty years old, and no one knew anything about me. I shed the *lunatic* and *victim* labels that had weighed me down like winter clothes on a gorgeous summer day—they were smelly and utterly useless.

For an entire decade of my life, I had let someone else define my choices, my emotional state, my boundaries. On a ferry boat headed to the enchanted San Juan Islands, I made a pact with myself: If my twenties were about surviving a terrible mistake, my thirties were to celebrate that survival with true love. My sister imagined a tall, ripped lumberjack perched on a granite boulder. I didn't care what he looked like or did for a living. I had a different "must" list: He must cradle my heart and we must, every day, show that we are worthy of each other.

I spent another year immersed in my work, phone dating a PhD who lived in New York. It was the perfect solution as I eased into the decade of love. He was safe, romantic, kind, and, most important, far away. The Doctor taught me that men can be chatty, interested in my interests, and beguiled by my sensuousness—all things I'd long forgotten or never learned.

At the conclusion of a huge project I'd been working on for months, my upstairs neighbor invited me to a dinner party. Exhausted and moody, I tried to decline. She had none of it. I was to celebrate the season opener of *Star Trek: The Next Generation,* whatever that was. I was standing in her kitchen cutting vegetables when Michelangelo's David, wearing a backward baseball cap and jeans with ripped knees, bounced into the room. I'd never seen anyone with such vibrant buoyancy. The Free Spirit smiled with his whole body. This was the height of the alternative music scene in Seattle, the city of many alternatives, and it was as if he was the physical embodiment of them all. Dressed like a Midwestern librarian—my shirt had barn animals on it, no lie—I put my head down and chopped.

Much to my surprise, he sat next to me most of the evening, talking about music, theater, his son, vegetarianism. More shocking, he returned to my neighbor's the next morning to "get the recipe for those quinoa-stuffed peppers" and lingered at my door. Hideously shy, I didn't venture outside. I left that afternoon for New York to see The Doctor, a surprise visit to see how we handled each other unplanned and spontaneous. It didn't go well. As I flew out of LaGuardia to Seattle, I was relieved and saddened to end our relationship. He was a sweet man and a good friend.

My message machine was blinking when I arrived home. The Free Spirit was inviting me for coffee, because "everyone needs more friends and more caffeine." We met at a Starbucks and took a long walk. He kissed my cheek. It is practically impossible to believe it, but we've been kissing ever since.

It was vital, from the start, that The Free Spirit know the truth about my history of crazy, my defective ability to love myself sick. We sat under the moon on a languid canal and I told him the whole, bloody story. He cradled me and kept my gaze. He had his own tale of woe and a four-year-old more precious than air. We decided to love each other one day at a time, with all the grace we could muster.

Together, we've raised an amazing person, someone who fulfilled my deep desire to nurture a child. The Boy helped me to heal from my most tragic memories. I am honored and privileged to love him, to help him bloom.

Together, The Free Spirit and I agreed to say "Yes!" to dreams. *Yes* to his guitar playing. *Yes* to my healing practice. *Yes* to his music studio. *Yes* to my activism. *Yes* to his Zen Buddhism. *Yes* to my reverence for rocks and trees and stars.

Together, we've faced death or ruin time after time. I returned to the insane asylum; he struggled to overcome his own demons. We lost a business; we nearly lost our home. And through it all, imperfect and ugly, crippled and pigheaded, lost and depressed, humbled and full of grace, we cradled each other's heart and demonstrated, every day, our worthiness of each other.

I am sure we will face mayhem and ruin again. In fact, I can hear The Free Spirit saying, "Of course we will, Baby Doll. It's part of the whole. It's how we face it that matters." And, I am sure of something else. Leaving the Catholic Church and divorcing The Lawyer emptied me of everything I thought I was so that I could fill myself with who I truly am. My truth, not someone else's doctrine. That sounds so pompous, but it isn't. In one of those plot twists of life that leaves you thinking, I didn't see *that* coming, I have learned to hold my ancestral women in the highest regard for stay-ing in their marriages. And I realize now, it had much less to do with religion than I presumed. To the casual observer, The Free Spirit and I should never have made it. At times, our life resembled an afterschool special on steroids, or a Mexican *telenovela* gone awry. And that's more or less how I interpreted the melodramas of my Irish-German matriarchs. I didn't feel that genuine love coursed between them and their men. Respect flowed. Forgiveness passed from heart to heart. Everyone was perfectly flawed and mired in love.

The Lawyer never risked the dangerous rapids of true love. That was the difference. The Free Spirit risks himself every day, as do I. I'm going down in family history as the first Stein woman, crazy as a loon, to divorce. But I can hear a roaring cheering section behind me now . . . Tresa. Julia. Mary. Delia. Margaret. Emma. Mildred. Mary Kay. Under the mad, mad moon, in all her beautiful phases, I bless us all.

ABOUT THE CONTRIBUTORS

laura andré received her Ph.D. in art history from the University of North Carolina at Chapel Hill. She was an assistant professor in photo history at the University of New Mexico from 2003 to 2007. Currently she lives in Albuquerque and works for an independent bookseller specializing in rare and contemporary photography books.

sally blakemore, a children's book author, illustrator, award-winning pop-up book designer and marimbist, has spent the last twenty years in Santa Fe, New Mexico, with her husband, Rusty, and their menagerie of animals. She has traveled the world printing her pop-up books and enjoying the amazing cultures of our planet.

h. k. brown is a practicing litigation attorney specializing in brief writing, and a professor of legal writing. She is the author of a legal textbook for first-year attorneys, published by Thomson-West Publishing, now in its fifth edition. Ms. Brown won Honorable Mention in the WOW-Women-on-Writing Flash Fiction Contest, and wrote *The Ground Rules,* a screenplay that was optioned by a production company in Simi Valley, California. She has completed the manuscript for a divorce recovery memoir entitled *Even Good Girls Get Divorced.* Ms. Brown currently resides in Laguna Beach, California.

jessica cerretani is currently an editor at Harvard Medical School's award-winning alumni magazine, and a successful freelancer. Her work has appeared in Martha Stewart's *Body + Soul, Prevention, Natural Health, National Geographic's The Green Guide, The Boston Phoenix, Boston Home,* and—ironically—*Boston Weddings.*

teresa coates has written for a variety of publications over the years, covering topics as varied as international adoption, transgender children, apron history, and, not surprisingly, travel in Vietnam.

mary-charlotte domandi is producer and host of the *Santa Fe Radio Cafe* on KSFR 101.1 FM, a program of interviews on subjects including politics, the environment, literature, art, science, and the local Santa Fe scene. She holds degrees from Yale University and St. John's College. She is a Latin music DJ, has studied social and folkloric dance in Cuba, and has interviewed many distinguished Latin musicians.

julie hammonds is a freelance writer and the associate editor of *Arizona Wildlife Views* magazine. Hammonds enjoys writing about people, nature, travel, and adventure. Her writing has won national awards from the Outdoor Writers Association of America and the Association for Conservation Information. "The Love List" is excerpted from a completed memoir manuscript about her solo travels. To read further selections, visit www.juliehammonds.com.

sonja herbert is the author of *Tightrope!,* an award-winning, as-yet-unpublished novel about her German mother surviving the Holocaust in a circus, and *Cross and Carnival,* a memoir about her search for God while growing up in a traveling carnival. She has also published many other autobiographical stories. After thirty-five years in the USA, Herbert presently lives in Germany, where she is doing research and getting reacquainted with her mother and siblings. You can find links to her stories on her website, www.germanwriter.com.

r. m. hora is an Ayurveda clinician and freelance writer based in San Francisco. She is the author of *Inner Beauty: Discover Natural Beauty and Well-Being with the Traditions of Ayurveda* (Chronicle Books, 2004) and *Ayurveda: The Ancient Medicine of India* (Mandala Publishing, 2007). She writes for Green Options media, and also writes screenplays for film, TV, and the web. Born and raised in Mumbai, she loves writing about the Indian experience, and life both inside and outside of India. Check out her work at www.reenita.com.

amy hudock, Ph.D., founding coeditor of LiteraryMama.com, teaches English at an independent college prep school in South Carolina, where she lives with her daughter. She is the coeditor of *Literary Mama: Reading for the Maternally Inclined* (Seal Press, 2006) and *American Women Prose Writers, 1820 to 1870* (Gale, 2001), and the author of scholarly essays on nineteenth-century American women writers. Her memoir writing about motherhood has appeared in the anthologies *Mama, PhD: Women Write About Motherhood and Academic Life* (Rutgers University Press, 2008) and *Single State of the Union* (Seal Press, 2007). Her work has also appeared in periodical publications such as *Skirt!, ePregnancy,* and *Pregnancy and Baby.*

julie hutchison geen just finished her third screenplay. Her columns on astrology have been published in *Mamalicious* magazine, and she also writes pieces for mothering.com.

marrit ingman writes nonfiction, criticism, and documentation about dual-blade buffer robots. She is the author of *Inconsolable: How I Threw My Mental Health Out with the Diapers* (Seal Press, 2005) and has contributed to many anthologies, including *The Maternal Is Political* (Seal Press, 2008). Previously, she was a regular contributor to *The Austin Chronicle,* and she performs as part of the Dick Monologues (www.dickmonologues.com).

leigh anne jasheway-bryant is a humor writer and speaker who lives in Eugene, Oregon, with her husband and her giant wiener dogs. She is the author of fifteen published books, including *Not Guilty by Reason of Menopause* (Celestial Arts, 2008) and *Life Is Funny: A Riveting Tale of Comedy, Hairdressing, and Texas Politics* (Comedy Workout Publishing, 2007). For eight years, she was a humor and inspiration columnist for *Family Circle Magazine,* and has written for more than a dozen other national magazines. Her website is www.accidentalcomic.com.

melanie jones is an author, editor, columnist, and television personality. She is the author of four books on such topics as dating disasters, plastic ,surgery horror stories, and the life of ballerina Karen Kain. She appeared regularly on CityTV's *Your City* and *Breakfast Television* as the Dating Dame with her own brand of take-no-prisoners advice. She has worked as a magazine editor and a freelance dance writer. An avid endurance athlete, Jones finished Ironman Canada in August 2006 (twelve hours, baby!) and has run several marathons.

rozella kennedy lives and works in Santa Fe, New Mexico. She is the author of the novel *BecomingMom.com* (AuthorHouse, 2001) and is indebted to her mother-in-law for the handy expression "heck of life." Her mother-in-law has been married to her father-in-law since 1950.

elisabeth kinsey received her B.A. in Creative Writing at Metropolitan State College of Denver, home of the best rag-tag, adult student, undergrad writing program in Colorado. She has published poetry in *Wazee Journal, Metrosphere,* and memoir/creative nonfiction in *Emergency Online Journal* and *The Rambler*. She won first prize in Writes of Spring and was awarded a partial stipend to Summer Literary Seminars. She is pursuing her Masters in Creative Writing (she does want fries with that).

kate mcdade lives in Portland, Maine, with her daughter Nora and their incredibly destructive Maine Coon kitten, Hugo Chavez Gato. Kate is grateful to have her little story included in this anthology and would like you to know that she kept the rock, but not her end of the bargain.

theo pauline nestor's memoir *How to Sleep Alone in a King-Size Bed* (Crown, 2008), was a Kirkus Reviews Top Pick for Reading Groups, and soon will be translated into German. Her essay "The Chicken's in the Oven, My Husband's out the Door" was recently published in *Modern Love: 50 True and Extraordinary Tales of Desire, Deceit and Devotion* (Three Rivers Press, 2007). Her fiction and nonfiction have also been published in *The New York Times, Alligator Juniper,* and *Brain, Child,* as well as online at msn.com, austinmama.com, and happenmag.com. She teaches memoir writing for the University of Washington's Extension Program.

nine moved from Northern Ireland to Scotland in 1996, which did wonders for her already messed-up accent. She works at a project for sex workers, writes about sexuality for *The Skinny* magazine, and makes out with a colorful cast of characters. Her zine *If Destroyed Still True* is available from her website www.jinxremoving.org.

michele peterson's writing has appeared in the *Toronto Star,* the *Globe and Mail, Hispanic Magazine, MoneySense,* the *Boston Herald,* and several other publications. Her essays have been featured in the anthologies *Sand in My Bra* (Travelers' Tales, 2003), *The Risks of Sunbathing Topless* (Seal Press, 2005), *A Woman's Asia* (Travelers' Tales, 2005) and *Go Your Own Way: Women Travel the World Solo* (Seal Press, 2007). She divides her time between Toronto and Central America. Her website is www.michelepeterson.com

sabrina porterfield is an American ex-pat living in Finland with three cats, one French bulldog, a set of boy/girl twins, and "the best woman this side of the Atlantic." She has no regrets about relocating, even though it requires a great deal of down clothing and people keep forcing cups of coffee on her. (She still won't eat the weird fish paste, though.)

sue sanders lives in New Paltz, New York, with her husband, daughter, two dogs, and a rabbit. Since starting to write a little more than a year ago, she's had articles published in a variety of magazines. She's working on her first novel.

amé solomon is a Certified Professional Midwife (CPM), and a happily married mama of two living in Central Vermont. She scrawls out poetry at 2:00 A.M., contemplates and writes about the emotional complexities of motherhood, speaks out for the rights of mothers and children, and is thankful for the spiritual journey of motherhood.

elaine soloway is the author of *The Division Street Princess: a Memoir* (Syren Book Company, 2006). This coming-of-age tale of a young girl, a family grocery store, and an old neighborhood in the 1940s was named a *Chicago Tribune* Best Book of 2006. Currently, Elaine is putting the finishing touches on her second book, *She's Not the Type,* a coming-of-middle-age novel also set in Chicago.

susan carol stein is a freelance writer, a certified Jin Shin Jyutsu practitioner, and president/founder of www.TheGivingRing.com, a fair trade business that donates its net profits to global organizations benefiting women and children. Susan holds a B.A. in poetry writing and political science from the University of Pittsburgh and is currently writing a nonfiction book about her life-affirming experiences with alternative medicine. She and The Free Spirit make their home in Seattle, Washington.

kristin tennant has been making a living for fifteen years as a copywriter, journalist, brand consultant, and, more recently, a writing instructor for MediaBistro.com. A Michigan native, Kristin is now a prairie-dweller, living in Urbana, Illinois, with her husband Jason, her two daughters, and one stepdaughter, plus the extended family, which includes her ex-husband and his new wife, and Jason's ex-wife and her wife…and their new baby.

samantha ducloux waltz is an award-winning freelance writer and teacher of writing in Portland, Oregon. Her essays appear in the *A Cup of Comfort* series, the *Chicken Soup for the Soul* series, the *Ultimate* series, the *Hero* series, and a number of other anthologies, as well as the *Christian Science Monitor* and *The Rambler*. Her website is www.pathsofthought.com.

kathleen wiebe is a forty-five-year-old college student in Victoria, British Columbia. When her life was turned upside down by marital separation, she decided to go with the theme of change. Mother to two boys and a brand new wife to an old flame, she is writing a novel and is studying to become a teacher.

ACKNOWLEDGMENTS

many thanks to krista lyons, for plucking my proposal from the slush pile and making my somewhat impertinent dream into a reality that has been so healing and effervescent for everyone involved.

I'm very grateful to Laura, for holding my hand, guiding my gaze, losing sleep, and unstintingly giving hours, thought, attention, insight, and so much heart and soul to this project.

I owe so much to the writing teachers and mentors who kick-started and shone their sun on my development: Audre Allison, Grace Anderson, Judith Schutzmann, Stacy Hubbard, Charlotte Sheedy, Deidre Lynch, Beverly Baio, Susan Donowitz, Masani Alexis DeVeaux, Raymond Federman, and the late Robert Creeley.

Thank you to Tanya Taylor of Project Life Stories for helping me to unearth the germ of my story with your incredible process and laser-sharp eye for the nitty-gritty, and thanks to Amy Hudock for editing the editor.

Thank you to Peggy O'Mara, for your grace, generosity, and example, and for writing such a liberating, seminal essay on this topic in *Mothering* magazine and *A Quiet Place*. Thank you, Laura

Egley Taylor and Naomi Williams, for your indelible, incredible stamps on this book. Thanks to *all* of the writers who sent essays—I was enriched and blessed by the privilege of reading your stories of growth and transcendence.

Thank you to Ashisha, Kimber, Gia, Nancy, Susie, Sally, Alexis, Tej Kaur, Leanne, and Melissa, for taking all my late-night phone calls and being the kind, warm current, *and* the sparkling shore, *and* the beach towel, *and* the picnic lunch that awaited me.

Thank you, Julie. You made all the difference.

I want to thank my mother, Linda Graham, for both giving birth to me and midwifing my writer self, and my father, Peter Walsh, for his support, and for loving me, as his inscription in my high school yearbook asserts, "from sky's end to sky's end." Thank you, Susan, for all of the big and little things you have done for me; not one has escaped my notice or my appreciation.

Thank you, Lisa, for sharing the journey behind us and the one ahead. Pete and Jim, thank you for having my back. Thanks also to Honorée and Nathaniel for letting Mommy write.

And I want to thank Peter for every good thing he did give me, including the surprising knowledge that I could get there from here.

© Laura André

About the Author

✳

✳

candace walsh is a writer, poet, and editor living in Santa Fe. She is the articles and poetry editor at *Mothering* magazine. She cofounded and edited *Mamalicious* magazine. Her articles have also appeared in *Travel + Leisure, Sunset, Food & Wine, Entree, Newsday, Blender,* and *Details.* She recently cowrote *Stone Designs for the Home,* a New Mexico Book Award finalist, with John T. Morris (Gibbs Smith, Publisher, 2008).

Selected Titles from Seal Press

For more than thirty years, Seal Press has published groundbreaking books. By women. For women. Visit our website at www.sealpress.com. Check out the Seal Press blog at www.sealpress.com/blog.

Single State of the Union: Single Women Speak Out on Life, Love, and the Pursuit of Happiness, edited by Diane Mapes. $14.95, 1-58005-202-9. Written by an impressive roster of single (and some formerly single) women, this collection portrays single women as individuals whose lives extend well beyond Match.com and Manolo Blahniks.

Tango: An Argentine Love Story, by Camille Cusumano. $15.95, 1-58005-250-9. The spicy travel memoir of a woman who left behind a failed fifteen-year relationship and fell in love with Argentina through the dance that embodies intensity, freedom, and passion.

Dirt: The Quirks, Habits, and Passions of Keeping House, edited by Mindy Lewis. $15.95, 1-58005-261-4. From grime, to clutter, to spit-clean—writers share their amusing relationships with dirt.

The List: 100 Ways to Shake Up Your Life, by Gail Belsky. $15.95, 1-58005-256-8. Get a tattoo, ride in a fire truck, or use food as foreplay—this collection of 100 ideas will inspire women to shake things up and do something they never dared to consider.

The Money Therapist: A Woman's Guide to Creating A Healthy Financial Life, by Marcia Brixey. $15.95, 1-58005-216-9. Offers women of every financial strata the tools they need to manage their money, set attainable budget goals, get out of debt, and create a healthy financial life.

Go Your Own Way: Women Travel the World Solo, edited by Faith Conlon, Ingrid Emerick & Christina Henry de Tessan. $15.95, 1-58005-199-5. Paying tribute to the empowerment of independent adventure and discovery, women recount the thrills of traveling solo, from Borneo and Senegal to Argentina, Paris, Japan, and more.